Business Process outsourcing

Business Process outsourcing

The Competitive Advantage

RICK L. CLICK
THOMAS N. DUENING

WILEY

John Wiley & Sons, Inc.

For general information on our other products and services, or technical support, please contact our Customer Care Department within the United States at 800-762-2974, outside the United States at 317-572-3993 or fax 317-572-4002.

Wiley also publishes its books in a variety of electronic formats. Some content that appears in print may not be available in electronic books.

For more information about Wiley products, visit our Web site at *www.wiley.com*.

Library of Congress Cataloging-in-Publication Data:

Click, Rick L.
    Business process outsourcing : the competitive advantage / Rick L. Click, Thomas N. Duening.
       p. cm.
    Includes bibliographical references and index.
    ISBN 0-471-65577-5 (cloth)
    1. Contracting out.   I. Duening, Thomas N.   II. Title.
  HD2365.C48 2004
  658.4'058—dc22

                                     2004008608

10 9 8 7 6 5 4 3 2 1

contents

Foreword   vii

Preface   ix

Acknowledgments   xiii

PART ONE

  BPO Overview   1

CHAPTER 1
What Is So Revolutionary about BPO?   3

CHAPTER 2
Who Is Using BPO and How?   27

PART TWO

  To BPO or Not to BPO?   45

CHAPTER 3
Identify and Select the BPO Opportunity   47

CHAPTER 4
Identify and Manage the Costs of BPO   70

PART THREE

  BPO Vendor Selection   91

CHAPTER 5
Identify and Select a BPO Vendor   93

CHAPTER 6
BPO Contracts   112

PART FOUR
Executing an Outsourcing Project   **133**

CHAPTER 7
Managing the BPO Transition   **135**

CHAPTER 8
Managing the Buyer–Vendor Relationship   **154**

CHAPTER 9
Infrastructure Considerations and Challenges   **172**

CHAPTER 10
Business Risks and Mitigation Strategies   **189**

PART FIVE
The Future of BPO   **207**

CHAPTER 11
Future Potential for BPO   **209**

Endnotes   **223**
Index   **233**

foreword

The topic of business process outsourcing (BPO) has become controversial and the subject of a great deal of media attention over the past year. As an executive who has been using outsourcing as a business strategy for more than a decade, the recent upsurge in interest in the topic was unexpected. Perhaps the fact that 2004 is an election year has something to do with it. Or maybe, as the authors point out, the convergence of a number of social and technological factors has only recently made BPO an option for organizations of nearly any size.

My experience with BPO ranges over a number of business processes. Organizations that I manage as Chief Engineer of Occidental Oil & Gas have taken advantage of specialized labor pools around the world. As a multinational enterprise in a highly competitive industry, Occidental must be aggressive about controlling costs and employing the highest quality labor it can find. Occidental's experience with outsourcing has mostly been positive, but there have been many lessons learned.

From time to time I have considered the prospect of writing about the lessons I have learned in initiating and managing a BPO project. Time and business considerations have always intruded into those thoughts and made them unrealistic. Fortunately, Rick Click and Tom Duening have taken the time to write this book, which is a fine presentation of how to organize and manage a BPO initiative.

Click and Duening's book is a comprehensive guide that managers and executives in nearly any size organization will find valuable. The mix of insight and practicality that is evident in the writing will provide most readers with the confidence to launch into the BPO waters. The tools and tips contained in this book will make even the most experienced outsourcing manager think again about the methods he or she uses and whether they can be improved.

Of course, no book is without its drawbacks. At times Click and Duening take their discussions to levels of detail that are more appropriate for an academic work. For example, their discussions of change management and interorganizational relationships are long on detail but a little short on examples. Still, the book reads very well and most managers and executives can usefully be reminded of the importance of effective change management to the success of transformational initiatives such as BPO.

Overall, I believe this book will be of tremendous benefit to anyone or any company currently undertaking or considering undertaking a BPO initiative. The complexities of working with offshore partners and the potential risks to the business make the investment in this book well worth the purchase price.

Leading thinkers in the area of global economics assure us that free trade is a good thing for people everywhere. It is likely that the world will not reverse the course of the past several decades of ever broadening trade relationships among nations. In short, BPO is here to stay and it will be a disruptive force in many industries. Managers and executives who want to take advantage of BPO should get this book to help them become successful. Managers and executives who do not want to take advantage of BPO should get this book so they understand what their competitors are doing. In the end, no one can ignore BPO since it will surely affect the cost-structure of nearly every industry. I predict that the hype around BPO will subside quickly, but the business advantages it will bring to many are here to stay.

ROBERT E. PALMER

Chief Engineer, Worldwide Operations
Occidental Oil & Gas
June 2004

Business process outsourcing (BPO) has emerged as one of the leading business and economic issues of our time. A natural extension of the free-trade juggernaut that has dominated global economics over the past two decades, BPO has been met with mixed emotions. Workers whose lives have been disrupted because their jobs have been outsourced to lower-wage workers overseas have understandably decried "offshoring" as a threat to their way of life. Others, especially those in the foreign locations where new jobs are rapidly being created, are elated about the opportunity to apply their hard-earned and high-value skills.

Presidential politics have also weighed in on BPO—with both parties articulating their positions on the issue. Rarely has there been such high-level discourse about a legal business activity that, in the long run, promises lower prices on a wide range of goods and services for U.S. consumers.

In this book, we attempt to examine BPO from the perspective of its application and implementation in businesses of all sizes. We do not address the political or economic controversies swirling around outsourcing. Instead, we assume that the movement of service work to lowest-cost providers, no matter where they may reside, will continue in some form. It seems wholly unlikely that new barriers will be erected that will seriously limit global free trade. With that in mind, we have developed a rigorous methodology that businesses can use to analyze the outsourcing opportunity, to make informed decisions about choosing a vendor, and to manage change and execute an outsourcing project.

The team-based approach to BPO project analysis and implementation is based on the fact that BPO is a socio-technical phenomenon. That is, a well-executed outsourcing project must involve both social and technical resources of the organization. BPO is transformational to the organization and requires attention to the social and human impacts that accompany business transformation. At the same time, one of the primary enablers of BPO is the set of technologies that have emerged to connect the world in a global communications network. As a socio-technical phenomenon, effective BPO management requires a diverse skill set that is not likely to be present in any single individual. Thus, we recommend a team-based approach since the necessary skills are more likely to be available in a group of people united to achieve common objectives.

We also develop the concept of the BPO Life Cycle to denote clear milestones in development of the BPO project and to provide more specific management and leadership guidelines to be applied at different stages of the Life Cycle. The BPO Life Cycle applies to any type of outsourcing project and to any size company.

It has become clear that BPO provides far more than mere cost savings to firms that use it. BPO has become a strategic business choice that can be leveraged for competitive advantage as well. When a business outsources a process to a vendor whose core competence is centered on that process, the buyer is likely to experience service enhancements that can be turned into competitive advantages over rivals. Furthermore, when the buyer–vendor relationship evolves into a business partnership, both sides will be motivated to look for mutually beneficial ways to leverage the combined asset pool.

We have divided this book into five parts to mirror the various stages of the BPO Life Cycle. Part One is intended to provide an overview of BPO. Chapter 1 highlights the primary drivers and the various types of BPO that are in use today. Chapter 2 provides several case examples of firms that use BPO in a variety of ways.

Part Two asks the question "To BPO or not to BPO?" Firms of all sizes are faced with a decision about whether outsourcing can help them achieve cost savings, or scale or competitive advantages. Chapter 3 introduces the concepts of core competence identification, process mapping, and our recommended team-based approach, beginning with the BPO Analysis Team (BAT). Chapter 4 provides a framework for analyzing the costs associated with a BPO project, both obvious and hidden.

Part Three examines the variables and factors associated with BPO vendor selection. Chapter 5 describes a systematic approach to vendor selection and recommends appointing a Vendor Selection Team (VST) to manage that process. Chapter 6 examines the considerations and nuances involved in developing a workable BPO contract, including service level agreements, penalties, rewards, and remedies.

Part Four is the largest of the five parts, discussing the various aspects of effectively managing an operating BPO project. Chapter 7 deals with the transition phase, where the outsourced process is formally migrated to the vendor. Chapter 8 provides tips and insights into effectively managing the buyer–vendor relationship on an ongoing basis. Chapter 9 examines the organizational infrastructure issues that arise during the transition and operating phases of the BPO project. Chapter 10 explores the various business risks inherent to a BPO project and suggests mitigation strategies.

Finally, Part Five briefly explores the future of BPO and the likely implications it will have on business, economics, workers, and education. Chapter 11 provides extrapolations and educated guesses about how BPO is likely to unfold in the coming years.

Each chapter is populated with inserts that provide additional insights into the BPO revolution. Inserts include case studies, ethics and governance, and executive viewpoints.

As this book is going to press, outsourcing has become an important new force in the global economy. It is our hope that the prescriptions, guidelines, concepts, and tools provided in this book will be useful to managers in organizations of all sizes as they struggle to determine their best opportunities for outsourcing. With the rapid evolution of outsourcing techniques and methodologies, we are certain that this book only makes a dent in the growing understanding of the BPO revolution. At the same time, there are timeless change management lessons in this book that apply to outsourcing and global, interorganizational business relationships. We hope that readers will enjoy this book and that it provides managers with insights and concepts to make informed decisions and choices.

The BPO revolution is upon us, and we are hopeful that the global economy will become more tightly integrated and interdependent as a result. We cannot expect that all will be made well as a result of a more tightly integrated and more prosperous global economy, but it might make things a little better than they are today. Who could ask for more?

RICK CLICK
TOM DUENING

June 2004

acknowledgments

This book has been an incredibly stimulating challenge and has introduced us to many fascinating people on several continents. Any book ultimately is the result of input and feedback from a wide range of people, and this one is no exception. We thank everyone who contributed his or her time and efforts to this project. Especially notable has been the contributions of the executives and outsourcing professionals that we consulted time and again to understand more deeply the nuances of an effective project. We also want to acknowledge Mr. David Piper of the law firm Boyer & Ketchand for his contributions to Chapter 6; Mr. Lalit Ahuja of Suntech Data Systems for his assistance on Chapter 8; and Mr. Matt Castleman for his exceptional work on the graphics and exhibits in this book. Our Wiley editor, Mr. Sheck Cho, is to be commended for his vision in signing this project before outsourcing became a household word. Of course, we take full responsibility for any errors that remain in this book.

Foremost among those we feel compelled to acknowledge are the members of our families. This project consumed many hours over the course of the past year and meant that vacations, weekends, and family dinners were placed on hold as the relentless pressure of deadlines kept us at our writing tasks. Amy Click and Charlene Duening, our wives, were, as usual, our strongest supporters along the way, and we could not have written this book without them.

one

BPO Overview

Part One of this book provides readers with an overview of business process outsourcing (BPO). BPO has been both hailed and vilified during the 2004 presidential campaign, and it is likely to be a topic of controversy for some time. This book takes a neutral political stance on BPO but assumes that it will survive in some form regardless of which party dominates U.S. politics in the coming years.

Chapter 1 consists of an analysis of the primary drivers of BPO and the various types of BPO that are being practiced today. The chapter includes some of the latest projections of the size of the outsourcing industry and the number of jobs that are likely to be affected. It also points out that BPO is a socio-technical phenomenon that impacts both technical and social systems of the organization.

Chapter 2 provides examples of successful and unsuccessful outsourcing projects implemented by a wide variety of firms. The brief case studies examine decision-making processes, BPO implementation challenges and tactics, and outcomes. The case studies are derived from the popular business literature or from actual experiences and provide a broad look at how companies are using innovative approaches to BPO to reduce costs and to improve their strategic advantages.

What Is So Revolutionary about BPO?

We ought not be over anxious to encourage innovation, in case of doubtful improvement, for an old system must ever have two advantages over a new one; it is established and it is understood.

—C.C. Colton, British author

The Internet bubble bursts, and the world keeps on turning. Terrorists attack the World Trade Center, and the world keeps on turning. The global economy reels in the throes of a major recession, and the world keeps on turning. Despite their unpredictable—and sometimes despicable—natures, humans are nothing if not innovators and perpetual optimists. In the face of doubt, ambiguity, and even terror they continue to strive to build a better world. We are fortunate to be so resilient.

And so, as our hopes for an easy peace and "new economy" prosperity in the twenty-first century were dashed within months of its arrival, humans have continued to strive to create a better world. Part of that striving is based on the technological breakthroughs that seemed to arrive breathtakingly fast during the 1990s. Standing on the shoulders of those innovators, a new generation of visionaries has created compelling new business opportunities. Among the vast array of novelties introduced in the past few years, none is more important than the creation of the global communications and information infrastructure that has now burrowed into nearly every city, village, hamlet, and encampment around the world. Fiber-optic cable spans oceans and continents. Low-earth-orbit satellites provide streaming images, data, and voice to the most remote locations. Tragedy and joy each mark the onset of this communications revolution. A doomed climber places a phone call from the top of Mount Everest to say goodbye to loved ones as he succumbs to the elements in that unpredictable environment.[1] A Russian astronaut staffing the orbiting international space station is joined in marriage to a terrestrial-based bride.[2] No place on earth, or in near-earth, is now beyond the reach of the information and data nervous system that was constructed over the past few decades. This *is* revolutionary, and this nearly universal telecommunications infrastructure is a major part of what gives life to the business innovation called *business process outsourcing*.

Business process outsourcing (BPO) is defined simply as the movement of business processes from inside the organization to external service providers. With the global telecommunications infrastructure now well-established and consistently reliable, BPO initiatives often include shifting work to international providers. Five BPO international hot spots have emerged around the globe, although firms from many other countries are specializing in various business processes and exporting services:

1. *India*. Engineering and Technical
2. *China*. Manufacturing and Technical
3. *Mexico*. Manufacturing
4. *United States*. Analysis and Creative
5. *Philippines*. Administrative

Each of these countries has complex economies that span the range of business activity, but from a BPO perspective they have comparative advantages in the specific functions cited.

Because of the job shift that accompanies the quest to employ the highest-value talent, BPO has been both hailed and vilified from different quarters. Business executives and owners hail BPO as a means of eliminating business processes that are not part of the core competence of their organizations. Back-office functions such as payroll and benefits administration, customer service, call center, and technical support are just a few of the processes that organizations of all sizes have been able to outsource to others who specialize in those areas. Removing back-office functions from their internal operations enables organizations to reduce payroll and other overhead costs. In an era when executives have been admonished from a wide range of business commentators and analysts to focus on core competence, BPO offers them an opportunity to finally achieve that goal in a dramatic new way.

Like appliance manufacturers that moved production from the Midwest to Mexican *maquiladoras* or apparel firms that moved production to the Far East, businesses of all types and sizes are now shifting back-office jobs to international locations such as China, India, and the Philippines where the labor is inexpensive and highly skilled. In the past several years, companies have turned to these regions for increasingly sophisticated tasks: financial analysis, software design, tax preparation, and even the creation of content-rich products such as newsletters, PowerPoint presentations, and sales kits.[3]

With the increasing education levels around the world, BPO is no longer confined to routine manufacturing jobs or boiler-room telemarketing centers. Today's outsourcing involves complex work that requires extensive preparation and training. For example, Indian radiologists now analyze computed tomography (CT) scans and chest X-rays for American patients out of an office park in Bangalore. In the United States, radiologists are among the highest-paid medical specialists, often earning more than $300,000 per year to evaluate magnetic resonance imaging (MRI), CT scans, and X-rays. In Bangalore, radiologists work for less than half that. Not far from the radiology lab in Bangalore, Ernst & Young has 200 accountants processing U.S. tax returns. Starting pay for an American accountant ranges from $40,000 to $50,000, whereas in Bangalore accountants are paid less than half that amount.[4]

In the next 15 years, Forrester Research predicts that 3.3 million service jobs will move to countries such as India, Russia, China, and the Philippines. That is the equivalent of 7.5 percent of all jobs in the United States right now.[5] Exhibit 1.1 shows that the number of back-office jobs being outsourced will escalate rapidly in the coming years. The 2015 bar includes a breakdown of the projected numbers of jobs going overseas in common work categories.

The Gartner Group, a Stamford, Connecticut–based research firm, estimates that 85 percent of U.S. companies will outsource their human resources (HR) functions in the near future and that revenue from these transactions will exceed $45 billion in 2003.[6] Gartner also estimates that one in ten jobs

EXHIBIT 1.1   Jobs Expected to Shift Overseas

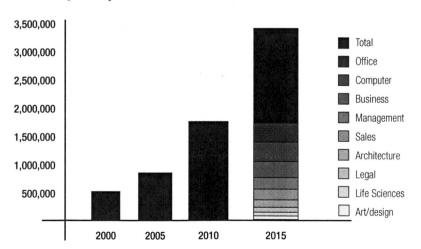

at specialty information technology (IT) firms in the United States will move abroad by 2005, along with one in twenty IT jobs at general businesses—a loss of about 560,000 positions. Gartner also predicts that BPO will reach $178 billion in revenues worldwide by 2005, representing a compound annual growth rate of 9.2 percent for the five-year forecast period.[7] Market research firm IDC predicts that finance and accounting outsourcing will grow to nearly $65 billion by 2006, up from $36 billion in 2001. Two-thirds of U.S. banks already outsource one or more functions.[8]

BPO has caught on as well with the venture capital community. In 2002, venture capital firms in North America poured nearly $3 billion into BPO firms and another almost $1 billion by June 2003. Some BPO providers currently enjoy operating profit margins as high as 40 to 50 percent. Even though margins are expected to level out to between 20 and 25 percent as the market matures, these returns are greater than are currently being experienced in nearly any other industry.[9]

Despite this increasing global adoption and capital inflow, BPO is not without its critics and naysayers. There is no doubt that the history of outsourcing in manufacturing has been black-marked by the many American workers who lost their jobs and cannot find new ones in the traditional manufacturing sector. Today, everything from electronics to home furnishings is being manufactured by low-cost labor in places such as Shanghai and Monterrey. American workers were told that free-trade agreements such as the North American Free Trade Agreement (NAFTA) would create a "giant sucking sound" as jobs moved to low-wage labor environments. That prediction has rung true for many U.S. workers. Factories across the country, including steel mills, paper mills, and other staple industries of America's industrial past, have gone silent—apparently for good. Families and towns have been broken apart, as workers have had to pack up and seek alternative work far from home. The Ethics and Governance insert addresses the issue of how outsourcing relates to the U.S. unemployment rate.

No doubt, such wrenching change at the level of individual human lives is painful and unsettling. At the same time, the resilience of the American worker to find new ways to create value in a global economy shows few limits. As the nineteenth century's Agrarian Age came to an end and workers moved from farms to factories, they adapted and built some of the greatest cities in the world. At the end of the twentieth century, the Industrial Age gave way to the Information Age, and workers were moving out of factory jobs into information-rich occupations and built some of the greatest technologies in the world.

Today we are faced with adapting yet again to a world that is only partly of our creation. There is no question that we funded and built the enabling technologies that make the BPO revolution possible, but we did not necessarily do so intentionally. As C.C. Colton asserts in the quotation at the begin-

ETHICS AND GOVERNANCE

BPO Increases U.S. Unemployment Rate?

The Labor Department, in its numerous surveys of employers and employees, has never tried to calculate the number of jobs that are shifted overseas as a result of BPO. But the offshoring of work has become so noticeable that experts in the private sector are trying to quantify it. Initial estimates are that at least 15 percent of the 2.81 million jobs lost in America since the recession began have reappeared overseas. Productivity improvements at home account for the great bulk of the job loss. But the estimates suggest that work sent offshore has raised the U.S. unemployment rate by four-tenths of a percentage point or more.

Among economists and researchers, one high-end job-loss estimate comes from Mark Zandi, chief economist at Economy.com, who calculates that 995,000 jobs have been lost overseas since the recession began in March 2001. That is 35 percent of the total decline in employment since then. Most of the loss is in manufacturing, but about 15 percent is among college-trained professionals.

Source: Adapted from Louis Uchitelle, "A Missing Statistic: U.S. Jobs that Went Overseas," *New York Times* (October 5, 2003).

ning of this chapter, be careful to encourage innovation because we do not really know where it will lead. Colton and many others would be distressed at the prospect of BPO. We, however, are hopeful that BPO will help create a more tightly integrated business world that will lead to a more tightly integrated cultural and economic world. BPO has the potential to create new prosperity for workers everywhere through participation in a BPO-based business super-culture that spans the globe. This book is designed to help you determine how BPO can work for your organization and to help you transition to BPO in a manner that considers the human implications of its adoption.

BPO: A SOCIO-TECHNICAL INNOVATION

A lot of executives and managers shy away from BPO because they wrongly believe it to be a technical innovation—one better left for the chief information officer (CIO) or other technology administrators. In part, this belief results from the IT origins of BPO. Many of the early adopters of outsourcing were those who needed software development expertise or who sought technical expertise to staff help desks and call centers. During the 1990s, the labor pool for such talent in the United States was very tight, prompting many leading companies to search abroad for the personnel they needed. These organizations turned to international labor markets, where they were able to identify and hire highly skilled technical workers who were far cheaper than their U.S.-based counterparts. Today, the talent shortage in the United States has abated, but the cost savings to be gained by using outsourced talent remains.

BPO has evolved far from these IT-specific roots and now encompasses nearly every business process. To be sure, the implementation of a BPO initiative will always involve a technology component, but for that matter so does implementation of an accounting system at the local beer distributor. The point is, nearly every modern business innovation comprises both a technical and a social component. Workplace teams use collaboration tools such as groupware or instant messaging to converse and work on projects; HR administrators train employees through e-learning systems; and executives monitor the entire organization using online balanced scorecards. Decision making, strategy setting, service delivery, and nearly every other business activity is now socio-technical in nature, involving humans interfacing with technical systems. BPO is like that.

Fundamentally, then, BPO is a socio-technical business innovation that provides a rich new source of competitive advantage. By socio-technical we mean that BPO requires skillful management of people and technology (hardware and software). The manager who initiates a BPO strategy must find effective ways to introduce people to technology and vice versa. If left solely in the hands of technical specialists, a BPO initiative is likely to fail for lack of paying attention to the soft issues of human relationships, change management, and organizational culture. If left solely in the hands of nontechnical managers, a BPO initiative is likely to fail for unrealistic expectations about the potential and limitations of the enabling technologies.

BPO is one of those interdisciplinary workplace innovations that require a diverse set of skills in order to be successful. The initiation and implementation of a BPO project in an organization requires focused attention on several human factors, both within the organization initiating the project and within the outsourcing vendor. These human/social factors cannot be ignored and must be handled correctly in order for the project to succeed. Human factors include the following:

- Developing various teams to manage the BPO initiative throughout its life cycle
- Reassuring staff of their role in the company
- Training people on the new way of doing business

■ Dealing with job loss and/or reassignment
■ Keeping morale high throughout the change process
■ Encouraging people to participate in decision making
■ Understanding cultural differences between the organization and BPO partner

The initiation and implementation of a BPO project also require attention to technology issues. Among these are the following:

■ Compatibility of systems between the BPO buyer and vendor
■ Data and system security
■ Backup and recovery procedures in the case of system failure
■ Data interface challenges and strategies
■ Software and database compatibility challenges
■ Data and knowledge management

These various issues are discussed in detail throughout the book. Next, let us examine the major driving factors of the BPO revolution.

DRIVING FACTORS

Scholars who study how complex systems change over time are familiar with two types of change: evolutionary and emergent. Evolutionary changes are those that a system is likely to produce based on its current design and goals. For example, living systems develop sensory equipment to help them react to what is going on in their environment. Because the goal of such systems is to live and procreate, it would be reasonable for us to predict that they would evolve sensory apparatus over time. It is not surprising that creatures that live in a lighted world develop eyes and that creatures that live in darkened worlds do not.

Occasionally, however, complex systems develop structures that are not predictable from their goals and current state. These phenomena are referred to as *emergent*. They are system features or capabilities that would not have been predicted in advance based on the understood design and goals of the system. They are usually the result of a series of parallel evolutionary changes that, when taken together, produce surprising or unexpected results. Consciousness in humans is often highlighted as an emergent phenomenon of increasingly complex and integrated brain systems, rather than as something that is a natural result of our evolutionary past.[10]

We contend that BPO is revolutionary because it is such an emergent phenomenon. It is emergent because, as far as we can tell, no one set out to design the potential for organizations to use BPO. BPO is emerging from a set of driving factors that have unintentionally converged in this particular time to enable the shifting of work to its lowest-cost/highest-quality provider regardless of the provider's physical location. BPO is a business innovation that leverages these driving factors and applies them to practical business problems. The main drivers at the heart of the BPO revolution are illustrated in Exhibit 1.2.

Each of these drivers is discussed in detail in the following sections.

Educational Attainment

The United States still dominates the world in the quality of its higher education, but the rest of the world is catching up quickly. As more and more Ph.D.-qualified faculty return to their home countries with their degrees from Harvard, MIT, Stanford, and other prestigious schools, they are helping to transform higher education worldwide. At the K–12 level, it has long been noted that the United States lags behind other countries, especially in technical areas such as math and science as measured by standardized test scores. The gap between the United States and many foreign nations has increased

EXHIBIT 1.2   BPO Drivers

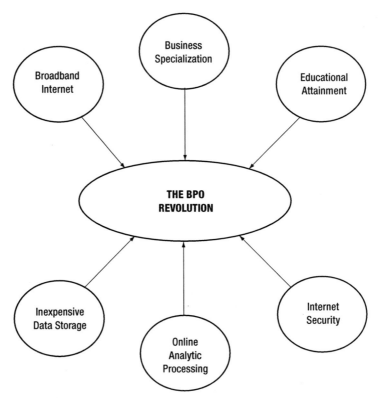

over time in technical education, which has now also translated into fewer U.S. students seeking college degrees in technical fields. Exhibit 1.3 compares the relative numbers of U.S. and Asian students pursuing science and engineering disciplines at the collegiate level. As illustrated in the exhibit, Asian students are increasing their engineering expertise in a world that increasingly appreciates and utilizes their new abilities.

Of the nearly 590,000 foreign students enrolled in U.S. higher education in 2002, more than 20 percent came from India or China. Ironically, the United States is not only relocating its coveted technical jobs to these foreign locations, but it is also preparing many of the workers who fill those jobs. The following list provides some sobering statistics on technical education

EXHIBIT 1.3 Comparison of Asian and U.S. Technical Education

Bachelor's S&E Degrees in the United States and Selected Asian Countries and Economies by Field (1975–1988)

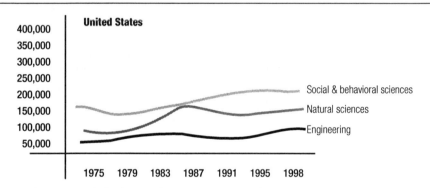

Natural sciences include physics, chemistry, astronomy, biology, earth, atmospheric, ocean, agricultural, as well as mathematics and computer science.

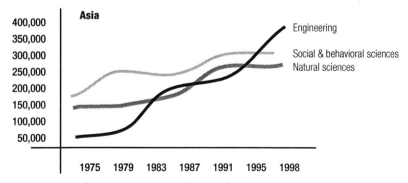

Asian countries and economies include: China, India, Japan, South Korea, and Taiwan. Data for China is included after 1983.

Source: Science and Engineering Indicators—2002.

worldwide that indicates why so many U.S. firms are looking abroad for the talent they need to compete in today's marketplace:

- In 2001, 46 percent of Chinese students graduated with engineering degrees. In the United States, that number was 5 percent.
- Europe graduates three times as many engineering students as the United States and Asia five times as many.
- In 2003, less than 2 percent of U.S. high school graduates went on to pursue an engineering degree.
- In 2001, almost 60 percent of those receiving Ph.D.s in electrical engineering in the United States were foreign-born.
- Among the more than 1.1 million seniors in the class of 2002 who took the ACT college entrance exam, fewer than 6 percent planned to study engineering, down from 9 percent in 1992.
- Less than 15 percent of U.S. students have the math and science prerequisites to participate in the new global high-tech economy.
- In the United States, more students are getting degrees in parks and recreation management than in electrical engineering.[11]

It now makes sense for U.S. firms to rely on foreign providers of highly skilled labor. The logic is simple: The quality of talent is high and the cost is low. Educational attainment around the world will drive BPO innovators to seek new ways to tap that talent for business purposes. There is no way to put that genie back into the bottle. It would be foolhardy to the point of malfeasance for managers not to seek and use the best available talent that fits the organization's budget—wherever that talent may reside.

Broadband Internet

In fall 2003, the *Wall Street Journal* published its annual report on telecommunications. In the front page article, the journal writer stated, "After years of hype and false starts we can finally declare it: The Age of Broadband is here."[12] The article reports that by the end of 2003, 21 percent of all U.S. households will have broadband Internet and about 50 percent by 2008. It is also expected that more than 7 million businesses will have broadband connectivity in the United States by the end of 2003.

Broadband refers to the growing pipeline capacity of the Internet, allowing larger chunks of information to flow with fewer congestion issues. *Broadband* is the term used to refer to Internet connectivity speeds that are in the range of 2 megabits/second (2 million bits/second). Leading semiconductor maker Intel has predicted that by 2010 there will be 1.5 billion computers with broadband connections.[13] High-speed Internet access is becoming commonplace in regions where dial-up was once the only option. With broadband, workers in different countries can share data, while consumers can surf the Web for the latest bargains.[14]

Growth in broadband connectivity is largest in regions where deployment is still scattered—Latin America (up 63 percent to 619,000), South and Southeast Asia (up 124 percent to 1.12 million), and the Middle East and Africa (up 123 percent to 107,000). The Asia-Pacific region is the runaway regional leader, with nearly 11 million digital subscriber line (DSL) users, followed by North America with 6.5 million and Western Europe with 6.3 million. Eastern Europe has the lowest level of broadband connectivity, with barely 70,000 DSL users. In relatively mature markets, the percentage of DSL subscribers who use the service at home is much larger than in new markets and smaller economies, where businesses account for a larger percentage. In North America 22.6 percent of users are businesses, and the figure for Western Europe is 16.5 percent.[15] Hong Kong tops the world in broadband connectivity with more than 66 percent of Internet users opting for the high-speed connection.[16] Exhibit 1.4 highlights broadband/DSL leaders around the world.

Broadband penetration around the world is driven by the creative and business behaviors of users. Research from the Pew Internet & American Life Project, the results of which are illustrated in Exhibit 1.5, found a correlation between specific online behaviors and demand for high-speed access. Pew found that broadband users are extraordinarily active information gatherers, multimedia users, and content creators. Internet users with six or more years online who engage in similar activities are most likely to switch to high-speed access. In fact, Pew found that of those dial-up users who are

EXHIBIT 1.4 World Leaders in DSL Broadband

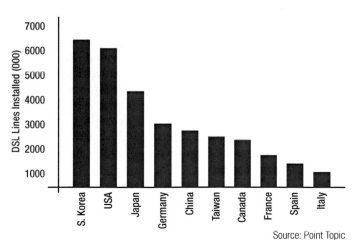

Source: Point Topic

EXHIBIT 1.5   Online Behaviors and Demand for High-Speed Internet

	Broadband Users	Experienced Dial-up Users	Dial-up Users
News	41%	35%	23%
Research for Work	30%	30%	15%
Participation in Group	12%	11%	4%
Content Creation	11%	9%	3%
Stream Multimedia	21%	13%	7%
Download Music	13%	3%	3%

Source: Pew Internet and American Life Project.

contemplating broadband, 43 percent logged six or more years online, compared to 30 percent of those online for three years or less. Greater disparities in these behaviors are seen between less experienced dial-up users and those with broadband connections.[17]

Although Western Europe currently lags behind North America, by 2005 the European market will match North America for size. Undeveloped telecommunications infrastructure and economic volatility continues to hamper broadband growth in Latin America.[18]

Abundant Data Storage

Data storage has always been a critical resource for business. In the days of paper-based record keeping, data storage was primarily accomplished via file cabinets, closets, and dingy overstuffed basements. The computerization of the workplace gradually replaced paper-based filing systems at first with punch cards and later with magnetic tapes and then disk-based storage. As the integration of the Internet and its related technologies into business processes and functions has progressed, data storage has gone from being a problem to one of oversupply. Firms that had envisioned growing rich by supplying online data storage on an as-needed basis have discovered that storage has become a commodity—it is nearly as limitless as the Internet. Advances in data storage, including sophisticated data retrieval, have driven down storage costs dramatically. Rare is the individual today who walks about with a floppy disk in his or her shirt pocket. Rather, most have learned to transfer files into a virtually limitless cyberspace storage room, where they can be retrieved whenever and wherever needed.

The elimination of the barriers to data storage has enabled new ways of thinking about what is possible in the structure and procedures of the workplace. In times when storage was scarce, difficult decisions had to be made about what data to collect, keep, and eliminate. Even more limiting, in times when storage was scarce, decisions had to be made about who had access to critical information and when.

In an era of storage overcapacity, an embarrassment of riches awaits savvy executives if they can move beyond the scarcity mindset. Data protection and access controls must continue to play a role in a storage-rich environment, but they play a different role. In the storage-poor past, data access was controlled in part because storage limitations affected the number of copies of data that could be made. That barrier has been lifted by digitized document storage that allows literally infinite distribution of key documents, forms, and plans. In the past, gatekeepers, whose approval was needed to acquire and use company information, managed data access. That barrier has been lifted by precision software-based systems that enable rapid access to very specific data sets based on prearranged approval levels. These systems are constantly being upgraded to be more user friendly and can adapt quickly to unique work processes and systems.

One danger of shifting work to a third party is the potential loss of organizational learning. When a process is executed internally, the organization's employees handle the related transactions and, over time, are able to discern and adapt to specific patterns or trends. Some of these patterns concern customer or competitor behaviors. When these transactions are no longer executed internally, there is potential for this vital learning to be lost. With nearly infinite data storage, however, each transaction that occurs remotely can be stored for independent analysis. As we discuss below, sophisticated analytical software can then be used to mine the transactional data to reveal customer or competitor patterns—preserving and even enhancing organizational learning.

Analytic Software

Software is a major source of business competitiveness, as well as a major source of headaches for anyone who has ever booted a computer. Originally invented as a tool for us to work *with*, software has increasingly been designed to perform work *for* us. Expert systems, decision support systems, and artificial intelligence all are software tools that perform analytic tasks. Business analysis tasks were formerly the domain of human logicians, administrators, and executive decision makers. The advent of analytic software capable of re-creating and possibly improving on human decision making has revolutionized the power of the desktop computer. Where the ideal of the Industrial Age was to eliminate the need for human thinking through mechanical design, the ideal of the Information Age seems to be to improve on human thinking through software design.

Online analytic processing (OLAP) has created a wide range of new possibilities in workplace structure, including effects on hiring practices, organizational design, and productivity. Although OLAP has enabled some human resources to be eliminated, it has also placed a premium on individuals who can use the sophisticated output and create new value with it.

Software that provides human-like data output has opened the door to the possibility for data and information to seek lower-cost labor in the same way that manufacturing has done. Computational systems that have replaced human analysts range from trend analysis in sales and marketing to workflow optimization on the shop floor.

Before the advent of sophisticated OLAP software, it was necessary for highly educated people to analyze a firm's data and information to make it useful. In general, the more highly educated the labor, the more costly it is. As software takes the place of humans in an ever-widening array of business analysis functions, the roles left to people are increasingly confined to implementation tasks. The training required to implement the results of processed data is usually less extensive than that required to analyze it in the first place. Reliable data analysis software can eliminate high-cost analyst labor and replace it with relatively lower-cost implementation labor. For many business processes, the outcomes of processed data are predictable within a range. Business rules can be developed to specify the actions required within a range of possible outputs. In the case of an outlier, it is simple enough for the data implementation specialist simply to escalate the output to a few management-level analysts for additional processing.

Analysts traditionally have been the white-collar middle managers who have served as the glue, gatekeepers, and information stewards in organizations of all sizes. The transition of analyst jobs from inside the organization to outsourcing partners will displace many of these middle-level roles in organizations. In fact, as the development of analytic software continues, it is likely that the swath of job shift in middle management will grow wider and reach ever-higher levels of the organization chart.

Internet Security

Internet security refers to the ability to send information and data (including voice) over the Internet without fear of leakage, espionage, or outright loss. It is critical for companies to be certain that their data integrity will be maintained despite its movement around the globe in the servers, routers, and computers that make up the World Wide Web.

In the past, many executives were reluctant to conduct any back-office business transactions over the Internet or beyond their own four walls because they felt the security risks outweighed the value proposition. However, in today's world of ever-changing technology advancements, most executives are more computer savvy and better understand the security protocols now available. With these new technical breakthroughs, companies can now work within virtual walls with the same level of security they enjoyed within physical walls.

One of the most significant enablers of this new virtual workspace is the use of Kerberos technology, developed at the Massachusetts Institute of Technology (MIT) as a cryptographic environment. This technology allows computer systems to use digital certificates for authentication within their transactions. Kerberos is just one piece of a much larger security framework that is now in place. Security systems today include proxy servers, passwords, authentication, firewalls, encryption layering, certificates, virtual private networks, open systems interconnection, and extranets. With these security advances, two companies can partner and safely share resources in the virtual world.

In addition to the security innovations at the technical level, there have been significant changes at the policy and regulatory levels. Most organizations have enacted internal policies to protect sensitive data and information, including institution of security access to physical facilities and requirements for employees to wear identification badges. At the regulatory level, national governments have instituted laws regarding data security. For example, the Indian IT Act of 2000 addresses privacy-related issues and attempts to define *hacking* and *computer evidence*. It also strongly prescribes the implementation of digital signatures and Public Key Infrastructure (PKI) for facilitating secure transactions. The Data Protection laws enacted by the United Kingdom and the European Union (EU) are considered to be benchmarks in international privacy laws.

In addition to federal legislation, several international certifications and standards mitigate security risks. Most BPO providers adhere to one or more of these standards and have received the appropriate certifications. Several global and national compliance benchmarks include the following:

- **BS 7799.** First published in February 1995, BS 7799 is a comprehensive set of controls comprising best practices in information security. BS 7799 is intended to serve as a single reference point for identifying a range of controls needed for most situations where information systems are used in industry and commerce, and to be used by large, medium, and small organizations. It was significantly revised and improved in May 1999 and a year or so later published by the International Organization for Standardization (ISO).
- **ISO 17799.** ISO 17799 is an internationally recognized information security management standard. The ISO first published it in December 2000.
- **HIPAA.** The Health Insurance Portability and Accountability Act (HIPAA) of 1996 establishes standards for the secure electronic exchange of health data. Health care providers and insurers who elect to transmit data electronically must comply with HIPAA security standards.

Even with these security standards, organizations should be aware of security best practices and ensure that the BPO vendor they choose has the capability and processes in place to meet and exceed security needs.

The new laws governing data protection, organizational policies, and new technologies have converged to create a highly secure—although still imperfect—communications infrastructure. Although hack-proof systems have yet to be constructed, the ever-more-complex barriers erected to prevent cyber-espionage and cyber-crime make them increasingly less attractive projects for weekend hackers and an expensive undertaking for anyone else.

Business Specialization

Since the days of Adam Smith, capitalist economists have touted the benefits of specialization as a key to productive exchange among economic agents. The famous example of the pin factory used by Smith has stood the test of time. His eloquent analysis of division of labor in the production of pins and the vastly greater output that would occur if people each specialized in a part of the process can be applied to nearly any product or service.[19] As it turns out, in a world where business-to-business (B2B) services have become as common a part of the economy as business-to-consumer (B2C) products and services, the basic economic agent can as readily be construed to be a business firm as it could be a person.

Business specialization has been urged for several decades. Former General Electric CEO Jack Welch, for example, famously stated that GE must be number one or two in the world in a given business or it should get out of that business. In their popular book *Competing for the Future*, Pralahad and Hamel called on businesses to focus on their "core competency." They urged companies to develop a "portfolio" of core competencies around the customers they serve.[20]

The idea of focusing on core competence, if pursued logically, leads to the idea that a business organization should operate as few non–revenue-producing units as possible. In the early days of a business, when the firm is small and everyone pitches in to do whatever is necessary for the business to succeed, it is easy to call everything core. However, as a business grows, and as administration and overhead grows with it, there are many things a business does that are expensive but not directly involved in revenue generation. Accounting, legal counsel, payroll administration, human resources, and other processes are all necessary for the business to operate but not tied directly to the top line of the income statement. If a business truly focused only on its core competence, it would not operate those units that are not tied directly to meeting customer needs and generating revenue.

This mind shift could easily be overlooked as a driving factor of the BPO revolution, but it is crucial. Transformational organizational changes—

paradigm shifts, if you will—often cannot occur until a sufficient number of managers and executives have changed their thinking about the form and function of their organization. Such mind shifts can occur through education and experience, but they are far more likely to be a result of competitive pressures.

As B2B operations have flourished, the potential for firms to shed more and more of their noncore activities has accelerated. For example, it is estimated that 2 to 3 million Americans are currently co-employed in a professional employment organization (PEO) arrangement. PEOs are operating in every state, and the industry continues to grow at an average of 20 percent each year. Today, it is estimated that approximately 800 PEO companies are responsible for generating more than $43 billion in gross revenues.[21] Many firms today have simply eliminated their personnel function by outsourcing their employees to a PEO.

The potential for B2B firms to exist and to provide the specific services they do is based entirely on their ability to add value to their clients' businesses. If these firms were not able to provide high-quality, lower-cost services, they would not exist. At the same time, they would not be in business without the relatively new concept of core competence driving management thinking and behavior. Just as quality and customer service seem to be patently correct ways to organize a business today, they have not always been important factors to business managers. Ford was an early adopter of quality management in the United States, but only because Japanese automakers had begun to erode Ford's domestic market share. Until then, American automakers and manufacturers in general did not pay attention to quality as a major factor in their production processes. Likewise, the idea of focusing on core competencies—really focusing—did not seem important and strategic until some organizations demonstrated that they actually were able to perform better by outsourcing their internal processes. Early BPO adopters among Fortune 100 companies include British Petroleum, IBM, American Express, AT&T, and General Electric. These pioneers were able to risk outsourcing noncore processes. In many cases they succeeded, and sometimes they failed. But the trail had been blazed by these pioneers, and the lessons they learned along the way now ensure a higher probability of success for those firms that follow the leaders.

Management behavior on a large scale resembles crowd behavior in a stadium full of people at a major sporting event. An innovator in the crowd decides to start the wave. Rising up out of his seat with arms outstretched, he implores those around him to join in. Some are reluctant, but others decide to join in. The wave spreads from section to section, each re-enacting the first instance with some early adopters and some reluctant doubters. The wave picks up steam after a few passes around the stadium until most people have decided to give up fighting its inevitability. As the BPO wave goes around several times, more companies will recognize its inevitability and join in. It will become less remarkable as it becomes the norm. And then the day will come when we wonder how we got along without it.

BPO TYPES

Business process outsourcing has usually been discussed in terms of the international relocation of jobs and workplace functions. In reality, there are three types of BPO: offshore, onshore, and nearshore. Exhibit 1.6 illustrates how these types are differentiated.

Organizations are prone to use any or all of these types, depending on their needs and the BPO initiative being implemented. In some cases, firms use a combination of types to achieve their objectives. The following sections look at each BPO type in more detail.

Offshore

Offshore BPO is the most challenging type of this relatively new approach to conducting business but potentially the most rewarding. It began with movement of factory jobs to overseas locations and has been made both famous and infamous with stories of suddenly prosperous geographic regions mixed with stories of exploitative labor practices. The so-called sweatshops identified in Vietnam, India, China, and elsewhere have stirred criticism for American companies, including Nike, Wal-Mart, and Walt Disney Company. Despite the criticism leveled at some companies that outsource processes and functions to international labor markets, the advantages of doing so continue to

EXHIBIT 1.6   BPO Types

Type	Location	Functions
Offshore	India China The Philippines Russia	Manufacturing Programming Financial Analysis Call Center
Nearshore	Mexico Canada Central America Latin America	Manufacturing Call Center
Onshore	U.S.A.	HR Administration Call Center

outweigh the disadvantages. By taking advantage of lower wages overseas, U.S. managers can cut their overall costs by 25 to 40 percent while building a more secure, more focused workforce in the United States.[22]

The complexity of business functions being moved offshore continues to increase. As such, organizations using the offshore approach have developed a variety of different models to ensure continuity. Some have utilized a model known as *offshore insourcing*. Under this model, the organization establishes a wholly owned subsidiary in the international market and hires local labor. An extension of this model is the so-called build-operate-transfer (BOT) model. Organizations build offshore companies (usually with a local joint-venture partner) specializing in a business process, operate them jointly for a year or so, and then transfer the firm to internal control (insource).

It is important to note that there is no one-size-fits-all approach to offshore BPO. With the growing list of companies outsourcing at least some business functions to offshore vendors, the range of possible approaches will grow as well. This makes it increasingly likely that the next adopter of offshore BPO will find a model suitable to its needs. The Case Study describes how GE Capital and Microsoft have utilized outsourcing for value-added services at low costs.

CASE STUDY

Two Giants Take the Offshore BPO Lead

GE Capital's International Services unit, which provides everything from risk calculation to IT services and actuarial analysis for GE worldwide, has grown from 634 employees to 17,000 during the past five years. More than half of those workers are in India, and they are not being used for mindless data entry—in India every employee has a college degree, and more than 1,200 have Master's degrees in Business Administration (MBAs).

Microsoft has about 200 employees developing software in Bangalore, where it opened its first non–U.S.-based product development center five years ago. In July 2003, the company announced it will be shifting more currently U.S.-based jobs to India as it seeks to lower technical support and development costs. Microsoft will increase its staff in India in the coming years, as the country continues to turn out tens of thousands of English-speaking engineers each year.

Sources: Adapted from Reed Stevenson and Anshuman Daga, "Microsoft Shifting Development, Support to India," *Reuters News Service* (July 2, 2003); and Nelson D. Schwartz, "Down and Out in White Collar America," *Fortune* (June 23, 2003), p. 82.

Onshore

It would be a mistake to conceive of BPO only as an international business phenomenon. Many U.S. businesses are outsourcing back-office functions to firms based in America. One of the more prominent examples of this is payroll outsourcing, which is managed by several large U.S. companies. Automatic Data Processing (ADP) provides a range of payroll administration services, time sheets, and tax filing and reporting services. The firm has more than 40,000 employees and, as an indication perhaps of the future potential of the firm, has seen Warren Buffett steadily increasing his company's position in its stock.[23]

There are many reasons that a firm will use BPO. The cost savings that result from moving back-office processes to low-wage environments is the most oft-cited one. However, firms can also use BPO to transfer service functions to best-in-class performers to gain competitive advantage. A firm that outsources customer service functions to a firm that specializes in and provides world-class support in that area will perform at a higher level in that function than its competitors. Moving to a best-in-class provider may actually increase costs in the short run in the interest of developing competitive advantage. Under this rationale, BPO is a strategic investment that is designed to upgrade service levels at a cost, with the intent of increasing revenues through enhanced competitiveness. What matters most is the acquisition of partners that provide market-shifting capabilities for the firm doing the outsourcing.

Many U.S.-based outsourcing firms use the world-class provider strategy to acquire business. Staked to a head start over their low-cost international rivals, U.S.-based outsourcing firms must continuously innovate and seek new ways to provide value to remain in front. They are worth considering for services, even if their costs are higher, if strategic advantage is the goal of an organization's BPO initiative.

Nearshore

Nearshore outsourcing is a relatively new term that is used to refer to the practice of outsourcing on the North American continent. International issues will arise when American firms outsource to Mexico, Canada, or Central America, but they are likely to be less complex than those that attend outsourcing arrangements in, say, India or China. Nearshore outsourcing allows companies to test the BPO waters without the level of risk associated with going offshore. Firms that go with a nearshore strategy are often seeking cost savings, but they are also occasionally able to find best-in-class providers of the services they need.

For example, Mortgage Electronic Registration Systems, an organization created by the mortgage banking industry to develop systems for mortgage tracking, is moving its customer relationship management (CRM) function from Michigan to Nova Scotia. The move is expected to save the group 15 percent annually on CRM costs.[24] The firm could have saved even more by outsourcing with firms in India, but it wanted to keep its CRM operations closer to home.

TO BPO OR NOT TO BPO? A STRATEGIC QUESTION

BPO has managers around the world asking what it can do *for* them and what it might do *to* them. They are excited about the potential for BPO to help them manage costs and improve their balance sheets. Under constant pressure from analysts to control headcount, outsourcing back-office activities to contract laborers in remote corners of the world can provide welcome and quick relief. Whether the labor source is in India, Pakistan, China, or some other international port, the prevalence of high-speed Internet provides opportunities for real-time back-office support regardless of location.

At the same time as these new possibilities are opening up as a result of the BPO revolution, new questions are being asked and new challenges in organizational design and leadership are arising. Many organizational leaders remain skeptical about BPO because of the lingering aftereffects of the tech bubble burst. Their memories are still fresh with images of the "change the world" mentality of the tech bubble and its dismayingly rapid crash. The very thought of investing in new business models right now—especially those with a technology or Internet component—is very difficult for many managers and executives.

Many leaders are also concerned about the risks of BPO. They are unsure about the information security issues associated with outsourcing back-office processes. For example, in order for a BPO vendor to assist a client in managing employee benefits, the vendor must have access to some of the most sensitive and mission-critical information the organization possesses. The thought of shipping this data overseas to be managed and used by individuals who are not bound by the organization's formal and informal controls is enough to keep a manager awake at night.

BPO is based on the fundamental proposition that organizations should focus on what they do best and outsource everything else. If your company markets and sells sporting goods, it should spend substantially *all* of its time doing that and as little time as possible managing its accounting, customer service, and employee benefits plans. In theory, the concept makes a great deal of sense. In practice, it still seems to invite a new set of challenges that may cost more than the problems that are supposed to be solved.

It is critical to point out that BPO is not a technology or a technology system; it is a business strategy. In that regard, to BPO or not to BPO is a

EXECUTIVE VIEWPOINT SME's Board the BPO Express

Lalit Ahuja, CEO, Suntech Data Systems, Bangalore, India

From my perspective as a provider of BPO services to companies all over the world, the decision to use BPO is actually a decision to focus on core competence. There are only so many things that any company can do well. Whether their core focus is on price, cost, quality, or innovation, a firm can leverage BPO to dedicate resources more intensely on what it does best. Of course, initially firms chose BPO for cost savings. Today, they recognize that an outsourcing partner whose sole business is to service a specific business process can develop unique and highly competitive domain knowledge. Harnessing this knowledge has become an important source of competitive advantage for the BPO buyer.

Today, we are seeing a shift from primarily large companies using BPO to SME use of BPO as well. While the large firms develop exclusive relationships with providers, many SMEs use a shared-services model. This approach enables SMEs to realize many of the same BPO benefits as the larger organizations. BPO providers are meeting the marketing challenge by increasing their risk-management capabilities, and by placing agents in the buyers' markets using a dual-shore strategy. These agents not only educate and acquire SME customers, but they help them reengineer their business processes and manage the BPO transition.

question nearly anyone who manages a business process must now confront. As a strategic choice, the BPO option is a live one for anyone with a budget, limited resources, and decision rights over a business unit. In the Executive Viewpoint insert, Mr. Lalit Ahuja, CEO of outsourcing vendor Suntech Data Systems in Bangalore, India, notes the growing ranks of small- to medium-sized enterprises (SMEs) using BPO. For some managers, the decision may even involve the continued existence of their own departments and their jobs. No one is likely to decide to eliminate his or her own job, so managers must learn to understand how BPO may fit into their overall responsibilities and develop the skills to manage the BPO transition and maintain it once it is up and running.

Taking advantage of business process outsourcing will be a challenge for managers in all types of organizations and at all levels within those organizations. As we move into an age of greater accountability among organizational leaders, boards of directors, and others with fiduciary responsibility, it is imperative for those leaders to ask the question of whether the firm could perform better by adopting new business models like BPO. Furthermore, as firms within an industry adopt BPO, others will be forced to consider it as the traditional cost structure of their industry comes under pressure.

The competitive and regulatory pressures that will compel managers to take a serious look at their BPO options are only beginning to be felt in some industries, but the revolution is upon us, and its will is relentless. Competitive forces that drive each industry to seek the most effective cost-control measures are as irresistible as a river of water seeking its level. No earthen structure has yet been proven to be able to hold off a persistent river, and no management or organizational structure will be able to hold off the BPO revolution. This means that adoption of BPO in whatever industry you are in is virtually inevitable. Managers must prepare for the changes that are coming by understanding the factors that go into making a sound BPO decision.

In addition to the basic choice of whether to use BPO, a host of technological, business process, and HR issues follow in the wake of an affirmative decision. The technological issues will range over the type of electronic infrastructure that will be required to communicate effectively with BPO partners to the integration of new technologies with legacy systems throughout the organization. These difficult issues require the skillful assembly and management of a team of diversely talented individuals. Because BPO is fundamentally a strategic issue, managers cannot simply call upon their firm's CIO or systems administrators to decide how to achieve an outsourcing relationship. The web of relationships that make up successful BPO initiatives will be based on a range of managerial actions and skills that is unlikely to be present in any single manager or executive.

SUMMARY

- Business process outsourcing (BPO) is simply the movement of business processes to the highest-skill/lowest-cost provider.
- There are talent hot spots around the world, including India, China, Mexico, the Philippines, and the United States.
- Gartner Group estimates that 85 percent of U.S. companies will outsource their HR functions and that BPO will reach $178 billion in revenue by 2005.
- BPO is a socio-technical revolution in that it is both a social shifting of jobs and a technology-based method of doing so.
- BPO is an emergent phenomenon to the extent that it is a result of several driving factors, none of which was intended to create the potential for BPO.
- There are six primary driving factors of the BPO revolution: educational attainment, broadband, data storage, analytic software, Internet security, and business specialization.

- There are three types of BPO: offshore, onshore, and nearshore.
- To BPO or not to BPO is a strategic decision for organizations.
- A BPO initiative requires both technical and nontechnical managers in order to implement it properly.

CHAPTER 2

Who Is Using BPO and How?

Don't be afraid to take a big step when one is indicated. You can't cross a chasm in two small steps.

—David Lloyd George, British Politicain

The BPO revolution is evolving as we write, but many firms have already pioneered dramatic new ways of utilizing outsourcing to reduce costs, improve competitive position, and introduce new organizational strategies. The pioneers in outsourcing were predominantly the large, Global 2000 firms that were able to absorb the risks associated with doing business in radically new ways. Some of the early outsourcing efforts met with modest success and some with disruptive failure. Key lessons have been learned along the way, and new business models and ways of working together have resulted.

Today, much of the risk has been removed from basic BPO arrangements because of the knowledge gained by buyers and vendors alike. For example, executives in firms of all sizes today are familiar with employee leasing and HR outsourcing arrangements. Firms that offer these services no longer have to spend time in early sales calls educating potential clients about the nature of the services they provide. Buyers and vendors have co-adapted to one another, and maturity is evident in this niche of the outsourcing industry.

As discussed in Chapter 1, BPO is increasingly being recognized as a strategic as well as tactical initiative. The usual reasons cited for outsourcing a business process (e.g, cost reductions, shedding noncore functions) are being supplanted by strategic benefits in even the most mundane business processes. For example, Brooks Automation, Inc., a Chelmsford, Massachusetts, manufacturer of semiconductor production equipment, sells a lot of its products to foreign buyers. Normally, the company relies on letters of credit (LOC) for payment. Brooks spent a lot of company time correcting discrepancies that often occurred in its LOCs. To reduce the time it spent managing and tracking LOCs, Brooks decided to outsource the responsibility to ABN Amro Bank, a leader in trade finance, which now handles most of Brooks's LOC activities. Brooks reports that the relationship is successful, saving the firm time and expense. More important, this operational efficiency has become strategic, enabling Brooks to pursue both higher-risk deals and a greater volume of business. The risks to its cash flow have been mitigated by its outsourcing arrangement with ABN Amro.[1]

This chapter examines case studies of companies that have taken the outsourcing plunge. There are a wide variety of permutations to the outsourcing theme. Some of these themes have become fairly commonplace and have developed a large base of popular writing and discussion around them. Some of these more common themes are as follows:

- Onshore, offshore, and nearshore outsourcing
- HR outsourcing
- Call center and help desk outsourcing
- Payroll and benefits outsourcing

In this chapter we explore outsourcing themes that are less well documented but that might be helpful to organizations and managers that are new to BPO. The various outsourcing themes and cases detailed in the following sections are intended to be helpful to firms interested in testing the BPO waters for the first time or in a new way. We have also provided bookends to the cases by examining a successful offshore initiative and one that was not successful. The chapter concludes with reflections on what can be learned from these cases and how to use other cases as models for your organization. These brief case studies highlight firms that have outsourced one or more business processes based on the following themes:

- Successful offshore outsourcing
- Competence co-development outsourcing
- Variable-price outsourcing
- First-timer outsourcing
- Reverse outsourcing
- Business transformational outsourcing
- Unsuccessful offshore outsourcing

Each thematic area is introduced, and a brief case study highlights key points and lessons learned.

SUCCESSFUL OFFSHORE OUTSOURCING

The exploration of how companies are using BPO will begin with a story about a successful offshore initiative. The popular media is currently alive with discussion about offshore outsourcing and its impact on U.S. jobs. Although no opinion is offered in this chapter regarding the macroeconomic advantages or disadvantages of offshore BPO, we examine the practice from a business perspective. In this case, the offshore strategy employed by Metropolitan Life through a domestic outsourcing consultant has achieved its cost-reduction and quality objectives.

Metropolitan Life Insurance (MetLife) is the largest life insurer in the United States with approximately $2.1 trillion in life insurance policies, nearly 50,000 employees worldwide, and serving 10 million households as well as 88 of the Fortune 100 companies. Despite its size and financial wealth, MetLife had not invested in IT upgrades to its back-office processes as of the late 1990s. As late as 1999, most of its claims processing was paper-based and accomplished manually. Its workflow was redundant, and its call center operated at less than optimal levels. According to Carlos Creamer, vice president of strategic operations, an average claim took 10 days to process. MetLife decided to look into outsourcing to improve its product offerings and overall claims-processing performance.

In 1999, when Creamer interviewed outsourcing candidates, he learned that Affiliated Computer Services, Inc. (ACS) of Dallas, Texas, processes the claims of eight of the top ten health-care providers in the world—a total of 500 million claims per year. ACS processes claims anywhere from three to nine times faster, from 25 to 75 percent cheaper, and from 35 to 40 percent more accurately than MetLife's in-house operations. After interviewing other candidates, MetLife chose ACS because it stood apart from the competition in mail imaging and data capture and was among the leading bids in terms of pricing.

ACS now processes a MetLife claim online in a matter of seconds, not days. MetLife claims arrive at ACS's mailroom in Lexington, Kentucky, where they are opened and prepared for scanning. As an example of how having claims processing as a core competence leads to process innovation, consider that ACS sands the edges off the envelopes it receives instead of slicing them open. Slicing envelopes tends to cut up internal documents, which then have to be taped together again before scanning, adding another step to the workflow.

Once the staff scans the document, the image is almost simultaneously sent offshore for data capture via ACS's proprietary satellite network. ACS has disaster prevention practices in place, including never sending more than 50 percent of a client's work to one offshore location. MetLife preferred this system to other BPO providers who were limited to a single location or who had no backup or recovery mechanism.

ACS has offshore operations in Ghana, Mexico, Guatemala, and China. When claims arrive at these centers, a single operator keys in the data from the digitized image of the claim and another operator independently keys it in again. The system automatically compares the two versions to verify that there is no difference in the information.

The ACS method has saved MetLife time and money. MetLife did not have imaging technology in-house, so it could not process the claims online. With ACS's imaging system, scanning and image routing happens in seconds. Also, ACS's automated workflow is so precise that it drives significant time and cost out of the processing cycle. ACS also pays less for offshore labor and passes on the savings to MetLife. The ACS solution includes a productivity-based compensation model that pays workers on a piece-rate schedule.

To gauge the improvement in processing, MetLife benchmarked its dental claims processing. Before outsourcing, the company was processing less than 80 percent of dental claims in 10 days. Now it is well over 95 percent during the same period. As a result, Creamer said MetLife experienced "a significant improvement in customer satisfaction." What is more, he concluded, "our ROI [return on investment] is huge and we are very pleased."[2]

In this case, MetLife is working with an onshore firm to leverage low-cost offshore labor, reducing overall processing costs. MetLife does not have direct interaction with the offshore team. This distance between the BPO buyer and the offshore vendor can be useful because it relies on the onshore vendor to develop the cultural sensitivities and management techniques appropriate to the offshore labor pool. At the same time, additional costs are associated with engaging an onshore intermediary. The BPO buyer must assess whether these additional upfront costs are offset by the costs that would be associated with developing the necessary international management expertise. Later, we look at a case where the BPO buyer did interact directly with the offshore vendor in an outsourcing deal that did not work as planned.

COMPETENCE CO-DEVELOPMENT OUTSOURCING

Companies often outsource business processes that have no clear match with potential vendors. This scenario happens most often when the buyer is considering outsourcing a complex process, the boundaries of which are ambiguous or touch on the buyer's core competence. In such cases, the vendors who respond to the firm's request for proposals (RFP) may not have competence directly in the buying firm's area of need. For example, the responders may have competence in a peripheral business, but they respond to the RFP because they want to extend their portfolio of competencies.

When that occurs, the BPO buyer needs to look beyond the experience factor to make a reasonable judgment about the vendor's capability to develop the needed competence. This is a risky strategy and, as discussed in more detail in Chapter 5, should normally be avoided. However, on occasion a buyer and vendor may engage in a BPO competence co-development strategy, in which each firm has an interest in developing the vendor's expertise in the business process.

Sears faced such a challenge when, in the early 1990s, it was struggling with how to handle merchandise returns at more than 2,500 retail locations. With more than 10,000 vendors providing products to the retail giant, the local stores were overwhelmed with the logistics of managing returns. Sears sent out an RFP to seek a vendor that would provide it with an efficient product returns system.

Unfortunately for Sears, none of the firms responding to its RFP had direct experience in handling returned merchandise. However, one firm, Genco Distribution Systems, Inc., of Pittsburgh, Pennsylvania, had related experience. At the time, Genco's business competence was centered on transporting expired-date grocery items from retail store shelves and either disposing of them or distributing them to food banks. Sears and Genco agreed to enter into a competence co-development outsourcing project, working closely together over time to extend Genco's capacity in the process area needed by Sears. Actually, Sears considered several firms that had such related competencies. However, Sears decided to work with Genco because of the latter's interest in a co-development approach in which both sides assumed some risk.

The value of developing a deep partnering relationship between buyer and vendor in process competence co-development is apparent in the deal struck by Sears and Genco.[3] To develop the necessary competencies, Genco worked with Sears and its vendors from the outset. The two firms worked together to map process flows, gather data on each supplier's return preferences and requirements, and develop a solution that would be able to handle the large volume of returns.

Today, Genco's custom R-Log software tracks several variables associated with each returned item. Data tracked include which store the product came from, the proprietary Sears item number, the stock-keeping unit (SKU) number, and the price Sears paid for the item. The SKU number identifies other attributes as well, such as the name of the supplier.

At Sears, most returns go back to suppliers. However, other potential paths include online auctions, discounters, resale next year, recycle, donate, or destroy. Decisions about which path to follow are made at Genco-run return centers in Sacramento, California; Columbus, Ohio; or Atlanta, Georgia. Genco's R-Log compares data on incoming returns against a database that tells how to route the hundreds of thousands of products Sears sells, including clothing, appliances, electronics, tools, toys, car parts, and home decor. For example, apparel maker OshKosh B'Gosh wants all returned merchandise back and then gives Sears full credit for it. OshKosh does not allow Sears to sell its products to secondary markets. In contrast, private-label clothing made for Sears can often be sold overseas at a discount, with the label ripped out.

And products such as gardening supplies can be stored and resold the next year.[4]

With the operational infrastructure expanded to handle not only Sears but others of its franchises as well, Sears and Genco teamed up to find additional ways to leverage the systems they had developed together. They now work together in managing an extensive recycling program. For example, plastic hangers are not accepted in landfills in many areas because of environmental concerns. Sears and Genco decided to recycle more than 100 million hangers each year, converting what had been an expense into a revenue stream. The two firms are also leveraging the Internet as a means of liquidating returned merchandise, including exploring B2C auction strategies.[5]

Clay Valstad, director of central return center operations for Sears, said, "Our reverse logistics strategy is to take the work, square footage, and expense out of returns for our stores by consolidating and handling returns offsite. . . . This allows our stores to focus on taking care of our customers."[6] Valstad said, "In addition to recovering significant dollars in vendor credits or through recycling, we are able to recover all of the costs of running our reverse logistics program."[7]

In this outsourcing scenario Sears was motivated to find a solution even though no existing vendor matched its needs exactly. The current era of B2B services that we discussed in Chapter 1 has opened up a new type of partnering option. Going beyond joint venturing, a business process co-development strategy leverages the competencies of both firms with the goal of improving operating efficiencies on the one hand, and extending the service portfolio on the other. Each side wins and no heavy negotiations about equity stake or profit distributions are needed. The competency co-development strategy allows both firms to focus on their core competence and to be rewarded for high performance.

VARIABLE-PRICE OUTSOURCING

There are a variety of pricing approaches to BPO. By far the most common approach is the fixed-price contract where a vendor manages a buyer's process and gets paid a fee based on meeting preestablished performance benchmarks. Fixed-price contracts, however, can be imposing for small- to medium-sized enterprises (SMEs) or for firms that are struggling to meet financial goals. Making a commitment to a large fixed-price contract when the benefits lie far off in the future can be difficult, if not impossible, for many SMEs or struggling firms. If there were no pricing alternatives, many firms would be unable to consider the outsourcing option.

To overcome this pricing barrier, outsourcing vendors have developed variable-pricing strategies that allow firms to pay only for the capacity they use or only for performance-related outcomes. This approach is reminiscent of the application service provider (ASP) approach to software distribution that captivated investors in the late 1990s.

When AXA Financial sought to outsource its data center, the worldwide financial services and insurance conglomerate wanted an IT services partner that would provide variable-level pricing. Like many financial services firms trying to weather the bear market, AXA, which employs 140,000 people worldwide and has 50 million client accounts, was looking to outsource its data center.

Rather than seek a traditional outsourcing arrangement with standard service level agreements and fixed-cost terms, AXA wanted to pay only for the capacity it actually used in a given period of time. For example, when Web traffic or transactions volume was high, AXA would pay for more capacity. When transaction volume was low, it would pay less. Potential vendors balked at this arrangement at the time because that was not how IT services companies historically structured their outsourcing deals. Although IBM Global Services eventually won the $1 billion deal, it was only after a year of trying to negotiate a fixed-price contract.

AXA's determination that it did not want a traditional outsourcing arrangement came early on in the process. The company—a France-based conglomerate of 60 companies that entered the United States with its acquisition of Equitable—felt those deals never worked out as promised. At the same time, AXA did not want to bear the cost of owning and maintaining its computing assets any longer.[8]

With on-demand storage and computing, clients get more out of existing IT investments and pay only for the resources used. For example, clients can change from ownership of multimillion-dollar storage systems that may only be 20 to 50 percent utilized to intelligent storage services that provide what they need, when they need it. In financial terms, this can mean a 15 to 50 percent cost improvement for used capacity.[9]

BPO buyers increasingly are demanding variable-pricing approaches, and vendors are responding. At the same time, pay-as-you-go pricing models have several drawbacks that managers must consider and monitor. For instance, counterproductive behavior could result if the pay-as-you-go chargebacks are mapped directly to business units. Under such a pricing scheme, a cost-conscious manager in the BPO buyer firm might encourage staff to minimize use of the vendor's services in an attempt to minimize their chargeback. This could result in less productive employee behavior over the long term, including the possibility of missed opportunities or an overreliance on legacy systems.[10]

FIRST-TIME OUTSOURCING

Many managers reading this book are employed by companies that have never undertaken a BPO initiative or whose culture is generally opposed to BPO. Closely held family companies, for example, may believe that it is contrary to their culture and values to consider outsourcing work to an external party. In such cases, additional effort may be needed internally to communicate the benefits of outsourcing to top executives. One way to introduce the idea of outsourcing in such a culture is by identifying a particularly inefficient or cumbersome business process. Finding a vendor who is willing to pilot an effort to take over this process and demonstrate new efficiencies is a powerfully convincing approach to the overall business case.

Kohler Company, in Kohler, Wisconsin, is a family-held business that has not been active in outsourcing. However, when Dan Theune, manager of cash management, ran into an accounts payable record-tracking problem, he turned to API, an onshore accounts payable outsourcing vendor, for help.

Kohler is a leader in plumbing and power systems products. The Kohler portfolio of businesses extends beyond kitchen and bath items, including furniture and accessories, cabinetry and tile, engines and generators, as well as resort, recreation, and real estate businesses. For nearly 25 years, each of Kohler's domestic divisions had its own accounts payable (AP) department and handled its own AP functions. And, for nearly 25 years, this approach worked fine: Invoices were processed, microfilmed, indexed by control number, and stored independently at each location. But in the late 1990s, with the Y2K problem looming, the company decided to not only update its computer systems, but also to centralize the AP departments of all ten of its domestic businesses then housed in various locations throughout the United States.

In addition to technology upgrades, a new building was constructed on the corporate headquarters site to house the new shared-service division. In the old building, the microfilm room was one floor below the AP department. With the move to the new building, however, AP staff lost its ability to simply run down to the film room to look up information. In addition, with the new enterprise resource planning (ERP) system it had recently installed, remote offices all over the U.S. needed access to the microfilm records.

As the process of installing the ERP system began, the AP team discussed using the SAP imaging system to create electronic files of invoices. However, with the ERP implementation dominating staff time, Theune's team did not have the resources to tackle the imaging problem. It decided to seek an outsourcing vendor who could provide the needed competence. Kohler had no prior experience with outsourcing, so it needed to find a vendor who would help it ease into this new approach to doing business.

After reviewing several potential vendors, Kohler decided to work with API on an outsourcing pilot program. Kohler chose API in part because the company has developed a preoutsourcing analysis known as a Requirements and Definitions (R&D) study. The R&D study is an in-depth evaluation of the BPO buyer's business process, costs associated with outsourcing that process, and expected performance outcomes. API performs such an analysis with each new customer before beginning service.

API's R&D report helped the Kohler team develop a business case for its outsourcing vision. The report spelled out all of the processes and procedures of the process handover and described details such as what the indexing parameters would be. The report also provided details on costs and benefits. Theune said, "Initially, our most difficult task was to convince management that we should outsource the imaging function. We're a privately held family company, and we just don't outsource much. This was new to us, so the R&D study was very valuable and helpful to our management's decision-making process."

The turnaround time from the start of the R&D process until Kohler's AP department began sending data and documents to API was only 90 days. This included time for API to purchase a Kohler-dedicated server and to implement connectivity and data transfer capabilities. One of the greatest benefits of outsourcing for Kohler is the fact that API is responsible for purchasing and maintaining the server, which stores the AP images and requires limited assistance from Kohler's IT staff. Although the IT staff was involved initially, their overburdened resources were not further taxed because API handled much of the technical setup and maintenance.

With the technology and processes in place, Kohler now sends accounts payable data to API electronically and the actual invoices by FedEx daily. The invoices are scanned and match-merged to the related electronic data by reading the preprinted bar code on each SAP cover sheet. For documents with multiple bar codes, API uses zonal scanning to accurately pick up the right bar code by searching for a bar code positioned in a particular spot on the cover sheet.

Having access to electronic images has greatly improved the level of service Kohler's AP department provides to its internal and external customers without the challenges of managing an in-house imaging department. The central AP department and authorized remote locations can now retrieve, view, print, e-mail, and fax AP information in a matter of seconds. And, rather than search for invoices using a single control number, the documents can be retrieved using any one of ten index parameters.

Outsourcing has helped Kohler improve the process of tracking payables and shorten internal research time by providing immediate access to electronic images of AP documents. The increased efficiency has resulted in enhanced customer care and profitability, prompting Kohler to deploy API services to its accounts receivable department and to other subsidiaries.[11]

REVERSE OUTSOURCING

Another interesting twist on the outsourcing revolution is the conversion of a business competence into a revenue-generating business service, a process we call *reverse outsourcing*. This is not new, of course. Companies have developed new revenue lines out of business competencies developed from within for generations. What is new is that businesses are able to generate outsourcing revenue on an increasingly mundane set of back-office business competencies. From simple customized software sales to call center operations, firms that develop world-class competencies in a business process can now look beyond the competitive advantages those competencies provide to their potential for incremental revenue generation. As outsourcing noncore business competencies has become more common, two things have occurred to increase the opportunities for organizations to seek revenue from business processes they execute at a high level:

1. The "fear factor" about outsourcing has diminished.
2. The opportunities for outsourcing—even in highly specialized processes and business competencies—has greatly increased.

The outsourcing fear factor has been reduced as a result of some of the major BPO drivers discussed in Chapter 1. The improvement in Internet security has eased concern about data loss or theft. The fear factor has also been reduced as a result of the mind shift that has occurred among managers regarding the nature of the organization. Formerly, most managers believed in vertical integration and tight control of all business processes. Today, the prevailing wisdom is to focus on core competencies, while trusting market mechanisms and carefully crafted contracts to motivate business service providers to take care of noncore activities.

As the fear of outsourcing has diminished, the opportunities for outsourcing have increased, even in technical or nearly one-of-a-kind business processes. Many companies are now leveraging their best-in-class capacity in noncore business processes to earn additional revenue. For example, in June 2003, Amazon.com, the online retailer known mainly for discount books, announced the formation of Amazon Services, Inc., a provider of outsourced e-business solutions. The new outsourcing subsidiary offers hosting services using Amazon's existing storefront and shopping technology, but with complete branding control going to the retailer. It also includes fulfillment and customer support services.[12]

The formation of the business unit was not the beginning of Amazon's outsourcing business. Borders, the second largest U.S. bookseller, decided to abandon its online book sales effort in 2001, choosing instead to outsource its operations to Amazon. In turn, Amazon simply adopted its already well-established e-business infrastructure to generate additional revenue.

Amazon took over the Web operations of Borders Online and relaunched it as a co-branded site. The online retailer also handled inventory, customer service, and shipping services for book, music, and video sales. Ann Arbor, Michigan–based Borders Group Inc. receives a commission on each sale.

Based on the success of the Borders deal, Amazon has sought additional opportunities to outsource its application infrastructure to other Web-based retailers. Amazon has built its e-commerce outsourcing business with customers such as America Online, Target, and Virgin MegaStores. For example, visitors to Target.com will see the familiar Target bull's-eye logo, but Amazon is making it work.[13] Overall, the company has more than 30 such partnerships. It is interesting to note that when it comes to selling goods or selling online know-how and services, the services bring greater profit margins.

In its formal shift into outsourcing services, Amazon furthers its role as a technology innovator first and retailer second. The online retailer/outsourcer is reported to have spent $1 billion to date and spends $200 million annually on technology. This places its IT budget in a class with the largest firms in the world and rivals what any firm spends specifically on Web commerce capabilities.[14]

Neither Amazon nor its clients say much about how the deals are structured, but so far, Amazon seems to have made customers like Borders happy. In April 2003, its parent company, Borders Inc., extended its deal with Amazon, allowing customers to pick up Web purchases in Borders stores. Borders also said that Amazon.com would take over the site for its Walden Books subsidiary.[15]

In addition to being an outsourcing provider, Amazon also uses outsourcing to manage an increasingly complex IT infrastructure. In 2003 the company announced that it was outsourcing a new data center to Equinix Inc., a provider of data center and co-location services. Amazon already operates data centers in Seattle, Washington, and Chantilly, Virginia, but it decided to outsource the additional data center to Equinix.[16]

BUSINESS TRANSFORMATION OUTSOURCING

With years of outsourcing experience to bolster managerial courage to undertake even bolder projects, many are now using what is called *business transformation outsourcing* (BTO) to dramatically affect their firm's competitive strategies. In fact, 12 percent of chief technology officers in charge of IT outsourcing report undertaking BTO projects.[17] As research has shown, firms in volatile industries are more likely than those in stable industries to use outsourcing to help improve operations. Increasingly, these firms are turning to BTO to help them become more flexible and adaptable in a rapidly changing competitive arena.

Transformation outsourcing is defined as a long-term relationship through which an outsourcing vendor assists the buyer in stimulating continuous business change while also achieving operational effectiveness. BTO is generally distinguished from plain-old BPO on several dimensions, as shown in Exhibit 2.1.

BC Hydro is a Canadian utility with a traditional structure and organizational culture. Management change is typically initiated and executed only with great difficulty at the 140-year-old company. Nonetheless, in February 2003, Accenture and BC Hydro signed a ten-year agreement, valued at nearly $1 billion, designed to transform the way BC Hydro serves its customers. The new deal is projected to save BC Hydro customers $195 million.[18]

As part of the deal, Accenture formed Accenture Business Services of British Columbia LP, with more than 1,500 former BC Hydro employees. BC Hydro became the first customer of Accenture Business Services, outsourcing its customer services (including the development of a new customer information system), IT services, network computing services, HR services, financial systems, purchasing, and building and office services.

The agreement marked the completion of a process begun with a Request for Expressions of Interest that BC Hydro solicited from the private sector in October 2001. In April 2002, after BC Hydro reviewed 19 proposals, it announced to its employees that the discussions had narrowed to Accenture. The final terms of the agreement were reached after a negotiation and due diligence process that began on July 18, 2002. Accenture Business Services began operations in Spring 2003.

EXHIBIT 2.1   Key Distinctions between BPO and BTO

BPO	BTO
Operational focus	Business focus
Focus on cost cutting	Focus on value creation
Impose tight controls	Manage uncertainty
Fixed-bid fees	Performance-based fees
Offload noncore functions	Create business change

Transformation outsourcing is a bold approach to organizational change. Rather than the incremental, go-it-slow approach that many firms use in outsourcing business processes, the transformation approach is based on a forthright recognition of competitively disadvantageous processes within the company and a desire to eliminate them with the help of an experienced vendor. BTO can be the fastest route to achieving operational parity with best-practices providers or to vault beyond them through creative synergies between BTO buyer and vendor. In fact, if both parties are committed to leveraging the relationship beyond service provider and buyer, revenue opportunities may lie in reverse outsourcing the new competencies. BC Hydro and Accenture have done this with their joint venture, which was launched primarily to transform BC Hydro's outdated systems and service levels.[19]

UNSUCCESSFUL OFFSHORE OUTSOURCING

This chapter concludes by examining an offshore outsourcing initiative that did not work as planned. Although it may give the impression that we are ending the chapter on a downbeat, the story of the failed offshore outsourcing venture has a redemptive quality to it. The leader of the initiative was discouraged by the outcome of the particular project, but he is not discouraged by the prospect of using an offshore strategy in the future. Quite the contrary, he believes that the lessons learned as a result of the failed project provide greater prospects for success for the next project. Not all BPO projects work as planned, but the promise that BPO holds for most companies makes the hard knocks of failures and lessons learned worth tolerating.

Wesley Bertch and his team learned a few lessons about offshore outsourcing through the hard knocks academy. Bertch leads the software development group at Life Time Fitness, a high-growth, national health and fitness chain. Life Time offers its customers health clubs; spas and salons; member services, such as personal training and swimming lessons; a nationally distributed magazine; and energy bars, powders, and other consumer goods. Life Time also has a corporate wellness unit that sells products and services to thousands of companies. In addition to supplying these various divisions with information technology systems, Life Time provides services to its internal real-estate group. Keeping pace with the growing software needs of so many diverse business units is a huge challenge.

Bertch's internal staff of 15 programmers was able to produce only about one-third of the output he needed. With a limited budget and demand for greater output, he reasoned that offshore software development was the ideal solution. Bertch needed to augment his internal team in a cost-effective way, without sacrificing quality.

From an organizational perspective, Life Time met the key criteria for offshoring: centralized IT, process maturity, and years of experience working with Indian companies and technical workers, both in the United States and offshore. Life Time had executive sponsorship and commitment. It even had the perfect project to test the outsourcing waters: a small, low-risk Web application for its real-estate division. The application's purpose was to provide screens for entering new location information.

The vendor Life Time invited to implement the project was an Indian firm that had been successfully supporting the company's sales-force automation implementation. With this prior history of working together, both sides thought the Web application project would be relatively easy. The vendor agreed to take on the project for a fixed fee of $20,000, with a nine-week timeline.

Both parties agreed that the vendor should perform all phases of the project, from gathering business requirements through quality assurance. Life Time's internal staff was to monitor and participate as necessary. If the project proved successful, Life Time promised the offshore vendor that there would be much more project work in the future. The two organizations established a project team to manage the project. Exhibit 2.2 shows the roles that were established on the project management team.

EXHIBIT 2.2   Life Time's Offshore Development Team

On-site Liaison	Supplied by the vendor, acted as a bridge between the Life Time team and the offshore project manager. This person was on a senior level technically and had strong communication skills.
On-site Business Analyst	Supplied by the vendor, completed the application's functional requirements, then returned to India to act as offshore project manager.
Offshore Project Manager	Tracked tasks and schedules for three offshore team members: a Java developer, a JSP developer, and a tester.
Offshore Technical Manager	Supervised the Life Time project, as well as three others.
Life Time Software Manager	Coordinated Life Time team with the on-site liaison to provide code reviews, database design, and general advice.
Life Time Project Manager	An individual in Life Time's real-estate division served as the internal business champion.

The project got off to a good start. The vendor's business analyst met frequently with the real-estate division's users and, with the on-site liaison, worked to document all of the functional and user interface requirements within four weeks.

By week three, however, Life Time's software manager noticed problems in the software. His review of the functional specifications revealed problems in the requirements, particularly in the interface specifications. For example, the user interface as laid out forced the users to reenter data they had previously entered, and the screen flow was confusing. The on-site liaison countered that although the interface had problems, it complied with the documented business requirements.

To ensure that Life Time would get what it needed, Bertch extended the project timeline, agreed to a cost increase of $7,000 to allow for additional analysis and better interface design, and dedicated internal Life Time analysis and user interface experts to guide the final version of the documentation.

After the vendor's business analyst finalized the documentation, he returned to India and, in an effort to exploit his knowledge of the project requirements, was reassigned as the offshore project manager. By this point, the offshore technical manager had lined up the offshore project team, so the coding design began in earnest.

Once offshore, however, the project started to unravel. Upon receiving the offshore vendor's database design, Life Time's lead data architect declared it to be the worst he had ever seen. There were so many critical database flaws—more than 100—that Life Time's architects were unable to log them all within the scheduled one-week review period.

The database was not the only problem. Determined to impress Life Time with their programming prowess, the offshore developers insisted on completing the entire code design before allowing Life Time to review it. Confident in their original code design, the offshore team had launched immediately into writing Java code before Life Time's review. Unfortunately, the eventual review determined that the offshore team's design patterns were not in accordance with the standards Life Time follows, invalidating all of the offshore team's Java code.

In two weeks, the offshore team had gone from proud and eager to embarrassed and dejected. Once the reality of the logged defects sank in, the team knew there was no way it could straighten out the code design and then code and test the applications within the set time frame. Frustration levels were high on the offshore team, and the on-site liaison became increasingly defensive. The internal Life Time team was disappointed and annoyed as well, but accepted the fact that mistakes were bound to happen on the first end-to-end offshore project. The Life Time team valued a quality final product much more than timeline precision. Nevertheless, as Life Time learned later, the offshore team began working extra-long hours to avoid asking for a time extension.

Given all the problems up to that point, Bertch sensed the project was at risk, so he flew to India to meet with the offshore team. The visit was informational and warm feelings prevailed, but by this time the application was in the testing phase and nearly complete. Not long after Bertch's trip to India, the offshore team delivered the tested and "finished" application. According to the on-site liaison, all Life Time needed to do was perform a user-acceptance review and sign off on the project's successful delivery.

Instead, Bertch decided to perform some quality assurance with his internal team. In less than a day, one Life Time tester and one developer found more than 35 defects, many of them fatal. The offshore team categorized the hundreds of newly found defects as "in scope" (these they fixed) or "out of scope" (these were deemed Life Time's problem). Even after the vendor fixed the "in scope" defects, the application was unusable. And fixing it meant it would be late and even more over budget. At this point, Bertch decided the best course was to take delivery of the application and overhaul the code internally.

Reflecting on his offshoring experience, Bertch said:

You might assume that, given our dismal experience with offshore development, we have written off this model completely. Not so. Offshore may still hold promise as a way to cost-effectively extend our current team. What would we do differently? Instead of relying on the vendor to institute the offshore processes and team, we would set that up ourselves. Ideally, we would have a developer from our internal team relocate to India to build and manage a competent offshore team, perhaps within leased space at an existing development facility.[20]

This case is a good example of the challenges associated with working with an offshore development team. Offshore vendors are often overconfident of their own abilities and eager to take on new projects, the scope of which may lie beyond their current level of expertise. The overconfidence of the vendor also leads to a desire to impress the buyer with rapid turnaround and seemingly impossible schedules and deadlines.

To avoid that problem, companies working with offshore vendors must control the pace of the project and must ensure that specifications are carefully developed and understood before allowing the work to begin. Then, it is advisable to work on projects in stages, reviewing the work produced by the offshore team in discrete stages. Controlling the pace of work and reviewing the finished product as it is delivered will enable the buyer to stay in control and avoid additional costs and time.

CONCLUSION

This chapter provides only a glimpse at who is using BPO and how they are using it. Obviously there are many more permutations on the outsourcing theme than we are able to cover in a single book chapter. With BPO becoming an increasingly accepted business innovation, its coverage in the media and by specialty publications is also increasing. The informed manager can keep in touch with new innovations and variations on the BPO theme through these publications, which are updated regularly. In the meantime, this chapter can serve as a reminder that BPO can be practiced in multiple ways, and that there is probably a model out there somewhere that fits the unique structure and culture of nearly every organization.

SUMMARY

- Much of the risk has been removed from basic BPO arrangements because of the experience gained by buyers and vendors alike.
- Firms of all sizes are realizing both tactical and strategic advantages from outsourcing.
- Some firms use an intermediary to take advantage of the labor-cost savings associated with offshore outsourcing.
- Some firms use a competence co-development approach to outsourcing if they cannot find a vendor that provides services targeted directly to their area of need.
- Fixed-price outsourcing contracts can be prohibitive to SMEs and firms struggling financially, whereas variable-priced contracts might enable them to undertake BPO initiatives.
- First-time BPO buyers can benefit from using vendors who are willing to conduct pilot studies and/or pilot projects as a way of introducing outsourcing to the executive team.
- Many firms develop competence in a noncore business activity and reverse outsource that activity to develop an incremental revenue stream.
- Business transformation outsourcing (BTO) is a means by which organizations can radically transform their business. This is an especially effective approach for large, difficult-to-change companies or for companies in highly volatile competitive environments.
- Offshore outsourcing can be compromised by the overconfidence of some offshore teams and the failure of the buyer to control the project's pace and quality.

two

To BPO or Not to BPO?

Part Two of this book asks the question: "To BPO or not to BPO?" An increasingly wide range of companies is asking this question as they struggle to deal with profit margin pressures through operating and production cost reductions.

Chapter 3 provides a set of analytic tools and decision-making guidelines to help organizations explore their BPO opportunities. Nearly any organization has processes that are amenable to some type of outsourcing. The chapter recommends establishing an internal BPO analysis team (BAT) to explore opportunities and to build a business case.

Chapter 4 provides another set of analytic tools to help the BAT analyze the costs associated with a BPO project. Costs are divided into financial and strategic, overt and hidden. A total cost management (TCM) model is provided as a guide to list and quantify the costs associated with the BPO initiatives being considered.

CHAPTER 3

Identify and Select the BPO Opportunity

No sensible decision can be made any longer without taking into
account not only the world as it is, but the world as it will be . . .

—Isaac Asimov, science writer

BPO is not right for every company, nor is it right for every process in a given company, but its promise makes it imperative that managers seek out BPO opportunities and exploit them where possible. Whether or not your company has formal functional boundaries, it has processes that may be suitable for outsourcing to third-party providers. BPO was pioneered primarily by large companies, eager to reduce their costs and bloated payrolls. Today, many small- to medium-sized enterprises (SMEs) have discovered BPO advantages that enable them to compete with the larger firms that have been using outsourcing for years. In 2001, 75 percent of BPO users were firms with greater than $500 million in revenue. By 2002, that number had dropped to 64 percent.[1] What is indisputable is that any business that has grown to more than about $25 million in sales has begun to encounter growth-related challenges in back-office processes that may be suitable for handing over to an outsourcing partner.

For example, an exhibits design company in Illinois has 25 employees. To control costs, the firm had whittled down its health care coverage over a period of years. As a result, it had begun to struggle to attract and retain talented employees. In an effort to remedy the situation, the company outsourced its HR and benefits processes to a professional employer organization (PEO). By outsourcing to the PEO, the company now can offer a lower-deductible plan with better health care and dental coverage, while gaining the use of a professional claims manager. The firm was able to offer its employees these additional benefits while saving 40 percent overall on its health care costs.[2]

Without question, the decision to implement a BPO solution for any organization has far-reaching consequences and risks. At the same time, these implications of the decision-making process should not lead to paralysis—there are too many possible benefits to fall into the trap of doing nothing. It is important for decision makers to recognize that undertaking a BPO initiative is a *strategic* action. With the increasing sophistication of BPO providers, the decision to outsource is no longer one of mere cost savings or headcount reduction; it is also one of performance enhancement in critical functional areas. Is your technical support team overwhelmed by customer inquiries? *Consider a BPO provider.* Is your new-product development cycle too slow? *Consider a BPO provider.* Is your accounts receivable department tardy in tracking down late payers? *Consider a BPO provider.* In each of these examples, and many others, the choice of adopting a BPO solution is based on improving the company's performance in that process. In each case, performance enhancement may mean much more to the firm than simple cost reductions. Exhibit 3.1 highlights some of the reasons that decision makers have cited as grounds for choosing to implement a BPO initiative.

With these potential advantages, it is not difficult for organizations to justify a decision to at least investigate BPO opportunities. At the same time, inquiring into BPO has potential organizational consequences in the short term that must be considered and addressed. The most effective way to analyze and select a BPO opportunity is to utilize a deliberate, systematic approach that minimizes risk each step of the way. We have developed and recommend a six-step process for analyzing and selecting the BPO opportunity. This process has been designed to integrate and align the decision-making process with long-term organizational strategic objectives and near-term organizational needs. If handled systematically, the BPO analysis and selection process can be an effective way for an organization to examine itself. Whether a decision to undertake a BPO initiative is made or not, this process will shine a light on organizational processes and activities. This illumination will, at a minimum, help the organization identify and change underperforming processes and activities. We'll discuss the BPO analysis and selection process later in this chapter, but first we need to introduce the team structure that we recommend to explore, initiate, and manage an outsourcing project.

EXHIBIT 3.1   Reasons for Adopting BPO

BPO PROJECT TEAM STRUCTURE

The value of using teams in the workplace has been elaborated at length by a number of scholars, consultants, and executive-authors. All we can add to that discussion in the context of outsourcing is to reiterate the socio-technical nature of most outsourcing projects. That basic characteristic of outsourcing highlights the need for interdisciplinary skills to manage an outsourcing project effectively. Since such interdisciplinary skills are rarely present in a single individual, effective management of outsourcing projects will almost always require a team structure.

The team structure we recommend begins with an executive-level BPO Steering Team. The BPO Steering Team is responsible for initiating the outsourcing project, communicating its links to corporate strategy, and seeing to it that project goals are being achieved. The steering team should be comprised of individuals representing the major functional lines of the organization, including finance, human resources, information technology, and strategy.

The team structure we recommend for effective end-to-end BPO project management is represented in Exhibit 3.2. As you can see, the other teams illustrated include the BPO Analysis Team (discussed in this Chapter), the BPO Vendor Selection Team (see Chapter 5), and the BPO Project Management Team (see Chapter 7).

EXHIBIT 3.2 BPO Project Team Structure

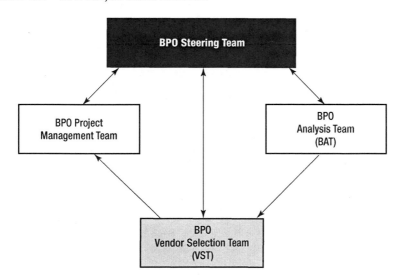

With the desirability of a team-based approach articulated and the team structure we recommend illustrated, we now turn to the six-step process that is recommended to identify BPO candidate processes within the organization.

SIX-STEP PROCESS

Analyzing the BPO opportunity for your organization means identifying core competencies and determining the most effective way to support high performance in those activities. As many organizations have discovered, an increasingly effective way to support core competencies is by outsourcing non-core functions to third-party providers. We have developed a six-step process for organizations to use to analyze and select BPO opportunities. Each step in the process is designed to help organizations link BPO decision making to overall organizational strategy:

1. Establish a BPO analysis team (BAT).
2. Conduct a current state analysis.
3. Identify core and noncore activities.
4. Identify BPO opportunities.
5. Model the BPO project.
6. Develop and present the business case.

Although these steps seem transparent, many organizations overlook opportunities or misunderstand the true value versus risk proposition by skipping steps in the analysis. An organization can also find itself managing confusion if a nonsystematic approach is used. This six-step process is not the only known approach to analyzing the BPO opportunity. However, this proven process can increase the likelihood of success and minimize the risks associated with a BPO initiative.

STEP 1: ESTABLISH A BPO ANALYSIS TEAM

As discussed in Chapter 1, BPO is a socio-technical business innovation that requires a variety of skills and expertise to be managed effectively. The multi-disciplinary nature of a BPO initiative requires a multidisciplinary team to adequately assess the opportunity for the organization. We use the term "BPO Analysis Team" (BAT) to designate the group that will undertake the opportunity analysis. With the expertise the BAT will develop, the organization may later want to assign some of the same people to implement the BPO initiative. We mention that point only to highlight the fact that, in this chapter, we are focusing on the process of *analyzing* and *selecting* the BPO opportunity. We discuss BPO *implementation* at length in Part Four of this book.

The BAT should be chartered by the organization's top executive team, which will also serve as the Steering Team for the BPO project. The BAT should consist of four to seven individuals who represent a range of organizational functions, including information technology, finance, human resources, and strategy. It is also wise to include individuals who have demonstrated an ability to adapt and change through previous organizational upheavals. These individuals may be important champions of the eventual BPO implementation and may be able to play a key role in minimizing resistance that will inevitably arise. The Case Study highlights the use of multidisciplinary teams and the creation of champions in a major HR outsourcing initiative undertaken by AT&T.

CASE STUDY

AT&T Uses Team Approach to Outsource its HR Function

When AT&T opted to outsource human resources, the telecommunications company signed a seven-year comprehensive outsourcing agreement with Aon Consulting. A team of functional experts in AT&T's human resource (HR) and finance departments orchestrated the outsourcing initiative. Each department challenged the other to prove the merits of the outsourcing strategy, resulting in a well-thought-out, appropriate, and cost-effective outsourcing initiative.

AT&T's finance and HR departments also developed an atypical process for determining which HR activities would be best served by outsourcing. Rather than ask respective managers to prove why their activity should be outsourced, the team asked them to provide evidence that their activity should continue to be retained in-house. In doing this, managers became more cognizant of the benefits of outsourcing, less adversarial and threatened by the strategy, and potential champions of it to the employee population. Ultimately, managers designated virtually every HR function for outsourcing.

Aon Consulting now provides AT&T with HR administrative, transaction, and payroll services, including the oversight of existing benefit plan providers, for AT&T's 70,000 U.S.-based employees.

Source: Russ Banham, "Long Distance HR," *HRO Today* (September 2003).

Preparation and training of the BAT is imperative to its success. Team members may be unaware of the potential benefits of BPO, and a crash course in BPO and its implications may be necessary. In addition to educating the BAT about BPO, the team must be knowledgeable about the organization's overall strategic intent. Because BPO is a strategic issue, the team must be prepared to build a business case for a recommended BPO initiative that is aligned with the strategic direction of the organization. Equally important, the BAT must be convinced that it has complete support from the executive team in its mission to identify and select internal business processes as outsourcing opportunities.

The formal charter offered to the BAT should include a clear statement of its objectives: to identify core and noncore business processes, to analyze which noncore processes may be good candidates for BPO, and to recommend whether to undertake a BPO initiative. An example of a BAT charter is provided in Exhibit 3.3.

Developing the BAT will be much the same as developing other cross-functional work teams. Scholars have reminded managers that teams go through developmental stages, often defined as: forming, storming, norming, and performing. Managers who charter the BAT must allow the team to develop interpersonal relationships and group norms. This can be facilitated through appropriate preparation and training. Occasionally, it may also be a good idea to provide the team with a training session on team dynamics and effective team performance. At any rate, savvy managers realize that the storming and norming phases are best handled using a hands-off approach as the team develops an identity and operating norms that will eventually lead to performing. Establishing a detailed charter and setting clear goals will help develop team independence yet keep it focused on results. The first performance task for the BAT is to conduct a current state analysis, as described in Step 2.

EXHIBIT 3.3   Charter XYZ, Inc. BPO Opportunity Analysis Team

---

Purpose: To undertake a process of organizational discovery dedicated to determining if internal processes could be beneficially outsourced.

Goals:
1. To identify, map, and classify core and noncore business processes.
2. To select which, if any, of these processes can be beneficially outsourced.
3. To prepare a model of the business costs and benefits of outsourcing identified internal processes.
4. To prepare and present a business case for specific BPO opportunities.

STEP 2: CONDUCT A CURRENT STATE ANALYSIS

Current state analysis is the term used to refer to the exercise of examining, mapping, and categorizing internal business processes. Typically, this exercise involves rolling up the sleeves and mapping business processes step by step on a white board or other erasable medium. The goal is to develop an understanding of how work flows within the organization. This is often a difficult task, requiring hard thinking and involving individuals from outside the BAT. Done correctly, a current state analysis can unveil hidden bottlenecks and expose sloppy procedures that have become entrenched within the organization.

At times the BAT may find that mapping the current business architecture is akin to trying to map geographic terrain—boundaries and borders are not always clear or obvious. A geographer standing in the Northern Rockies would have a difficult time identifying the border between Canada and the United States. Without a global positioning system, it is nearly impossible to tell where the border is exactly. There is no line on the ground that conveniently divides one side from the other. Yet, the border *is* there, and it does divide clearly distinct political entities.

The situation is often the same in modern organizations. Over the past two decades, scholars and consultants have implored managers to break down barriers between departments and to create "boundaryless" organizations. As a result the clarity of functional divisions within some organizations has diminished.

In their work on reengineering, Hammer and Champy asserted that most companies contain no more than ten principal business processes.[3] In the book *The Process Edge,* Keen identifies more than 100 processes, depicted in Exhibit 3.4, that he refers to as "the process swamp."[4]

The arrangement of processes within the organization constitutes its logical architecture. This logical architecture is often documented in the organizational chart, illustrating authority structure, reporting relationships, and business units. However, understanding the firm's formal structure is only a surface feature of the logical architecture of the organization. Underlying the organizational chart are the actual processes, activities, and behaviors of how things *really* get done.

The notion of an organizational process is similar to the concept of a system. Systems theorists have pointed out that the boundaries of a system are in part a function of the observer's point of view.[5] For example, the organization as a whole constitutes a system with its various inputs, outputs, and feedback mechanisms. Within the organization are other systems, which also have easily identifiable inputs, outputs, and feedback. The observer decides how to carve up the system into subsystems, usually based on practical concerns. With this analogy in mind, it is recommended that the BAT should not

EXHIBIT 3.4   The Process Swamp

customer service   inventory management   shipping
warehousing   investment planning   acquisition
channel management   team rewards   security
public relations   regulatory compliance   safety   communication
hiring   supplier relations   training   decision making   budgeting   R&D   legal
production planning   organizational design   downsizing planning
product launch   promotion   risk management   payments branding
risk management   quality control   forecasting   governance   shareholder relations
manufacturing   credit control   performance evaluation   corporate governance   tax
lobbying   personnel records   medical   freight
management development   records management   sales support   warranty claims
travel management   insurance   office management   outsourcing alliance
divestment   information systems planning   project management   competitive assessment
executive compensation   purchasing   cash management   invoicing   product launch
pricing   customer retention   marketing   change management   cost control
salary policy   benefits management   loans   technology assessment
financial control   global financing   benchmarking   innovation
executive compensation   capital investment   pension administration
negotiation   engineering   market research   accounting
management succession
catering   account management
environmental
data center
learning

be constrained to using the formal boundaries identified in the organization chart to identify work processes. Instead, it should use an approach similar to the systems theorists. The BAT should use a pragmatic approach to identifying organizational processes. That is, it should identify processes that produce meaningful results in the organization, not just those that are formally identified on the organization chart. One way to prime this mind-shift is by developing a working knowledge of the types of processes BPO vendors are addressing. This knowledge will help the BAT identify similar processes within the organization. Beginning with a list of common processes in mind provides the BAT with a starting point for the next task, which is to develop a process map of the organization.

Business process mapping (BPM) has been used by organizations over the past decade as part of reengineering and continuous quality improvement. Many of the tools and steps used for those purposes can now be turned to analyzing the BPO opportunity. BPM has been well documented and is routinely used by top firms to maintain a lean operation. The objective of BPM is to define clearly the activities within a process and to identify activity owners. Identifying activity owners is a critical element of BPM because these individuals or groups can dramatically influence the effectiveness of the overall BPO project. Gaining their buy-in and support at this early juncture will ensure a more accurate process map, as well as enable a smoother transition if the process is selected for a BPO initiative. This point is amplified in the Executive Viewpoint, which features a discussion with Renee Baker-Arrington, one of A.T. Kearney's top recruiters of BPO project leaders. Arrington points out that successful BPO project leadership requires soft skills to work with people throughout the organization.

EXECUTIVE VIEWPOINT Soft Skills Required in BPO Leadership

Renee Arrington, Vice President, Executive Search, A.T. Kearney Inc.

There are a wide range of skills that companies are seeking today in executives and/or managers recruited to execute BPO projects. Among the most important skills is the ability to communicate. That term means a lot of things, including team building skills, listening skills, political skills, and interpersonal skills. In addition, one skill that is very important to successful BPO projects—but one that is often overlooked—is empathy. Since BPO affects so many aspects of the organization, it is important for project leaders to be able to empathize with individuals as they adapt to change. Organizations have realized that BPO requires quite a few so-called soft skills to be managed effectively.

Skills needed to lead a BPO project actually may differ depending on the project, and the phase of the project. For example, the skill set that is necessary to develop and maintain the outsourcing vendor relationship is different from the skill set needed to identify and select a BPO opportunity. Managing the vendor relationship requires individuals skilled in negotiating, cross-cultural management, and controlling and measuring project outcomes. Often, the individual who leads the BPO opportunity identification and selection process does not have the skills needed to manage it once it is underway.

My hunch is that interest in hiring executives or managers with BPO project experience as a primary qualification is just beginning to grow. We seem to be at the beginning of a wave that could grow to significant size. As the implications of BPO are better understood and as more firms realize benefits of recruiting executives with BPO experience, I am projecting a significant rise in demand for such experience. I also expect that there will soon be more formal education programs aimed at developing executive skill-sets in BPO. As I stated before, I think we are only at the beginning of the BPO revolution, and it might have a large impact on executive recruitment and hiring practices in the next few years.

The business process map should be developed using what we call a three-tier analytic structure. Tier 1 analyzes the process at the highest level, using the common business unit terms of the organization chart and linking these units into a logical structure. For example, the accounting department and the marketing department are Tier 1 process names. A Tier 1 map of a manufacturing company is given in Exhibit 3.5.

Tier 2 features are the activities that occur within those departments to accomplish various tasks. These Tier 2 activities are also often referred to as subprocesses. We use the term *activities* to align the mapping process with the popular activity-based costing (ABC) approach to accounting. Many companies have discovered that while it may not be in their interests to outsource at the functional level, many *activities* within a *function* can be effectively outsourced.[6]

Analyzing the structure and flow of activities within a function usually requires that individuals working within the functional area be involved in the mapping process. At this stage of the analysis, the BAT is seeking activity-level details that will help identify cost, productivity, and mission criticality. Exhibit 3.6 illustrates a map of our example manufacturing company with Tier 1 and Tier 2 architecture displayed.

Finally, Tier 3 refers to the process of identifying the resources that support the Tier 1 and Tier 2 processes—including the human resources. This is the part of the analysis where activity and function costs are identified. It is also the part of the analysis where individual responsibility is linked one to one with the various activities. Exhibit 3.7 shows a process map with all three tiers of analysis.

The BAT should be aware that it might be difficult to recruit individuals to help it analyze organizational processes. If rumors of possible outsourcing are in the air, people may be reluctant to openly share information. To counteract this threat, the BAT should be encouraging about the opportunities of

EXHIBIT 3.5   Tier 1 View of Manufacturing Company

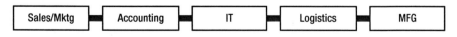

EXHIBIT 3.6   Tier 2 View of Manufacturing Company

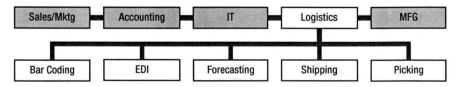

EXHIBIT 3.7   Tier 3 View of Manufacturing Company

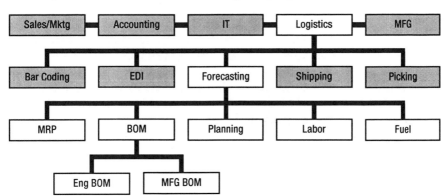

a BPO initiative—it does not necessarily mean that people will be losing their jobs. Often, outsourcing results in workers being hired by the third-party provider—as in an employee-leasing arrangement. It also often leads to improved work processes and greater opportunities for higher-value work.

The BAT should be aware that individuals brought into the mapping process might be skeptical about the intent of the analysis. Although it is not possible to provide complete reassurance that all jobs will be preserved, the BAT should work with the HR department to assure employees that their needs will be considered regardless of the outcome of the analysis. As counterintuitive as it may seem, it is possible for people to be willing to help restructure themselves out of a job if the appropriate support mechanisms are in place.[7] We will discuss the challenges of managing internal change associated with the BPO initiative in far greater detail in Chapter 7.

With the process map in hand, the next step for the BAT is to identify which of the processes are core and which are noncore activities.

STEP 3: IDENTIFY CORE AND NONCORE ACTIVITIES

Some consultants and business scholars have made it seem as if identifying an organization's core business is a complicated affair. They offer example after example of organizations that have experienced decline in market share because they did not focus on their core competences. Often, the prescription for returning to a healthy core competence is to engage in a series of high-level meetings that may involve scenario planning or other efforts to forecast the future and focus the organization on seizing competitive advantage. In reality, such meetings can be useful in setting strategy, but they are not useful in identifying core competence.

Other scholars have made identification of core competence a far less complicated task. For example, in his book *Managing on the Fault Line*, Geoffrey Moore said, "Any behavior that can raise your stock price is core, everything else is context."[8] Another simple definition is that core competence consists of "those capabilities that permit the firm to make the best response to market opportunities."[9] Pralahad and Hamel were a bit more sophisticated, but they limited their definition of core competence to a process that exhibits three traits:[10]

1. It makes a contribution to perceived customer benefits.
2. It is difficult for competitors to imitate.
3. It can be leveraged to a wide variety of markets.

Another widely held view, based on the so-called resource theory, holds that there are four elements of a firm's core competence:[11]

1. The resource is valuable.
2. The resource is rare.
3. The resource is difficult to imitate.
4. The resource is difficult to substitute.

In our view, a company's core competence is the process or processes that the front office, and especially the sales and marketing team, is emphasizing to customers. This customer-centric conception of core competence suggests a way out of the endless debate about how to define that term. It seems obvious to us that an organization ought to be telling its customers what it believes it does better than its competitors. If it is telling them something else, either the message needs to be changed or the firm needs to focus on that something else.

The customer-centric definition of core competence that we encourage distinguishes it from organizational strategy. Strategy defines how an organization defends, builds, and transforms its core competence over time. Deciding how to do *that* is a matter for scenario planning and forecasting—techniques usually practiced by upper management teams. The BAT must be careful not to get caught up in strategy discussions when the task in this step of the BPO opportunity analysis is to clarify and articulate the organization's core competence.

Once the organization's core competence has been identified, those processes that are noncore should also be identified and classified. Some of these processes will be more crucial in their support of the core competence than others. For example, if the organization's core competence is manufacturing, one crucial business activity may be logistics. This function may be more important to the support of the core competence than is, say, payroll administration. We have developed three classification categories for business processes that are not part of the organization's core business:

1. Critical
2. Key
3. Support

Critical functions are those that are very important to a company's core business activity. In the example just cited, logistics is a critical function to the manufacturing firm. Critical functions are those that must be performed nearly flawlessly and are potential candidates to become a future core competence if competitive conditions change. For example, a firm that excels in logistics to support manufacturing may one day eschew manufacturing and become a logistics firm.

Key functions are those that are important to the organization's pursuit of its core business, but are not tightly coupled to the overall pursuit of excellence in the core business. For example, a firm's benefits administration function must perform well to create satisfied employees, but flawless performance is usually not expected. Most employees, especially those on a fixed salary, will continue to function at high levels despite flawed performance in benefits administration. They may be annoyed or dissatisfied with a problem in their benefits program, but most will be tolerant and expect that the problem will be fixed to their satisfaction eventually. A key function, by our definition, is one that people within the organization can readily identify and usually also know who is responsible for it. Despite its relative proximity to the core, however, a key function is one that is unlikely to become the company's core competence.

Finally, support processes are those that are essential to the operation of the business but will never become the organization's core competence. Support processes are the most routine and fault-tolerant of the three types. These functions include such processes as call center, payroll administration, and mailroom activities. In large organizations, most people do not know who processes their paychecks—and most do not really care. They are aware when a paycheck is late, but they are also forgiving because they know they are under contract and will receive their check when the mistake has been identified and cleared. Such support functions are necessary for the organization to function effectively but constitute those elements often derided as bureaucracy or overhead.

As business processes are identified and classified, the BAT begins to develop a feel for which processes may be candidates for BPO. The task of identifying BPO opportunities is the next step in the analysis.

STEP 4: IDENTIFY BPO OPPORTUNITIES

This step in the process of analyzing the BPO opportunity requires that the BAT decide how the organization can use BPO to support the core competence in the current and projected competitive environment. In a highly competitive environment, where fast action is required, it may be necessary to consider outsourcing key and support functions immediately to a best-in-class provider in a winner-take-all strategy. However, in a less competitive environment, it may be prudent to take a more cautious approach to BPO, beginning only with support activities in measures designed more for margin enhancement rather than competitive positioning. Selecting the business process to outsource must take multiple factors into consideration:

- Goals of the outsourcing initiative
- Ability to recruit a motivated internal project sponsor
- Business case supporting the initiative
- Timing of the project
- Culture of the unit slated for outsourcing
- Amount of work required to implement the outsourcing initiative
- Expectations of senior management
- Risk to business

The decision process involved in selecting which organizational functions to outsource must necessarily be a collaborative one. Because BPO is a strategic choice for an organization, it must be determined if and how BPO fits into the overall strategy. This can only be done through broad, collaborative discussions at all levels and across all functional and process boundaries. Of course, no one gains if the BPO decision-making process gets bogged down endlessly in meetings and discussions. The general rule should be that, at minimum, people involved in functions potentially targeted for BPO should be included in discussions about the implications of outsourcing and the schedule to be followed.

It is likely that these decision-making discussions will be difficult and will often include some levels of conflict. Managers in charge of facilitating these meetings can help them stay on track by reminding participants of the organization's mission and strategic plan. These guiding ideas and documents should underlie each conversation and should help drive the BPO selection process to a conclusion. That outcome is more likely to occur if clear and measurable goals have been established.

We have developed a three-dimensional BPO Selection Matrix to help organizations decide which functions or activities may be best suited for an outsourcing solution. The matrix is a three-dimensional model of the key factors involved in evaluating a business process for outsourcing: process costs, process productivity, and process mission criticality. As shown in Exhibit 3.8, there are eight primary process types.

Each type on this matrix requires a unique approach and involves different factors to become a viable BPO selection. The BAT should place the various functions and processes examined in Step 2 at their appropriate location within the matrix. It is advisable that the BAT considers using the Tier 2 or Tier 3 levels of granularity in its distribution of processes within the BPO Selection Matrix. Analyzing processes only at the Tier 1 or functional level creates the potential for many costly or inefficient activities to slip past the BPO analysis. Although some activities may be too tightly coupled to the process as a whole to allow them to be outsourced, their placement on the BPO Selection Matrix exposes their relative efficiency and effectiveness. This alone can be useful in making necessary changes to processes that are overly costly or unproductive.

The following list examines each functional type and the issues to consider when deciding whether the function or activity is a good outsourcing candidate:

■ *Type 1.* Those processes within the organization that are high on each of the three dimensions are difficult to outsource. The only factor that suggests such a process be outsourced is the high cost. However, most organizations accept that highly productive labor that deals with mission-critical information is expensive. These functions are usually at the high-

EXHIBIT 3.8 BPO Selection Matrix

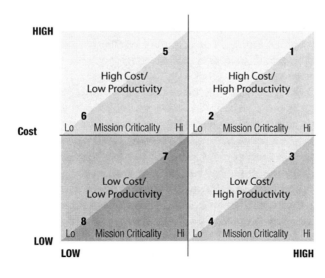

Productivity

est levels of organizations, and often include C-level titles such as CFO, CIO, or CEO. This level of the organization is likely to be a last bastion of untouchability for management-level employees and will be the most difficult to address with an outsourcing solution.

- *Type 2.* This type encompasses all of the technical workers whose skills are so highly valued and high priced, but who work on non–mission-critical systems. Such a process is a prime candidate for BPO. Individuals working in this type of process possess skills that have become more commonly available through lower-cost outsourcing alternatives. The major consideration in outsourcing this type of process is the high productivity demonstrated by the employees who comprise the function. The outsourcing decision must ensure that the high productivity levels will be maintained throughout the transition process and afterward.

- *Type 3.* Type 3 processes are characterized by clerical employees who deal with mission-critical information. Their low cost makes them unattractive outsourcing candidates as long as productivity remains high. Reasons for outsourcing such processes are confined to the identification of BPO partners who can provide competitive advantages over the internal unit. In this instance, the decision to move forward with a BPO initiative would be primarily strategic. For example, if the outsourcing partner can provide market-shifting capabilities in the process area, it may be worth the effort to outsource the process.

- *Type 4.* This type of process is a prime candidate for outsourcing even though it already has relatively low cost. The low productivity and low mission criticality of this type of process suggests there are few impediments to moving the function to an external provider. With the labor costs in some offshore outsourcing relationships reaching levels as low as 20 percent of internal costs, it may be the case that outsourcing such processes not only increases productivity but also actually reduces the already low costs.

- *Type 5.* Processes with high costs and low productivity are always good candidates for outsourcing. In this type, the process also has high mission criticality, making the outsourcing decision slightly more complicated. There are techniques for limiting a firm's risk exposure to outsourcing mission-critical functions. Choice of vendor becomes extremely important, as does the potential for backup and recovery. Fortunately, BPO vendors come in a wide range of capabilities and competencies. There are those that specialize in dealing with clerical-type activities and those that are familiar with and have built systems to deal with mission-critical functions. Organizations should perform due diligence on outsourcing firms that will be handling mission-critical processes. The due diligence should include reference checks and, if possible, site visits. Top internal

BPO champions should also attempt to establish personal relationships with the executive team of the BPO provider.

▨ *Type 6.* High cost and low productivity, combined with low mission criticality, make this process type among the most likely to be outsourced. Technical workers who are in short supply here in the United States, but who are in abundant supply in other regions, staff these types of processes. The greatest challenge to implementing BPO with processes of this type is that they are likely to be labor intensive and may result in large-scale employee displacement. Measures must be established to handle re-assignments or layoffs in a manner that minimizes resistance to change.

▨ *Type 7.* This process type is probably not worth considering for a BPO solution unless the company can identify a BPO provider that has strategically dominant services. Furthermore, the provider would have to ensure that the services are proprietary and protected to provide sustainable advantage. The only other scenario in which this process type should be considered is in the instance where competitors have established a strategically dominant position through an outsourcing partner and the organization is playing catch-up.

▨ *Type 8.* Low-cost processes are always less than ideal candidates for outsourcing, unless they are also low in productivity and mission criticality. Such processes are likely to be underperforming competitors, making them candidates for outsourcing to at least gain parity within the industry. Many organizations actually begin their investigation of the BPO opportunity by shedding Type 8 processes to outsourcing vendors. This enables the organization to experiment with a low-risk process and work out any kinks that may exist in transferring data back and forth with the vendor. If BPO is in your organization's future, beginning with a Type 8 process may pave the way to a smoother rollout for more complex and risky processes in the future.

This eight-type BPO Selection Matrix provides additional insight into processes that may be outsourced for organizational advantage. The costs associated with a process will be explored as part of the Tier 3 analysis in Step 2. The productivity of a process should be assessed using standard industry benchmarks. If no metrics are available (which, unfortunately, is often the case), qualitative assessments and judgments can be used to categorize a process on the productivity scale. Finally, mission criticality is simply the identification of a process as critical, key, or support, as analyzed in Step 3.

Many business activities will not fit perfectly into one of these eight category types. For example, some activities are neither high nor low in productivity, but rather are aligned somewhere in the middle. In such cases, it is suggested that the activity be categorized as low because it is likely that a third-party vendor could improve performance in the activity for the organization. In essence, if the organization is not performing at best-in-class levels in the activity or function, whether on a cost or productivity basis, the activity or function should be classified as low. However, our three-way classification of mission criticality (critical, key, support) does have a middle ground, and most noncritical activities should be closely examined for outsourcing. Exhibit 3.9 is an example of a manufacturing firm's activities placed within the BPO Selection Matrix.

STEP 5: MODEL THE BPO PROJECT

BPO is similar to any other strategic business initiative in that it is imperative to establish performance metrics before implementation. In the case of BPO, some of the metrics will be quantitative (hard) and others will be qualitative (soft). Hard data include such things as project costs, time involved, and opportunity costs. Soft data include such things as employee displacement, effects on morale, and impact on community goodwill.

In order to establish appropriate performance metrics for a BPO initiative, it is critical to first establish the objectives of the project. The BAT's char-

EXHIBIT 3.9   Example of Manufacturing Company

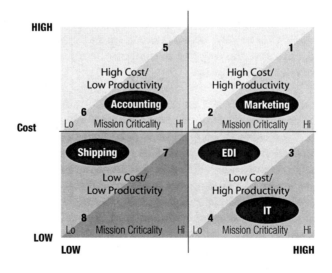

Productivity

ter charges it with defining the objectives of the initiative. Objectives should be identified both for the BPO initiative and for the transition process. At minimum, project objectives should include the following:

- Timing
- Costs
- Risk mitigation
- Deliverables

The timing of key events metrics will help identify if the BPO initiative is on track during the implementation phase. Event timing will include identifying realistic milestones for both the organization and its outsourcing partner. For example, developing a relationship with an HR outsourcing partner might involve shifting benefits administration and employee training responsibilities. For large firms this shift could be managed in phases, with each phase evaluated according to its time to implementation. At these critical deadlines, the project should be evaluated for effectiveness on a variety of measures. The metrics established by the BAT should include performance targets that are to be maintained once the BPO implementation is completed. These will establish the baseline standards that should be used in the selection of a BPO partner.

There will be costs involved with the BPO initiative, both cash and resource costs. The BAT should model the costs involved with both the BPO transition and with its ongoing maintenance. Implementation costs should be carefully detailed to include consulting or professional support required during the BPO analysis and implementation, personnel time, and opportunity costs involved with tying up key people during the transition. The organization should also monitor the noncash costs involved in the BPO rollout, including resource costs, downtime costs, and risk mitigation costs. A much more extensive discussion of the costs associated with a BPO opportunity is provided in Chapter 4.

Mitigating risks is a primary concern for a BPO initiative. Outsourcing necessarily entails ceding control of formerly internal processes, a prospect that is frightening to managers on many levels. Risks associated with outsourcing range from concerns over data security to a loss of organizational learning. Each specific risk can be mitigated, but there is no way to remove all risk from a BPO project. Thus, organizations need to weigh the risk of undertaking the project against the risk of not doing it. Risk mitigation tactics that should be modeled include provisions for what to do if the BPO provider fails outright. Having such contingencies in place will add to the complexity of the overall BPO project. Risks associated with BPO and mitigation tactics are discussed in greater detail in Chapter 10. The Ethics and Governance insert discusses how the international drive for consumer privacy has led to innovations in data security.

ETHICS & GOVERNANCE

Outsourcing Reduces Privacy Risks?

The drive to develop better means of protecting the privacy of individuals has led to international innovations in data security. Although not yet perfect, these innovations should help reassure companies considering outsourcing projects that involve sharing of sensitive data.

One of the primary drivers of information security is the need to protect medical records, resulting in the Health Insurance Portability and Accountability Act (HIPAA). This Act includes stringent data management standards to ensure that patient records are securely monitored and maintained. Nonetheless, medical transcription is a process that many hospitals, and even many transcription service providers, have elected to outsource. Today, medical records are being relayed around the world, and transcription is undertaken in places like Pakistan and India.

Although this might give some hospital administrators fits, it is possible that medical data are more securely managed through outsourcing than through in-house services. For example, if a hospital employee transcribes medical records, there is little recourse short of termination if the employee threatens to post the records on the Internet. However, a commercial provider that stands to go out of business if the records are improperly handled has a greater risk. Thus, the market-based governance of the third-party provider may be a more effective security management mechanism than organizational policies.

This principle holds true for data security and BPO in general. The digitization of corporate data has created security concerns in every industry. These concerns are real whether work is done in-house or outsourced around the world. Organizations considering BPO should mitigate data security risks through effective contracts. They should also be aware of the power of market-based governance mechanisms. The more a BPO vendor stands to lose by being sloppy with data, the more likely the vendor is to be a practitioner of leading-edge means of protecting that data.

Finally, the BAT should also develop clear expectations for the ultimate results or deliverables to be achieved through a BPO initiative. Many BPO projects are initiated with a pilot effort before a full rollout. The expectations for the pilot will likely be less ambitious than those for the full implementation, but they should be rigorous enough to test what is likely to occur when the switch is finally thrown. Results that fall short of expectations should provide insight into where the problems lie and how to fix them. They should also be used in a Go/No-Go decision strategy. One of the few tendencies in social systems that can be predicted with accuracy is the phenomenon known as "escalation of commitment" or the "sunk-cost effect."[12] This well-documented effect occurs as a result of the tendency for people to continue to invest in a project that is going poorly based on their past investment, rather than on forward-looking prospects. People tend to escalate their commitment to a project that is going poorly because they have already invested substantially in it and do not want to lose the investment. Organizations implementing a BPO initiative should be aware of and avoid this trap. They can do so by having clear Go/No-Go decision points established ahead of time.

Once the BPO initiative has been modeled for timing, costs, risk mitigation, and deliverables, the BAT next must build a business case for those processes that could benefit from outsourcing.

STEP 6: DEVELOP AND PRESENT THE BUSINESS CASE

The final step in the BPO opportunity analysis is to develop a business case for decision makers that will include direct recommendations on which, if any, business processes within the organization are suitable for outsourcing. A business case is a written document that presents the methodology and findings of the BAT.

The methodology section of the business case should include a review of the process the BAT used to reach its conclusions, including:

- The people who were consulted during the analysis phase
- The research documents reviewed, books read, conferences attended, and so on
- An overview of analytic tools applied to opportunity identification and selection (e.g., process maps)
- Copies of any research instruments (surveys, etc.) used to gather original data
- Minutes of the BAT team meetings

It is imperative to be concise in developing a business case, but the methodology should be clear about the thoroughness of the BAT's investigation. Often, top executives will fail to act on recommendations if they believe the findings are biased or likely to lead to internal bickering or resistance. The greater the level of involvement and thoroughness that can be demonstrated in the business case, the more likely that actions can swiftly and surely be considered and taken.

The findings section of the business case should include copies of the process maps developed by the BAT showing the three tiers of analysis. Gaps and inefficiencies in processes should be highlighted. In the end, if decision makers elect not to undertake a BPO initiative, the process maps developed by the BAT can at least assist the firm in reengineering processes that have serious gaps and/or inefficiencies.

The business case should also include the business model for each process recommended for outsourcing. The model will highlight in summary fashion the costs, timing, and deliverables associated with each process. Detailed transition models should be kept on reserve for those decision makers who wish to have more information.

Finally, the business case should make explicit the goals of outsourcing for each process. The goal may be to reduce operating costs, but it may also include the opportunity to develop world-class capability in a critical process, to reduce cycle times, or simply to free up business resources for other applications. Whatever the reason, the business case should clearly state the goals of outsourcing for each process and the likely improvements that may be attained through a BPO provider.

CONCLUSION

The six-step approach to analyzing the BPO opportunity outlined in this chapter provides a systematic framework for decision making. The importance of developing and managing a cross-functional BPO Analysis Team (BAT) cannot be overstated. An effective and committed BAT will be the focal point for BPO-based organizational change, including internal challenges to the BPO analysis process. Team members must be carefully chosen for their commitment to organizational strategy, ability to deal with and manage change, and capability to communicate and work with persons from a range of disciplinary backgrounds. Implementing the decision-making process and developing a business case should be done deliberately, with attention to deadlines and resource constraints. The systematic process we recommend is not foolproof, but it is likely to assist the organization in identifying inefficient or unproductive business processes, some of which can be outsourced and others of which can simply be fixed.

SUMMARY

- BPO is not right for every company, nor for every noncore process in a given company.

- SMEs are increasingly getting involved in BPO.
- Reasons for undertaking a BPO initiative include cost savings, reduced time to market, improved scalability, increased market flexibility, and acquisition of third-party expertise.
- The BPO analysis and selection process has six steps: (1) establish the BPO Analysis Team (BAT); (2) conduct a current state analysis; (3) identify core and noncore activities; (4) identify the BPO opportunity; (5) model the BPO project; and (6) develop the business case.
- The BAT should be chartered by top decision makers.
- The current state analysis maps business functions and activities using a three-tier approach.
- An organization's core competence is the process or functions that the organization's front office emphasizes to customers.
- The three critical factors to analyze in assessing an activity's BPO suitability are cost, productivity, and mission criticality.
- The three factors that should be considered in developing a model for a BPO initiative are timing, costs, and deliverables.
- The business case should include the BPO analysis methodology and clear recommendations.

CHAPTER 4

Identify and Manage the Costs of BPO

There are risks and costs to a program of action. But they are far less than the long-range risks and costs of comfortable inaction.

—John F. Kennedy, U.S. President

Make or buy? That is the fundamental decision that faces all organizations considering their alternatives for managing a business process. The decision involves many factors, not least of which is the cost associated with developing internal capabilities (making) or outsourcing them to an external provider (buying). As illustrated in Exhibit 3.8, the BPO Selection Matrix, in Chapter 3, cost is one of the three primary elements of the BPO decision, along with productivity and mission criticality. Each must be weighed when analyzing BPO opportunities for the organization. In a perfect world, where all other things are equal, the decision to undertake a BPO initiative would be based purely on cost-of-labor arbitrage—firms would simply source business processes to the lowest-cost labor, wherever it may be.

But our world is not perfect, and the various costs associated with a BPO initiative are not always easy to identify or forecast. The cost savings that are most often associated with a BPO initiative stem from the elimination of overhead, including jobs, capital assets, and real estate. However, the true costs of BPO involve far more than headcount and capital investments.

Identifying and assessing the costs associated with a BPO initiative are essential parts of the outsourcing decision. In this chapter we analyze the costs of BPO in two primary areas of concern: financial costs and strategic costs. The financial costs of BPO are the hard costs associated with the activities that must be undertaken to assess, launch, and maintain a BPO project. Strategic costs are the soft costs that are difficult to quantify but that can profoundly affect the firm's ability to compete. For example, one strategic cost of outsourcing that is often cited is loss of organizational learning in the out-sourced activity. This can lead to strategic blunders if the outsourced activity is important to the organization's core competence and the organization is not working closely enough with its vendor in mutual exchange of knowledge. Strategic benefits can arise from a deep partnership arrangement between BPO buyer and vendor. Such a relationship focuses not just on cost-effective performance on the outsourced activity, but also on knowledge sharing, innovation, and reciprocal exchange across business processes, including the outsourcer's core competence.

The total costs associated with BPO cannot be forecast precisely, but organizations seeking to undertake BPO can lessen the potential for expensive surprises by using an approach called Total Cost Management. By understanding the types of costs associated with BPO and techniques for mitigating them, organizations can budget appropriately and intelligently. The next section develops a Total Cost Management model for a standard BPO project.

TOTAL COST MANAGEMENT

Total Cost Management (TCM) is a term used to refer to the process of identifying, forecasting, and developing mitigating tactics for costs associated with a project. Individuals familiar with the initiation and implementation of information technology (IT) projects will recognize that this concept is similar to the Total Cost of Ownership (TCO) approach used for software and hardware investments. TCO is designed to focus attention on the total costs involved with a major IT investment and the organizational changes that are usually associated with such an undertaking. The approach helps organizations anticipate and evaluate all of the costs associated with an IT project, including the long-term maintenance and upgrade costs that are a part of nearly every IT investment, the human factors associated with adopting and adapting to a new technology, and costs associated with risk mitigation measures that need to be established.

As used in this chapter, TCM refers to the process of identifying and developing a strategy for managing the costs associated with initiating and managing a BPO project.[1] Exhibit 4.1 provides a high-level view of what we call

EXHIBIT 4.1   BPO Life Cycle

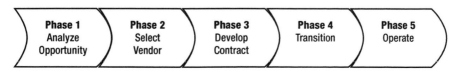

Phase 1	Phase 2	Phase 3	Phase 4	Phase 5
Analyze Opportunity	Select Vendor	Develop Contract	Transition	Operate

the BPO Life Cycle. Each phase of the life cycle has a variety of costs associated with it, some obvious and directly attributable to the project and others hidden and less easily attributed. For example, the BPO analysis team (BAT) will often require that non-BAT employees assist with the business-process mapping task. This means the employees will be pulled away from their normal jobs, if only briefly. Although it may be possible to attribute time-away costs to the BPO project, it is more difficult to attribute costs associated with disruptions in the work unit from which the employees came. Such disruptions can linger long after the individuals who assisted the BAT have returned to their work units. Questions about the security of their jobs, doubts about the intentions of the BAT, and work-time rumor exchange all sap productivity from the work team. These hidden costs are associated with the analysis phase of the BPO project. Using a TCM approach, these costs are identified, estimated, and attributed to the BPO project.

TCM involves the overt or direct costs that can be linked to the BPO project, hidden costs that are quantifiable but less easy to identify, and opportunity costs that are nonquantifiable but capable of being identified and estimated. Exhibit 4.2 shows a BPO Project TCM model that includes these varieties of cost categories.

In the following discussion, we examine in greater detail the financial costs associated with each phase of a BPO project. The chapter is concluded with an examination of the strategic costs associated with a BPO initiative.

EXHIBIT 4.2 BPO Total Cost Management

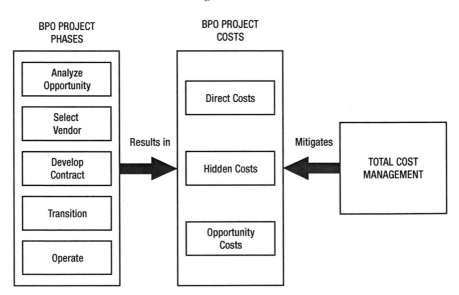

FINANCIAL COSTS

The financial costs associated with BPO are ongoing, as long as the project is active. Each project phase has predictable costs that can be forecasted, budgeted, monitored, and mitigated. In addition to these phase-specific direct project costs, each BPO initiative has a variety of less obvious yet insidious hidden costs. Project managers will do well to include these costs in their analyses because many initiatives accumulate unanticipated costs that can prove to be threatening to projects—and careers. In the next section, the direct and hidden costs associated with each phase of a BPO project are examined. We also discuss mitigation tactics that can be used to control costs in each phase.

Phase 1: Analyze Opportunity

The first direct cost to consider in the analysis phase of the BPO Life Cycle is associated with the internal staff that will be enlisted to conduct the analysis. As discussed in detail in Chapter 3, organizations should use a team approach to identify and select BPO opportunities. Organizing a BAT means that employees from diverse units will take time away from their normal duties to serve on the team. The time these individuals spend away from their normal duties is a direct cost.

Costs associated with removing individuals from their normal job functions can be calculated in several ways. One standard method is to count the hours spent on the BPO analysis for each BAT member (and anyone else they bring in on a transitory basis) and multiply this figure by the hourly wage for that individual. The result of this calculation is then attributed to the BPO project. This approach is often referred to as *transfer pricing*. For example, if the HR director is on the BAT and she has an hourly wage of $75, that figure would be multiplied by the number of hours she dedicated to the BAT. The product of this calculation would be attributed to the BPO project. Project managers commonly use what is called a task based costing estimate to forecast personnel costs associated with a project.[2] An example of such an estimate is given in Exhibit 4.3.

This technique is commendable but may not tell the entire story. For example, it is inevitable that BAT members will spend hours outside of their formal meetings thinking about BPO, analyzing opportunities in their minds, and talking with others informally about what the BAT is doing and learning. These extra hours are usually not calculated and attributed to the project. A technique that can be used to account for this hidden cost is to apply a standard multiplier to the hours that are logged as officially attributable to the BPO project. For example, a person may spend one hour outside formal meetings working on the BPO project for every two hours spent

EXHIBIT 4.3 Task-Based Cost Estimating Model

Assumptions:	
HR Director day rate cost	$600
Material day rate cost	$150
Information from Project Plan:	
Task start date	10/1/04
Task finish date	10/9/04
Computations:	
Task duration (days)	9
Outputs:	
Total personnel cost	$5,400
Total materials cost	$1,350
Total Project Cost:	$6,750

in formal meetings. A multiplier of 1.5 would capture that informal project time and provide a more realistic estimate of actual costs. In general, a multiplier between 1.0 and 2.0 applied to formal meeting time is appropriate in estimating BAT member time spent on the BPO project during the analysis phase.

Another direct cost associated with the BPO analysis phase involves third-party professional support that may be required to assist the team. BPO consultants, market research specialists, and change-management consultants are just some of the outside professionals the BAT may want to consider utilizing. This cost can be estimated at the beginning of the project using several heuristics, including:

- Prior BPO knowledge among BAT members and the organization as a whole
- Organizational history with BPO, reengineering, or other transformational change programs
- Top management support for BPO in the organization

The BAT member knowledge of BPO is a factor because lack of such background will usually require investment in outside support. It is simply unrealistic to expect individuals with no BPO knowledge or experience to be effective BAT members. Thus, training and preparation costs should be estimated. A good rule of thumb estimate is one week of person-time for each BAT member to read, review, and discuss what BPO is and how it can be utilized by the organization.

Organizational history with major change efforts can also reduce the costs of the BPO analysis. Firms that have such a history, whether with reengineering, TQM, or something else, will likely be better suited for the self-examination process that is required for effective BAT performance. Prior history with transformational change, especially if such change had positive consequences, can ease the burden of the analysis process. Individuals throughout the firm will be more willing to cooperate and work hard to analyze BPO opportunities if they believe that the process will result in positive changes. Estimating the costs associated with a lack of history in transformational change will be a subjective affair. In general, the analysis phase cost estimates should include an extra week of BAT member time if the organization has no history with transformational change.

Top management support is critical to the success of any organizational transformation. Individuals enlisted to be members of the organization's BAT must perceive that they are empowered to dedicate their time to the analysis process. If top managers badger them about time spent away from their central duties, they will feel conflicted and the BPO analysis process is likely to take longer and be less effective. Top managers must clear the space necessary for BAT members to undertake their analysis, while maintaining reasonable expectations about performance in their regular duties.

Hidden costs associated with the BPO analysis phase include those that arise from a lack of organizational capability to analyze the BPO opportunity. Reliance on third-party consultants to assist with the BPO analysis is common and in many cases recommended. However, overreliance on consultants can lead to additional project costs throughout the implementation, transition, and maintenance phases of the BPO initiative. To avoid these hidden costs, BAT members and others should strive to learn as much as possible from the third-party professionals. Failure to concentrate on organizational learning and building a knowledge base for managing BPO projects will lead to additional costs at some point in the project. Thus, the organization should seek to develop BPO champions within the organization. These champions will be responsible for absorbing, analyzing, communicating, and documenting knowledge gained from third parties and through the BAT's internal research process.

The opportunity costs associated with the analysis phase—as with all phases of the BPO Life Cycle—center on employee time and organizational resources that could have been put to some other use. Opportunity costs are notoriously difficult to measure. However, organizations should directly confront the issue of whether it makes sense to pursue BPO opportunities prior to and during the analysis phase. At this point in the BPO Life Cycle, commitment is still relatively low and a decision to cut losses and exit the project would not be as difficult as later in the project. Beyond this point, it gets increasingly difficult to shut down the BPO initiative and accept the sunk costs.

Costs associated with the BPO analysis phase can be mitigated through a variety of tactics. For example, the exercise of mapping organizational processes in the interest of determining their suitability for BPO also reveals opportunities for reengineering. Processes that have gone unexamined for a period of time almost assuredly have become bloated and inefficient in a number of ways, some subtle and some not so subtle. The process maps developed during the analysis phase should be used to catalyze reengineering efforts directed at those inefficient or unproductive processes that are not outsourced. The organization will derive benefits from the analysis phase if it is prepared to use its findings for organizational improvement regardless of whether a BPO project is initiated. The organizational learning that is a consequence of process mapping is not confined to BAT members. As stated in Chapter 3, the BAT should invite participation from individuals working within processes to assist with the mapping. These individuals can be encouraged to initiate changes to process inefficiencies when they return to their work units.

Another cost mitigation tactic that can be applied to the analysis phase includes the potential for a general elevation in work productivity levels as a natural result of organizational self-examination. The phenomenon of increased performance as a result of being observed is commonly referred to as the Hawthorne effect.[3] The reference is to the famous studies conducted between 1924 and 1932 at the Hawthorne plant of Western Electric, wherein employee performance was increased merely because of the presence of the researchers.[4] Organizations can encourage operating performance improvement during the course of the BPO analysis based on this effect. Communicating the process improvement objectives of the analysis phase to everyone in the units under scrutiny is a means of circumventing the potential for fear-induced performance declines. Getting people involved in the change effort is a classic technique to mitigate the hidden costs associated with the common human tendency to resist change.

The result of the BPO analysis phase is a decision about implementing a BPO project. Implementing a BPO project has several subphases associated with it, including:

- Identifying a suitable outsourcing vendor/partner
- Negotiating a contract
- Establishing a project map for the transition

Phase 2: Vendor Selection

One of the first decisions any organization must make after identifying a BPO opportunity is whether to hire a third-party intermediary to assist with the vendor selection. The decision about whether to use an intermediary during vendor selection can be an important one. Obviously, conducting the vendor selection in-house can reduce costs in the short run, but that choice may add costs in the long run. Especially for large and complex outsourcing initiatives, the vendor selection phase can be time-consuming and highly detailed. Third-party intermediaries that specialize in request for proposal (RFP) drafting, distribution, and response evaluation can reduce the time it takes to identify a suitable outsourcing vendor and allow internal staff to stay focused on internal issues.

For companies that decide to manage the vendor selection phase in-house, financial costs will include the time spent in crafting an RFP, distributing it to vendors, managing and responding to queries, and evaluating the completed proposals. Every RFP generates questions from potential responders. And the international distribution of many BPO RFPs raises the likelihood of misunderstandings and requests for clarification. Staff time will be needed to field questions—some legitimate, some maddeningly trite or irrelevant— from all over the world. A fair response process that limits the potential for liability requires each inquiry to be managed with equal care and interest.

Depending on the complexity of the BPO project, it could take anywhere from a month to several months to write a comprehensive RFP—one that clearly articulates the scope of the BPO initiative, the expectations for service delivery, the qualifications of the outsourcing firm, and the range of services that will be needed to fully outsource the process. On the vendor side, responding to the RFP can also be a time-consuming and labor-intensive process. As such, the responder may require additional information and clarification throughout the response period. The response phase of the RFP process may take another one to three months.

All told, it may take anywhere from two to six months or longer for the RFP process to be completed. Of course, at the end of that process the initiating organization will have an inbox full of complex and comprehensive proposals. These proposals each must be examined to identify which of the potential vendors is best suited to carry out the BPO initiative. For many outsourcing RFPs, there may be upward of 50 proposals from highly qualified vendors. If the initiating organization is merely seeking the low-cost provider, the process of selecting the vendor may (emphasize *may*) be made easier. However, even that approach to vendor selection can be deceiving. For example, a vendor that submits the low-cost solution may have scrimped on certain critical services or it may have suggested reduced service levels. Evaluating proposals on price alone may in fact lead to higher costs later.

The process of evaluating the RFP responses from potential vendors can take a month or longer. Typically, the evaluation process moves from scrutinizing the written proposals to actual meetings with the leadership teams of the top candidates, including site visits. These meetings can add another month to the selection process because some of the vendor facilities may be in faraway corners of the world.

Organizations that manage the RFP process in-house should assume that the process can take anywhere from three to six months, depending on the complexity, scope, and range of services involved in the project. They should also assume that the process will occupy 50 percent or more of the work time for at least one management-level individual during the process. Thus, estimating the cost of in-house management of the RFP process begins with the cost of one-half to one person-year of management-level personnel. The cost estimate does not end there, however. The decision to in-source the RFP process carries hidden costs associated with the risk of going it alone. No matter the experience of the individuals managing the RFP process, going it alone likely means additional costs associated with writing an incomplete RFP, establishing an ineffective response-management plan, and selecting a less-than-optimal vendor. Each of these is a reflection of the fact that RFP

CASE STUDY

GE Real Estate Understands Total BPO Costs

Realizing cost savings from offshore outsourcing often takes years of effort and a huge up-front investment. For many companies, it simply may not be worth it. "Someone working for $10,000 a year in Hyderabad can end up costing an American company four to eight times that amount," says Hank Zupnick, CIO of GE Real Estate. Yet, all too often, companies do not make the outlays required to make offshore outsourcing work.

"You have to bring people to America to learn your applications, and that takes time, particularly if you're doing it with a new vendor for the first time," explains Zupnick, who maintains a handful of three-year contracts with offshore vendors. In GE Real Estate's case, the transition time for each vendor was up to a year in some cases, in addition to the money-draining vendor selection period of several months.

Zupnick, who has seven years of offshore experience, says most of his peers do not appreciate the time and money it takes to get a relationship up and running. "The vendors say you can throw it over the wall and start saving money right away. As a result, I have heard of CIOs who have tried to go the India or China route, and nine months later they pulled the plug because they were not saving money," Zupnick says. "You have to build in up to a year for knowledge transfer and ironing out cultural differences."

At GE Real Estate, managing the offshore vendor is such a big task that Zupnick assigned someone to handle it on a half-time basis at a $50,000 salary. The individual makes sure projects move forward and develops and analyzes vendor proposals against the RFPs when it comes time to bid out new work.

Source: Adapted from Stephanie Overby, "The Hidden Costs of Offshore Outsourcing," *CIO* (September 1, 2003).

writing, distribution, and management is not part of the initiating organization's core competence. This hidden cost can be estimated based on the relative experience of the project's lead individual(s). An inexperienced project leader could double the costs of the implementation phase over the cost of using a professional service provider. A highly experienced leader may increase costs by far less, but such a person probably commands a far higher salary. The Case Study points out that GE Real Estate hired a manager who dedicates half his work time to managing the BPO of the organization's offshore outsourcing relationships.

The costs of selecting the BPO vendor can be mitigated using a variety of tactics, depending in part on whether the vendor selection is handled internally or externally. Handling the vendor selection internally will provide the value-adding benefits of increased levels of organizational learning and capability. The internal outsourcing manager or management team will be involved in drafting and distributing the RFP, responding to vendor inquiries, and selecting the vendor. Developing internal knowledge of these aspects of a BPO implementation means the organization has developed the capacity for additional BPO initiatives at some future date. The greatest value-added benefit is likely to be the reduced time required for future vendor selection.

Cost mitigation benefits associated with hiring a consultant to conduct the BPO implementation include a faster process and, quite likely, a more effective vendor relationship. Professional service firms skilled in matching client needs with vendor capacities are likely to be able to provide significant value to the BPO buyer. The BPO buyer can derive even greater benefits if the consultant is compensated in part based on vendor performance. This is just one example of contracting mechanisms and innovations that can be used during the implementation phase to reduce risks and increase benefits.

Phase 3: Contract Development

The principal cost of the contract development phase concern those associated with negotiating a contract with the vendor. It is highly recommended that the BPO buyer work with an experienced legal team when developing the BPO contract. There is simply too much at stake in the specification of services, deliverables, and remedies to cut costs in this area. We take up the issue of BPO contracting in detail in Chapter 6. Here, we simply suggest a rule of thumb contracting cost estimate. The rule is that contracting costs, in terms of internal time and legal review, should be less than 5 percent of the size of the outsourced project. Thus, a $1 million project may have contract development costs up to $50,000.

Hidden costs associated with contract development include the dangers inherent in failing to specify appropriate penalties, remedies, and exit strategies. These ticking-time bombs don't go off unless something goes wrong during the transition or operating phases of the BPO Life Cycle. Since not every contingency can be covered in a BPO contract, general problem-resolution terms should be included along with more specific problem situations and types. A legal team with experience in BPO can be vital to help buyer and vendor alike avoid downstream cost-traps via carefully constructed contract terms.

Ongoing BPO project needs and requirements will evolve over time, and the scope and nature of the buyer-vendor relationship must adapt as well. The typical BPO relationship will last four to six years and will involve ongoing negotiations and deal making. Each of these encounters presents the possibility of incurring undue costs resulting from poor negotiating skills, an incomplete or poorly designed original contract, or a rotating lead-person tango by either the BPO buyer or vendor. Poor negotiating skills can lead to less than favorable terms on changes in the original contract or in the provision of new services. Poorly crafted original contracts can lock in an organization to low service levels or draconian pricing. A rotating lead person by either party can mean a loss of organizational learning and a need to return time and again to the fundamentals underlying the relationship. This process is time consuming and can eat the cost advantages that are commonly part of a BPO relationship. Stability in the buyer-vendor relationship is built on the foundation of a carefully constructed contract. Hidden costs associated with a poor contract can destroy a relationship. BPO buyers shouldn't scrimp on direct contract development costs and risk the potential for project-threatening hidden costs in the later stages of the BPO Life Cycle.

Phase 4: Transition

The transition phase is one in which the business process that formerly had been handled in-house is wholly or in part shifted to the outsourcing vendor. The costs associated with the transition phase are driven by five primary characteristics of the BPO buyer–vendor relationship, as illustrated in Exhibit 4.4.

The "asset ownership and location" driver concerns which firm will be better able to leverage people, technology, and other assets for competitive advantage, and where those assets should be located. In some situations, a BPO buyer may want to retain all or part of its existing assets to continue to develop internal competence in a process. For example, a firm may elect to outsource a part of its call center to a vendor as a means of freeing internal call center staff time to make improvements to the in-house operation.

The decision about how asset ownership will be allocated between buyer and vendor has direct cost implications. For example, by outsourcing asset ownership, an organization can turn capital into expense: Assets that had previously required maintenance and continuing investment of time, money, equipment, and people are converted into a variable or fixed cost on the income statement, depending on the type of BPO contract.

EXHIBIT 4.4   Cost Drivers of the BPO Transition

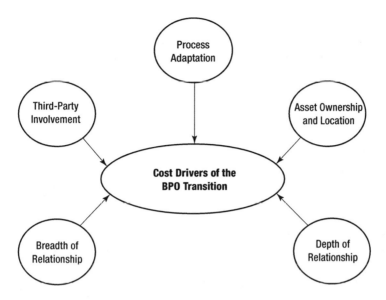

The decision about where assets will be located also has cost implications. Retaining a process on the buying organization's premises usually means that the transition can be completed more quickly than moving assets off-site, but not necessarily. There are many advantages to keeping assets on-site. One of these is that it is far easier to retain existing personnel, many of whom would be unwilling to relocate to the vendor (especially if the vendor is overseas). Employees involved in a process that has been outsourced can become productive members of the vendor organization, but the transition must be handled with care. It is not unusual for the BPO buyer to experience attrition, staff cuts, and reassignments during the transition phase. The vendor will often reengineer the outsourced process, reducing inefficiencies and enhancing individual productivity levels. This means that staff who remain may harbor lingering fears for their own job security—fears that may slow the transition and affect productivity. Proper management of the in-house transition to vendor management and process ownership will reduce these potential costs.

Regardless of whether the process remains on-site or is moved off-site, there will be a need to transfer process-related information, knowledge, and controls. In addition, during the transition phase it will be necessary to establish information exchange and data interface protocols that mesh the existing standards and information management architectures of each firm. It is nearly inevitable that this integration process will have a variety of workflow disruptions. Data needed for routine day-to-day tasks may be unavailable from time to time during the transition. New interface procedures, such as logins or passwords, may create confusion and frustration. The better the organization communicates with employees about these potential disruptions and their duration and scope, the less costly the transition phase will be.

Depth of relationship refers to the costs associated with developing and maintaining a strategic relationship with the vendor. We discuss the nature of a strategic relationship between buyer and vendor in detail in the "Strategic Costs" section that follows. Here, we mention only that a commitment to developing a strategic relationship will be more costly depending on the expectations for value extraction. The greater the value expected to be extracted from the relationship, the more time and resources will be required to develop and maintain the relationship.

The breadth of the relationship between buyer and vendor refers to the range of processes that are outsourced. In some cases, organizations outsource multiple functions to a single provider. On other occasions, multiple providers are used for a range of different processes. The decision about the breadth of processes to outsource to a particular vendor has both direct and hidden costs. In fact, working with a single provider for multiple processes may reduce costs as familiarity and trust develop over time. At the same time, the potential costs associated with vendor failure increase as dependence on the vendor increases.

A potentially significant cost associated with the transition phase of the BPO initiative is based on the need for third parties to assist in the integration of the vendor and initiating organization's systems. For example, it may be necessary to bring in specialists if the two firms have complex databases built on different platforms. This is more likely if the initiating organization has legacy systems that have not been upgraded in several years or if it has homegrown applications that are known to only a handful of individuals. The vendor should be expected to provide transition management expertise for most systems, but it cannot be expected to have expertise to manage a smooth transition if the initiating organization has outdated or, at least, very old databases and information architectures. In that case, third parties may be necessary to assist in upgrading and migrating the buyer organization's data to the vendor's system.

Hidden and opportunity costs associated with the transition phase center on the effects of outsourcing a process on employees who work outside the process. They may experience a period of adjustment as the process is transitioned. Adjustments include not only the need to understand and work with a reengineered process but also the need to interface with new people and unfamiliar systems. As usual for organizational change of this magnitude, some people will take longer than others to adjust, and some will simply resist the changes altogether. In general, organizations initiating a BPO project can expect some productivity dropoff in personnel who work internally with the outsourced process. Of course, the expectation is that after the period of adjustment, the productivity levels will reach their previous norms and may reach new highs as the efficiencies of the newly outsourced process kick in.

Transition phase costs are mitigated by the fact that the BPO decision has been taken and the wheels of change have been set in motion. Throughout this chapter we have been warning about the possible productivity-sapping dangers of organizational change. This negative effect is usually reversed once the decision to change has been made and the organization is clearly pursuing its new objectives. Those who had resisted the change will either adjust or, at least, stop resisting. Resistance to organizational change—or, for that matter, to nearly any type of personal change—usually reaches a peak just before the decision to move forward. Once the decision is taken, the mental energy that had previously been applied to blocking or resisting the change is now committed to adapting and adjusting to the new way of doing business—or to moving on to a new employer.[5]

Other cost mitigation strategies during the transition are associated, again, with whether the process is handled internally. Internal management of the transition increases the organization's operational capabilities for additional BPO projects or other major change efforts. The transition phase is characterized by complexities of integrating management styles, information systems, and work cultures. Third-party consultants can assist in making the BPO transition easier and less time-consuming. In the short run, hiring third-party support for the BPO transition can reduce costs. Organizations that are initiating BPO for the first time may want to hire a service provider, but they should assign a high-ranking insider to work closely with the consultant to siphon off the knowledge that can be used to manage subsequent BPO projects internally.

Phase 5: Operate

The operating phase of the BPO Life Cycle refers to the period when the contract is being fully implemented and performance expectations drive the relationship. Among the endpoints that should be monitored as part of an ongoing BPO initiative, include both financial and productivity ratios. Financial ratios that should be monitored range from standard return on investment (ROI) to margin enhancement. Depending on the intentions of the BPO project, the financial ratios to be monitored will vary slightly. As mentioned, some BPO projects are undertaken primarily for cost-reduction purposes and others primarily for strategic advantage purposes. Cost-reduction BPO projects are intended to enhance margins through reduced overhead, a feat that can often be achieved within a period of 6 to 12 months after commencement of the contract.

In contrast, strategic BPO attempts to leverage the world-leading capabilities of the outsourcing partner and will focus more on new revenue over margin enhancement. Organizations must establish financial metrics appropriate to the intentions of their BPO project. Exhibit 4.5 identifies key financial performance metrics associated with each type of BPO project.

BPO implementation will not only have a financial impact on the organization but also a productivity impact. The productivity impact, it must be noted, will likely reach beyond the unit or function that is targeted for the outsourcing project. Most BPO initiatives result in some job displacement or layoffs within the organization. Other employees will be concerned about whether their unit is a BPO target in the future. Employees who are concerned about the security of their jobs are likely to demonstrate a dropoff in productivity—at least in the short term.

Productivity measures used to control the BPO initiative must account for these short-term fluctuations in overall productivity while keeping track of long-term objectives. The distinction in metrics between cost-reduction BPO and strategic BPO is less pronounced for productivity than it was for financial indicators. Productivity measures are fairly consistent for the organization regardless of the cost-cutting or strategic initiatives undertaken. Several important productivity metrics that organizations can use to control a BPO initiative include the following:

- Output/employee
- Overhead cost/unit of output
- Output/capital expenditure
- Output/asset

These standard productivity measures will enable the firm to assess the pre- and post-BPO impact. The measures must each include a time element to account for short-term variation. It would be a mistake to pull the plug on a BPO initiative based on early returns that showed a dip in overall organizational productivity. Such fluctuation should be anticipated and accounted for before launching the project. Still, normalization or improvement in

EXHIBIT 4.5   Financial Performance Metrics

Cost-Reduction BPO	Strategic BPO
ROI	ROI
Net Margin	Gross Revenue
Sales/Employee	Market Share
Inventory Turns	Customer Acquisition Cost

productivity should be expected within a pre-established period and adjustments made to the BPO initiative if those targets are not being met.

Qualitative measures of the BPO initiative are far-reaching, including internal, external, and vendor-related metrics. Internal qualitative metrics will focus on a variety of issues concerning the relative health of the organization. Effectively managing the BPO rollout will require data collection before, during, and after the process. Before the process begins, organizations should collect data on several characteristics of the internal environment, including the following:

- Employee knowledge of BPO
- Employee understanding of organizational strategy
- Employee morale and sense of job security
- Employee capacity to deal with change

These various data points will help establish appropriate information and communication programs during and after the BPO implementation process. For example, if it is determined that employee knowledge of BPO and its potential to help the organization is low, the organization may benefit from training programs aimed at reducing the knowledge gap. Research has clearly shown that people are more productive and likely to pitch in throughout a change process if they understand the rationale and direction of the change.

External factors to monitor for a BPO initiative include issues related to customers, competitors, and shareholders. Organizations as a general rule should be collecting data regarding customer satisfaction, so we will not allude to it here as a new metric to monitor. We do stress the importance of maintaining a close watch on customer satisfaction levels during the BPO implementation process, regardless of whether the BPO initiative involves a customer-facing function. Of course, normal variations in satisfaction levels should not precipitate corrective actions, but variations beyond the norm must be carefully analyzed in case action is required. The latter is especially important if the BPO initiative involves a customer-facing process such as a call center or help desk.

If the organization has undertaken a strategic BPO initiative, competitive response will be a crucial external variable to monitor. Strategic BPO is undertaken precisely to gain and, ideally, sustain competitive advantage. Competitors will respond to new moves within the industry, especially those that have potential market-shifting or disruptive capability. Organizations initiating BPO for strategic reasons will be wise to establish a rollout strategy that keeps them beneath competitors' radar screens, at least until a defensible position has been established. Careful monitoring of the competition can help determine whether the rollout strategy is working.

Organizations should also monitor the reactions of shareholders and other major organizational stakeholders to the BPO initiative. Because most investors have a conservative streak, extensive reengineering or restructuring that includes a technology component may meet with anxiety and doubt. Clear understanding of stakeholder knowledge of organizational strategy before and after the BPO initiative has begun can help circumvent unnecessary roadblocks that may arise as people hear about the outsourcing project.

The final qualitative data points that must be collected and assessed during the operating phase involve those between the organization and the BPO partner. This complex relationship will evolve over time as the BPO partner performs on its contract. Underlying each BPO partner relationship are the so-called service level agreements (SLA) that specify actions that will be taken to ensure customer satisfaction. Organizations often have only a few individuals who have read and understood the SLAs. In the event that something goes wrong—and it always will—the SLAs will detail how to make corrections. Organizations should carefully monitor performance on the SLAs—both its own capacity for enforcing them and the vendor's capacity for responding to problems. The costs associated with non-performance are obvious—direct loss of business. There are also hidden and opportunity costs associated with slow response times, including customer dissatisfaction if the outsourced process is customer facing, employee disgruntlement, and a loss of confidence and trust between buyer and vendor that may adversely affect the future of the relationship. The BPO buyer must ensure that it is monitoring the "temperature" of the BPO relationship and that it can respond if things begin to go awry.

STRATEGIC COSTS

The strategic costs associated with BPO are centered on the potential loss of organizational learning that results from moving a process under the control of an external service provider. Competitive advantage in most industries today is a moving target, and firms must seek it wherever they can. In some cases, competitive advantage arises in unexpected quarters, as a serendipitous result of decisions taken long ago and improved on over time. For example, the Sabre ticketing system developed by American Airlines was a source of competitive advantage for the air carrier. The efficiency of the system provided an advantage to American during a time when it was difficult for the major carriers to differentiate themselves. American created a profit center around the Sabre system by leasing it to other carriers. The system eventually became a profitable business unit and was spun off into Sabre Holdings. The software is now used throughout the industry to manage the ticketing process. Had American decided long ago to outsource the ticketing process, it would not have developed the Sabre system. At the same time, American never consciously set out to make Sabre the industry standard. The airline was merely trying to develop a system that enabled efficient ticketing.

Outsourcing so-called noncore processes must be undertaken with careful forethought because it is never clear how future competitive conditions will unfold and what types of competencies will be required. In Chapter 3, we indicated that firms must distinguish noncore activities as critical, key, or support. Those activities that are tightly coupled to the core and are fault intolerant (i.e., mission-critical processes) should usually be retained in-house. At the very least, they should be outsourced only when the interorganizational relationship is clearly focused on developing and deriving strategic advantages. Knowledge management should be transparent from one firm to the other, and reciprocal exchange of insights should be considered routine. Furthermore, a quest for innovation in the interlinking of the critical and core processes must be a paramount concern for both sides of the outsourcing relationship.

In fact, the major strategic component of a BPO initiative is the relationship between buyer and vendor. Relationship costs are those that are involved in courting, establishing, and maintaining a relationship with a BPO vendor.[6] This complex undertaking can be as far-reaching and comprehensive as a merger or joint venture. Such transactions are distinguished by the need to mesh information systems, governance structures, and, not least, organizational cultures into a unified whole. The complexity of the challenges of merging two formerly distinct enterprises is often too overwhelming for the executives who engineered the deal. One or more top executives are often either asked or forced to leave as they become increasingly disoriented amid the chaos of the combined entity. For example, the merger of Hewlett-Packard and Compaq in 2002 led to a quick departure of Compaq's then-CEO Michael Capellas.[7] Departures related to that merger continued well into 2003.[8]

A thoroughgoing BPO relationship can have many of the same complexities of a major merger or joint venture. Firms that determine to outsource back-office processes are entering into a relationship with a vendor that will have important implications for their ability to compete. The risk posed by this loss of functional independence requires careful prior analysis of the capabilities and integrity of the vendor. In the case of a BPO relationship, it is simply unacceptable for any breakdowns in performance or integrity to occur.

The directly attributable costs of a BPO relationship are those that are associated with identification, analysis, and selection of the various vendor candidates, controlling the vendor relationship, and developing strategic knowledge management capacities with the vendor.

Hidden costs associated with the vendor relationship are primarily centered on the impact of transitioning formerly internal processes to external control. For example, in many outsourcing relationships, employees of the BPO buyer become employees of the vendor. This is often the case in data center management where a large organization such as EDS simply acquires the existing IT infrastructure, including staff, from the outsourcer.[9] This transition from one employer to another can have ripple effects throughout the organization, as uncertainty and fear are typically associated with changes of this type.[10] Others near to or friendly with those who have a new employer may pick up on grumbling or criticism and wonder whether they will be next in line for such a transition. In other words, the social contract between employer and employee—whether explicit or tacit—has the appearance of being violated when employees are optioned to another firm. It does not matter that such optioning usually results in better efficiencies and working conditions. The perception of violation of the social contract is enough to send some employees scurrying to Monster.com to seek out a new employer. The disruption of the work environment will always have hidden costs as morale and productivity are negatively affected by change.

Strategic costs associated with outsourcing can be mitigated through appropriate vendor selection and contracting. Using stringent selection procedures ensures that the vendor chosen has the intellectual, technological, and social resources to become a true partner in the success of the BPO buyer. The buyer–vendor relationship should not become a cat-and-mouse game focused on price issues. Rather, both sides should constantly strive to create positive-sum outcomes from their deep relationship. That is, rather than constantly seeking to increase service prices, the vendor should seek ways to help the buyer grow and to participate in that growth. Likewise, rather than constantly beating down the vendor's price, the BPO buyer should seek to deepen the partnership and find ways to leverage the vendor's capacity for mutual benefit. This is not a typical buyer–supplier relationship as outlined in the standard strategy textbooks.

With the financial and strategic cost factors identified and estimated, it is possible to create a TCM project overview. We conclude this chapter with a discussion of this final part of the TCM process.

CONCLUSION

The costs associated with a BPO initiative are many, and they could easily overwhelm a project and the project manager if they were not anticipated in advance. The TCM approach that we recommend in this chapter places costs within the context of project phases. Thus, at different points during the BPO initiative, it can be determined whether costs are in line with expectations and/or whether adjustments need to be made.

Exhibit 4.6 illustrates how costs can be mapped to BPO project phases. In many cases, the costs incurred directly in one phase linger across the other

EXHIBIT 4.6 TCM Applied to BPO Project Phases

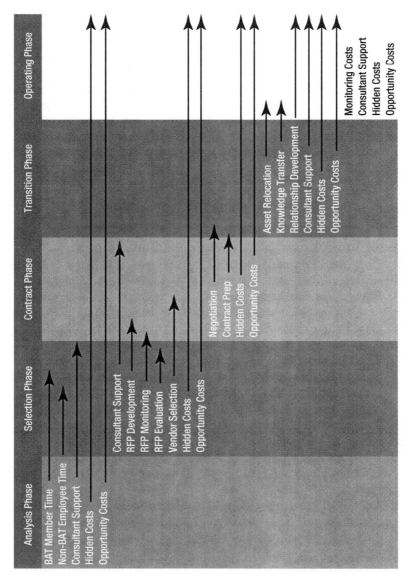

phases of the project. Note also that hidden costs and opportunity costs are present in each phase. These insidious costs have lasting effects that accumulate over time and must be estimated to get a true idea of BPO costs.

Finally, BPO project costs should be tracked throughout and adjustments in projected and actual total costs modified along the way. If savings have been achieved over anticipated costs, they should be noted just as well as cost overruns should be noted. Cost savings may be a good thing, but they may also be a warning indicator that an important consideration in the BPO project has been overlooked. Smart BPO project managers are cost alert and employ mitigation tactics wherever possible. They are also aware that every major change initiative carries risks and costs before benefits can be realized. This essential tension between moving forward and pulling the plug should motivate constant cost vigilance and a culture of appropriate frugality.

SUMMARY

- BPO costs involve far more than mere labor-cost arbitrage.
- There are five phases to the BPO Life Cycle: (1) analysis, (2) vendor selection, (3) contract development, (4) transition, and (5) operating.
- BPO costs can be understood as financial costs and strategic costs.
- Total Cost Management (TCM) is a term used to refer to the process of identifying, forecasting, and developing mitigating tactics for costs associated with a project.
- TCM involves the overt or direct costs that can be linked to the BPO project, hidden costs that are quantifiable but less easy to identify, and opportunity costs that are nonquantifiable but capable of being identified and estimated.
- The task-based cost estimating model calculates personnel time attributable to a BPO project.
- The transition phase is one in which the business process that formerly had been handled in-house is wholly or in part shifted to the outsourcing vendor.
- Transition involves consideration of five cost drivers of the buyer–vendor relationship: (1) asset ownership and location, (2) process adaptation, (3) depth of relationship, (4) breadth of relationship, and (5) third-party involvement.
- The operating phase of the BPO Life Cycle refers to the period when the contract is being fully implemented and performance expectations drive the relationship.
- The strategic costs associated with BPO are centered on the potential loss of organizational learning that results from moving a process under the control of an external service provider.

three

BPO Vendor Selection

This part of the book examines the challenges involved in selecting an appropriate outsourcing vendor and establishing an effective contractual relationship.

Chapter 5 recommends establishing a vendor selection team to conduct the initial search and to manage the request for information (RFI) and request for proposal (RFP) processes. The vendor selection team is chartered separately from the BPO analysis team described in Part Two. The vendor selection team is responsible for identifying a long list of potential BPO vendors and then systematically narrowing the field to a preferred provider.

Once the vendor is chosen, contract negotiations begin. Chapter 6 examines the major factors to consider when crafting an effective BPO contract. From service level agreements (SLAs) to dispute resolution to pricing, the contract is the legal foundation for the outsourcing relationship. Chapter 6 provides a thorough review of contract terms and how to avoid potential traps that could result in unexpected project difficulties.

CHAPTER 5

Identify and Select a BPO Vendor

Progress lies not in enhancing what is, but in advancing toward what will be.

—Kahlil Gibran, author of *The Prophet*

Finding the right BPO vendor is a critical step in an organization's outsourcing initiative and one of the most difficult to manage. The promise of BPO is always tempered by the perceived risks associated with handing responsibility for an internal business process—no matter how noncore or mundane it may be—to another firm. More than one manager has balked at launching a BPO project because of the occasional stories of vendor failure that appear in the media. Many would prefer to play it safe and stay with the status quo than to advance toward what will (or might) be.

With its implications for the long-term strategic direction of the organization, the vendor identification and selection phase of the BPO Life Cycle certainly must be taken seriously. When an organization enters into a BPO relationship, it is assigning a third party the responsibility of managing part of its business. When such a decision is made, the organization obviously is assuming additional risk.

The vendor identification and selection process has a life cycle of its own, beginning with scouring the Internet and other sources to identify potential vendors/partners, through the agonizing getting-acquainted stage, the evaluation stage, and, finally, selection. If all goes well, service delivery works as planned and may even continue beyond the original contract period. Both parties are satisfied. If things do not go well, the parties disassociate themselves, and the BPO buyer is forced either to find another vendor or to reestablish an internal version of the business process.

In some ways, the BPO vendor selection process is a highly subjective affair. For example, the decision about which vendor to select will ultimately be based in part on how well the buyer and vendor firms relate to one another. It would be unwise, and probably considered a bit absurd, to select a BPO vendor that was offensive or whose organizational culture was a clear mismatch with the BPO buyer's culture.

There undoubtedly are qualitative factors in vendor selection (as there are in romance), but the process can also be conducted systematically and with rigor. Large firms, such as Xerox, that pioneered BPO have well-developed systematic approaches for identifying and selecting outsourcing vendors.[1] Fortunately, the systematic approach that has been pioneered by the large early adopters of BPO has been refined and standardized over time. The basic steps of identifying and selecting a BPO vendor are now well known. This quasi-standardization means that vendors have developed expectations of how they will be approached and how they will be required to bid on projects. Becoming familiar with the standard procedures of vendor selection, then, can speed the vendor review and selection process for buyers and vendors alike.

AN EIGHT-STEP PROCESS

This chapter introduces readers to a systematic approach to identifying and selecting the right outsourcing partner. We have already discussed BPO opportunity identification in Chapter 3 and the likely costs of a BPO project in Chapter 4. This chapter assumes familiarity with the principles discussed in those chapters and focuses on the critical issues of BPO vendor identification, selection, and the initial stages of relationship development.

To help manage the BPO vendor selection process, we have divided this stage of the BPO Life Cycle into eight essential steps:

1. Appoint a vendor selection team (VST).
2. Establish qualifications.
3. Develop a long list.
4. Distribute the request for information (RFI).
5. Distribute the request for proposals (RFP).
6. Evaluate proposals.
7. Select a short list.
8. Select a vendor.

We recommend this systematic process for identifying a BPO vendor for several reasons. The most obvious is that the BPO vendor relationship can be strategically important to the BPO buyer over the long term. Getting the right vendor from the start can accelerate the realization of strategic benefits associated with an effective BPO relationship. Second, a systematic process is more likely to reveal the various alternatives in the market and will help the buyer distinguish among service options. As more and more outsourcing providers enter the market, they are developing increasingly sophisticated means of differentiating themselves, often around the services they provide.[2] The dynamics of the BPO vendor market, and the ease of entry for new firms with innovative new approaches, makes a systematic selection process nearly imperative.

Although the perfect BPO vendor may not come to the fore as a result of this systematic process, the buyer can at least avoid the negative consequences

CASE STUDY

Informal Vendor Selection Leads to Disaster

A large and well-respected company had a vision in the early 1990s of becoming one of the leanest and most profitable manufacturers in the industry. The company's CFO felt that the company could be much more efficient if it focused on what it was good at, as opposed to managing some of the larger support functions. After looking into its HR organization, the CFO determined that outsourcing this function would reduce a great deal of overhead and could fix several of the problems the company continually faced.

The CFO started the project by assigning himself to be the company's BPO champion. (This was mistake number one.) Next, he contacted the CIO and explained how this new outsourcing effort would allow the company to make its numbers in the next year and that he should be excited about assuming the role of change agent.

Recognizing that he had no experience in BPO, the CIO decided to go outside the organization for assistance. The first problem he faced was who to call. The CIO had a relationship with a local consulting group that specialized in outsourcing wide area networks. The firm was invited to a meeting to ask if they were interested in handling the BPO project.

The consulting group explained how outsourcing was one of its service offerings. However, as understood by the consultant, the project could not be completed quickly or inexpensively. Nonetheless, the CFO accepted the consulting group's statements and agreed to move forward.

The following Monday morning, a three-hour kickoff meeting began between the CIO, CFO, and the eager consulting company. The consulting presentation covered outsourcing at a high level and the financial impact it could have on a company. This presentation certainly reaffirmed the CFO's vision by capitalizing on the savings a company could anticipate. The unfortunate point was that no one in the room had any idea how complex this project was going to be.

(continues)

CASE STUDY (continued)

The CFO created a project team by assigning several subject matter experts to the team on a part-time basis. With everyone working part-time, no one really took responsibility for the project and simply assumed that the consulting group would handle it. The consulting group did not really understand the HR department functions and, therefore, could not structure the new process flow. Because the consulting group was not set up to handle the HR back-office functions, it found itself trying to outsource the process to another consulting group

This BPO project grew out of control within weeks. After wasting seven months and spending $800,000, the CFO became furious about the lack of progress. The CIO was fired for selecting the wrong consulting group, which apparently provided no added value, and the consulting group was released only to face a lawsuit.

This experience was a disappointment for the CFO, and he decided to revert back to the old way of operating the HR department. To this day the organization's HR function is as ineffective as it was before the BPO project debacle.

Source: Personal experience (RLC).

associated with hiring an ill-prepared vendor.[3] The Case Study highlights a situation in which an unsystematic process led to an unsatisfactory vendor choice.

Using the systematic approach to vendor selection suggested in this chapter should help BPO buyers avoid situations like the one in the case study.[4] Let us explore the recommended process beginning with the appointment of a Vendor Selection Team.

STEP 1: APPOINT A VENDOR SELECTION TEAM

There is far more to choosing an outsourcing vendor than there is to choosing a new supplier. Unlike the buyer–supplier relationship, the BPO buyer–vendor relationship involves a customized service, detailed agreement on service levels, and a strategically oriented long-term contract. Given our contention that a robust BPO relationship is strategic in nature, the BPO buyer and provider must have shared interests in key objectives and values. The relationship between BPO buyer and vendor will be more intimate than a standard buyer-supplier relationship. In general, BPO buyer–vendor relationships are characterized by regular senior management meetings and sharing of otherwise confidential information. Therefore, harmony among each firm's predominant management styles is a key prerequisite to success.

Using our BPO Life Cycle model and the team-based approach outlined in Chapter 3 as reference points, we are now at the vendor selection phase. The BPO Analysis Team (BAT) identified the BPO opportunity, estimated costs, and built the business case for an outsourcing project. A new team, or at least a new team charter, should be developed for the vendor selection process. We call this new team the vendor selection team (VST). Exhibit 5.1 shows the VST's relationship to the other BPO project teams.

Organizations may elect to keep the BAT intact for the vendor selection process or they may elect to develop a new team. Many firms decide to empower and charter a new team to manage vendor identification, selection, and development to introduce fresh ideas and to provide a clear endpoint to the BAT's efforts. It is recommended that, whether a wholly new team is established to manage this phase of the BPO Life Cycle or not, the organization should consciously select and develop one or, at most, a few individuals who will serve as the organization's BPO champions. One or more of these identified champions should be derived from members of the BAT. The BPO champions will be in charge of developing and deepening the outsourcing relationship over the long term. Experience has shown that it is better to have the BPO champion emerge from the vendor identification and selection team than to bring one in later to manage the ongoing relationship.[5]

EXHIBIT 5.1 Vendor Selection Team in the Context of BPO Project Teams

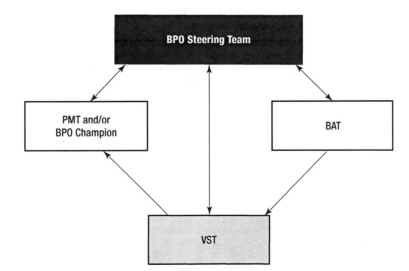

The VST should draw from the business areas that will be affected by the BPO project. Key staff members for the VST should include the following:

- Senior management
- Legal staff with contract expertise
- Technical staff and information systems analysts
- End users
- Financial staff

Consulting firms are available to help the VST with defining statements of work, evaluating internal needs, negotiating, evaluating vendor performance, and providing quality assurance. Although these services represent additional outsourcing costs, they can enable the organization to reduce outsourcing risks, accomplish goals, and select the right BPO partner.

As with any formally chartered team within the organization, the VST should establish a regular meeting schedule and set clear goals and objectives. A sample charter for the organization's VST is provided in Exhibit 5.2.

As shown in Exhibit 5.2, one task for the VST is to establish minimum standards or qualifications for potential vendors. Establishing qualifications is the next step in the vendor selection process.

EXHIBIT 5.2   Sample VST Charter

Purpose: To undertake a process of identifying and selecting a vendor to provide outsourcing services in the area identified by the BPO Analysis Team.

Goals:
1. To develop a list of qualifications that the BPO vendor will minimally require.
2. To identify a long list of potential vendors.
3. To gather information and evaluate the long list of vendors.
4. To develop an RFP and evaluate proposals from the long list of vendors.
5. To select a short list of vendors.
6. To select a final vendor candidate and evaluate its ability to meet the performance goals indicated in the RFP.

Objectives:
1. To complete the long list in 30 days.
2. To gather information and evaluate long-list vendors in 30 days.
3. To develop the RFP in 15 days.
4. To solicit and review vendor proposals in 60 days.
5. To review short-list candidates in 30 days.
6. To select a vendor within 6 months.

STEP 2: ESTABLISH QUALIFICATIONS

Similar to searching for a new manager or key executive, it is imperative for the BPO buyer to establish minimum qualifications for a BPO vendor. These qualifications may include standard items such as experience, price, and location. The qualification list may also include more strategic items such as the vendor's organizational culture, decision-making style, and reputation. According to extensive research into the needs of outsourcing buyers, the qualifications most often sought in a vendor are as follows:[6]

- Quality
- Performance history
- Warranties and claims policies
- Facilities and capacity
- Geographic location
- Technical capability

Customer service is another factor organizations may want to consider. This factor becomes more important the deeper and more strategic the relationship is intended to become. Deeper relationships will require more interorganizational communications and transactions and will be easier to manage if the vendor has a reputation for and knowledge of how to provide good customer service. BPO buyers must maintain a *customer* mindset during this phase of the BPO Life Cycle. A *partner* mindset in the BPO buyer should emerge only after the vendor has been selected and the contracting process has begun. By maintaining a customer mindset during the vendor selection phase, the BPO buyer avoids giving away too much too soon. In the partnership development stage of a BPO relationship, mutual compromise and cooperation is expected. During the vendor selection phase, the buyer is interested in deriving as much value as possible from the vendor and should not be making concessions on any of the provisions it has established as necessary for the project. It is important to maintain a customer mindset to motivate the vendors to work hard to demonstrate their capabilities to meet the project needs as they are. Compromise and cooperation will come later.

Process expertise is another relevant consideration for any outsourcing project. The consideration is lessened the further from the core the outsourced process is. Processes that are close to the outsourcing organization's core competence should never be outsourced to an inexperienced vendor.

Data sharing is a part of nearly every outsourcing relationship. Given that data sharing between the various commercial databases can be difficult, the technology platform of the vendor should be a qualification. If vendors do not have a system that is easily compatible with the buyer's existing system, they will be responsible for demonstrating how that hurdle can be overcome.

Understanding the emphasis of a vendor's business, or what drives their revenue, is essential in choosing an appropriate vendor. For example, large vendor companies are usually looking for extremely large contracts. Smaller contracts negotiated with large vendor firms are not likely to receive the same quality of treatment as larger contracts.

One of the main areas BPO buyers should look for with a vendor is industry specialization. Any vendor, other than the major consultancies, that claims to specialize in several outsourcing service areas should be treated with caution. Having a large base of multifunctional outsourcing expertise is rare, not to mention expensive to maintain. Many vendor companies will make the claim that the skills from outsourcing a function in one industry transfer to another. This may be the case; however, in general, if the vendor is not an expert in the field, it will not know about the hidden challenges associated with providing services in that industry.

In general, if a vendor has limited experience providing outsourcing services in the BPO buyer's area of need, selecting that vendor usually leads to unnecessary costs. Basically, the buyer will be paying for a BPO on-the-job training program. Selecting the BPO vendor that has proven experience in the buyer's particular industry will save headaches and a considerable amount of rework.

Whatever qualifications are established by the VST, those critical to the buyer organization should be decided at this early stage in the vendor selection process. At minimum, the requisite qualifications should consider both expected performance levels and strategic fit with the buyer organization. Many firms also distinguish qualifications between soft and hard issues. Soft issues include cultural and organizational values, mission and vision statements, and organizational history. Hard issues are more quantitative and are usually associated with performance and productivity. In addition to this distinction, some firms also use a weight system to distribute the relative importance of each issue over the decision process. An example of a weighting system is provided in Exhibit 5.3.

Operations research scholars have developed far more sophisticated decision models than the one in Exhibit 5.2.[7] For the purposes of outsourcing a well-defined business process, however, using a weighted system like that shown in Exhibit 5.2 and a systematic approach to data gathering and analysis will produce a qualified list of vendors. The next step in the process is to develop a long list of possible vendors.

EXHIBIT 5.3   BPO Qualifications Weighting System

Parameter	Weight
Quality: • ISO Certification • Six Sigman	.20
Performance History: • Experience with other, similar projects • Performance with other clients	.25
Warranties and Claims Policies	.10
Facilities and Capacity	.15
Geographic Location	.05
Technical Capability	.25

STEP 3: DEVELOP A LONG LIST

Launching the BPO vendor search can be intimidating. There are no Yellow Pages or magic oracles to consult when trying to identify qualified vendors. This is one of the reasons it is important to establish well-defined qualifications. Seeking vendors with specific qualifications versus considering all vendor generalists will make the search process far more efficient.

The VST's objective in this step is to build a qualified list of 15 to 20 potential BPO vendors. There are several good places to start the BPO vendor search. Believe it or not, the Internet is one of the richest sources for identifying BPO candidates. The VST can make headway in vendor identification by using the standard Internet search engines and keyword combinations. For example, if a firm is seeking to outsource its help desk function, its search may include keywords such as:

- Help desk outsourcing
- Help desk vendors
- Outsourcing IT functions

Another technique many organizations use to develop a long list is to search among their current suppliers to see if any are qualified and willing to bid on the BPO project. This type of relationship is referred to as *sole sourcing* or *single sourcing* and can be effective based on the experience gained in working together in other business areas. However, sole sourcing may lead to retaining a vendor that is not completely qualified to manage the business process under consideration. It also increases business risk. If the vendor experiences problems, more of the BPO buyer's processes will be affected. By searching for and evaluating multiple vendors, BPO buyers will better understand what the marketplace has to offer, are more likely to find the best vendor for their needs, and will distribute risk over multiple partners.

Many outsourcing magazines and online portals offer unbiased directories specific to outsourcing, such as OutsourcingCentral.com, Outsourcing Center, the Outsourcing Institute, and FirmBuilder. These organizations can assist in locating potential vendors. Some BPO buyers may want to consider third-party consultants to help them find vendors that match their requirements. These companies sometimes offer searches at no cost and often have built a list of vendors from which to choose.

A good way to begin fact finding on the long list of vendor candidates is by visiting their respective Web sites. Many BPO vendors have extensive detail on their Web sites. In many cases the vendor will include case studies for review and lists of partners, customers, and services offered. Although this information will undoubtedly reflect positively on the vendor, it can be scanned for indications of the vendor's fit with the qualifications established by the VST and for strategic fit with the BPO buyer organization.

The long list development process is generally conducted in a semi-clandestine (at least to the outside world) manner. If the BPO buyer reveals that it is in the market for a BPO vendor, it is not unusual to be overwhelmed with unsolicited proposals. In many cases a new BPO vendor search can generate three or more times the proposals desired.

The goal of the VST is to whittle down the long list to a single qualified vendor with whom the organization will develop an effective long-term partnership. The next step in the vendor selection process will begin to cull the long list developed in Step 3.

STEP 4: REQUEST FOR INFORMATION

After gathering the necessary data to build a long list of 15 to 20 potential BPO vendors, it is time to directly gather information from the candidates. A common technique to accomplish this is to send a scope of work (SOW) outline and request for information (RFI) to each vendor on the long list. The SOW should contain the broad intention of the outsourcing proposal and the time frame for responding. The RFI is a questionnaire-type survey intended to establish the level of vendor competence and interest. Organizations should send the RFI to the long list and track each vendor's interest in the project.

A common method used to make initial contact with long-list vendors is via a phone call to each vendor's sales department. This call will involve only a high-level discussion about the BPO project. It is designed to gauge the vendor's interest level before moving forward with the RFI. If there is interest, specific information should be gathered about where and to whom the RFI should be sent. The vendor should be informed whether the buying organization would allow an ongoing dialog before the RFI process.

The VST should set a firm deadline for responding to the RFI. After the deadline has passed, the VST will schedule and conduct capabilities interviews with acceptable respondents to determine their respective ability to meet project goals. Capabilities interviews are usually conducted initially via a telephone conference. Issues that need to be probed during the capabilities interview include:

- What are the vendor's core capabilities?
- What metrics does the vendor use to evaluate its effectiveness?
- How many clients is the vendor currently serving?
- Does the vendor have unused capacity or will it have to grow to serve new clients?
- Where is the vendor investing its resources?
- How well does the vendor rate with its current customers?
- Does the vendor fit with the buying company's culture?

During the capabilities assessment, the BPO buyer should determine if each vendor has the skills, technology, and personnel necessary to fulfill the project. A vendor site visit will assist with this determination. If a site visit is warranted, the VST should meet with vendor management teams and personnel, evaluate their workplace, and observe how they respond to requests and questions.

The long list of 15 to 20 vendors should be reduced by half as a result of the capabilities interviews, leaving 7 to 10 vendors who will advance to the next step. The contending vendors should be informed that they have been selected to receive the formal RFP.

STEP 5: REQUEST FOR PROPOSALS

The objective of developing a request for proposal (RFP) is to create a document that details the services, activities, and performance targets required for the BPO project. Beyond that, the RFP is also a sales document designed to interest vendors who can add value to the BPO buyer organization.

RFPs vary in format from organization to organization. At a minimum, the requirements for the BPO project should be clearly communicated to the vendors. Being detailed in communication of requirements at this stage ensures that initial responses will provide a full and clear picture of the vendor's ability to meet the needs of the organization. The requirements section of the RFP must reflect the sophistication and experience the vendor will need to complete the proposal successfully.

There are several general guidelines for developing an effective RFP. One of the most important is to be clear about the business process that is slated for outsourcing and the scope of work that will be required from the vendor. At the same time, RFPs should not be so long and burdensome that some qualified vendors will elect not to respond. Several items that should be included in any RFP are as follows:

- *Administrative.* This section includes information about the BPO buyer's company, business priorities, purpose of the RFP, deadlines for response, required format, assessment criteria, and contact information.
- *General requirements.* This section details expectations regarding the services to be provided, reporting and information sharing, customer service, claims resolution, contract implementation, training, and benchmarks for fees. For example, a firm that is seeking to outsource its help desk function might have a section including details about the function, as shown in Exhibit 5.4.
- *Pricing requirements.* This section outlines the expected pricing approach, including goals for net rates and volume discounts.
- *Contractual/legal.* This section provides details about expected contract terms and conditions, warranties, remedies, and any disclaimers.[8]

EXHIBIT 5.4 RFP Section on Outsourcing Help Desk Processes

- We currently have a 20 FTE help desk operating on a 24/7 schedule.
- Their primary responsibilities are to support 3,000 employees who are located around the world.
- The help desk operation center is located in our Ohio headquarters and provides all help desk support via our toll-free number.
- The applications supported are Microsoft 2000, Novel 6.x, Microsoft Office, and CAD 2.7.
- The help desk employees are also responsible for level-one troubleshooting via the toll-free number.
- The help desk tickets are managed in Helpdesk Pro software, and the average open ticket time is 12 hours.
- The help desk employees have, on average, two years of college and four years of IT experience.
- We do not currently have standard operating procedures.

Generally speaking, the VST should be able to eliminate two or three of the companies after reviewing their bids, because their skills will not be a match with the BPO project needs. A letter should be sent out immediately to the eliminated vendors. This will leave five to eight vendors in the running that will be evaluated for their potential to become the buyer's BPO partner.

STEP 6: EVALUATE THE PROPOSALS

The proposals that the BPO buyer receives from contending vendors will be extremely comprehensive. Initial screening of proposals may reveal interesting facts about the vendor. For example, the VST should scan each proposal to determine whether it addresses their organization's unique needs. Often, a BPO vendor will cut and paste material from another proposal and simply insert it in the current one. Although this practice is understandable and acceptable to an extent, an excessively cut-and-pasted proposal probably indicates that the vendor has not spent a lot of time thinking about the buyer's unique needs. The VST should read the proposal carefully and look for the signs of generic template use. A good BPO vendor must be customer oriented. The proposal should be directly written for the buyer's BPO project. Buyers should be wary of vendors that fill their proposals with boilerplate and puffery.

Those vendors that have submitted acceptable proposals should be scheduled for telephone interviews which, at this stage, are generally one-hour in length. The VST can expect that each of the vendors will suggest a face-to-face meeting. However, the opportunity to meet with the VST in a formal presentation should be reserved for the short-list candidates only.

Within the teleconference, the BPO vendor should explain in detail its submitted proposal, including addressing the following issues:

- Approach
- Company background
- Experience in the process area
- Strengths
- Availability
- Certifications
- Suggested solution

After the vendor has explained its proposal, the VST should request a submission of tender. The tender is a precise document that spells out exactly what the vendor intends to do and how it intends to establish fees and the invoice schedule. The vendor should also be requested to furnish the following:

- *Case studies*. Vendors should be able to provide case studies of BPO projects similar to the BPO buyer's project.
- *Copies of résumés*. Each vendor will probably send résumés of its best and most highly credentialed personnel. The buyer should ensure that these individuals are the ones who will actually be working on the project should any particular vendor be selected.
- *Copies of certifications*. BPO vendors often cite industry certifications, such as ISO or Six Sigma. BPO buyers should request copies of these certificates to verify their authenticity.
- *List of references*. BPO buyers should request at least three positive references and, when possible, one negative reference. It is important that the BPO buyer talk with at least one of the vendor's customers that experienced a negative result. The objective is to determine how the vendor handled the project when it was failing and why contingency plans did not correct the problems.
- *Proof of financial stability*. It is not unusual to request that vendors provide documentation showing their financial stability, how many employees they have, how long they have been in business, and the maturity of their facilities.

As with everything else in this process, the VST should establish firm deadlines for the submission of tender. With the vendor proposals and submission of tender information in hand, it is time to narrow the long list down to a short list of candidates.

STEP 7: SELECT A SHORT LIST

Once the first round of proposal evaluations is complete, the VST should now possess the necessary information to select three to five of the most qualified vendors. The selected vendors should be contacted directly and invited in for face-to-face formal presentations.

The VST should arrange meetings such that it will meet only one vendor per day. The vendor visits should be scheduled as close together as possible so the VST can compare notes on each vendor while they are still fresh. In general each presentation should be limited to four hours, and the VST should set the agenda for the meeting and share it with each vendor in advance. At the beginning of the formal presentation, the VST chairperson should communicate the following:

- Inform the vendor that it has made the short list.
- Explain that the vendor has four hours for its presentation.

- Express interest regarding the vendor's pricing model.
- Reiterate what the organization is looking for in a BPO vendor.
- Let the vendor know that there will be a final telephone conference to clarify the bid submitted.
- Ask the vendor to submit its best bid no later than the deadline you have established.
- Let the vendor know when the decision will be made.

During the presentation, VST members should look for the following:

- Who has the vendor sent to the meeting?
- Was the presentation developed uniquely or is it canned?
- Does the vendor include contingency plans?
- What performance data does the vendor provide?
- Who are the vendor's leading clients?
- How well does the vendor team *listen* to the buyer team?
- Does the vendor's presentation address issues in the RFP?

Special attention should be paid to the logical architecture outlined in the presentation. Many vendor presentations demonstrate their expertise with technology, but they lack deep understanding of workflows and process improvement opportunities (the logical architecture). Failure to address the logical architecture of the business process to be outsourced is one of the most obvious signs of a BPO vendor's lack of maturity in that business process.

After the vendor presentations have been completed, the final review of vendors begins. The VST should review all presentation material in great detail, along with the notes recorded by those who attended the presentations. Someone within the VST should be recording all questions the team may have because these questions can be answered during scheduled final phone conferences with each vendor.

The final phone conference is the time to clarify all outstanding issues about the vendor's proposal, service offering, and to discuss the formal presentation. During the phone conference, the BPO buyer should communicate the following:

- Explain to the vendor that it is among the finalists.
- Explain that this will be the final presentation.
- State that final pricing schedules must be articulated.

The vendor should be allowed to ask any questions it may have. The buyer should state that a decision will be made and a BPO vendor will be selected within a defined period (usually two weeks) after the telephone conferences. This helps motivate the vendor into making the best deal possible to win the buyer's business.

After the telephone conference, the BPO buyer should select two or three vendors for a second face-to-face presentation. Once this selection has been completed and the vendors have been informed, the meetings should be scheduled as soon as possible. Each vendor should be informed that it has four hours for the final presentation.

STEP 8: SELECT THE VENDOR

Final vendor selection should be completed shortly after the second round of face-to-face presentations. By now, it is usually clear which vendor has developed a proposal that best meets the needs of the buyer, both short term and long term. If the VST has established its vendor qualifications early on, weighted them appropriately, and observed both the quantitative and qualitative aspects of each vendor, it should be able to reach consensus on the final selection.

It must be stated that the VST may decide in the end that none of the vendors is able to meet the organization's needs as they have been specified. If that occurs, it is in the interests of the organization to abandon the BPO project. As stated, one danger associated with initiating a BPO project is the escalation of commitment phenomenon. For many executives and managers, the decision to abandon a project after such a large investment of personal time and other resources is exceedingly difficult. However, sound business decision making sometimes requires firms to cut their losses and move on. In this case, if none of the vendors can meet the organization's specifications after this systematic selection process has been followed, it would be unwise to attempt to either gerrymander the specifications or allow the vendor to alter its bid to try to force a fit.

If one of the vendors has emerged as the winner of the BPO project bid, there are still several steps to consider before moving on to the contract stage. For example, members of the BPO buyer's staff who are scheduled for transfer to the vendor should meet the new management team before any contracts are signed. Allowing employees to air their concerns and ask questions may help reduce the feeling among employees that they are being cast aside. Conflicts in style and personalities may emerge in these meetings that could affect the vendor's performance. During this precontract stage, the firms should also address issues of terms and conditions of employment, including appropriate compensation if vendor employment is not available or not required. If any additional training will be required as a result of joining the new organization, it should now be brought to light.

Leaders of the BPO implementation from both parties should discuss the objectives of the new work processes and what the organizations want to achieve. All members of the new interorganizational work team should understand their personal contribution to the team's success. Many problems can be avoided by communicating regularly and vigorously with employees at this early stage of the BPO implementation.[9] Up to this point the rumor mill may have been going full speed and people had no idea who or what to believe.

Another useful exercise in the precontract stage is to make certain that the contract will stand up to the rigors and complexities of the actual operation. A trial period is ideal for making adjustments before the contract becomes final and for judging the likelihood of the partnership breaking down.

In general, this precontract testing period should not be less than 90 days—long enough to allow anything unexpected to arise. For example, when Lehman Brothers decided to outsource its IT function to an offshore firm, it spent more than $8 million on 80 separate pilot projects with the various finalists.[10] Remember, the BPO buyer and vendor are attempting to develop a partnership, and there are going to be problems that must be worked through.

The main issue that needs to be addressed after the test period is the unexpected work that has surfaced and how it will affect the cost model in the vendor's proposal. At the same time, the buyer should be cautious about judging the service levels, because new people and processes will improve performance levels over time. As a result of the new BPO relationship, it is likely that a lot of responsibilities and processes will change in the buyer's organization. Despite these changes, the BPO buyer should be careful not to allow its corporate identity to change.

CONCLUSION

This chapter has been designed to help organizations approach the BPO vendor identification and selection process in a systematic way. Using the systematic approach outlined here does not guarantee a successful outcome, but it should help reduce the risk associated with making a bad vendor selection. As stated in other contexts in this book, to BPO or not to BPO is a strategic choice, and the risks associated with BPO should not lead to inaction. BPO buyers will not find the perfect BPO vendor no matter how systematic their selection process is. However, if buyers use this systematic approach to vendor selection, they will find a sound alternative that can help the organization achieve its aims.

Outsourcing is not a new phenomenon, although its recent popularity suggests that it is. In reality, companies have been outsourcing business processes for many years, and some generic lessons can be derived from this experience. The systematic vendor identification and selection process described in this chapter is a derivation of those lessons and is designed to help BPO buyers accelerate the BPO Life Cycle without compromising rigor. In the end, following a rigorous process of vendor selection will tell the buyer things about itself that it did not know and will more likely result in selection of a vendor that can become a true strategic partner.

SUMMARY

- A systematic vendor selection process can help accelerate the realization of strategic benefits associated with an effective BPO relationship.
- The eight steps of the vendor identification and selection process are (1) appoint a vendor selection team; (2) establish qualifications; (3) develop a long list; (4) distribute the request for information; (5) distribute the request for proposals; (6) evaluate proposals; (7) select a short list; and (8) select a vendor.
- The VST may be made up of BAT members, but it should have a separate and new charter.
- The VST should have one or a few individuals being groomed as BPO champions for the organization.
- Vendor qualifications should include both soft and hard criteria.
- The most often cited qualifications in vendor selection include quality, delivery, performance history, warranties and claims policies, facilities and capacity, geographic location, and technical capability.
- Customer service, process expertise, and data sharing are other key qualifications buyers should look for in the outsourcing vendor.
- Using keywords to search the Internet can launch the BPO vendor search.
- The long list of vendors generally comprises 15 to 20 firms that seem to have the requisite qualifications.
- The request for information (RFI) will help the VST narrow the long list to seven to ten potential vendors.
- The request for proposal (RFP) should provide abundant details about the nature and scope of the project, including information about the buyer firm's administration, general requirements expected of the vendor, pricing requirements, and details about legal matters.
- Proposal evaluation should include inviting several vendor firms to provide formal presentations to the buyer firm.
- A submission of tender will provide additional details about the vendor, including case studies, résumés of key personnel, copies of certifications, and a list of references.
- The short list will consist of three to five vendors who will be contacted for a telephone conference.

▧ Based on the telephone conference, two to three vendors will be invited back for a second formal presentation.
▧ Vendor selection should be followed by a precontract period during which the firms become acquainted, and a pilot project may be implemented to test the relationship.

CHAPTER 6

BPO Contracts

Even when laws have been written down, they ought not always to remain unaltered.

—Aristotle, author and philosopher

It is commonly believed that many outsourcing ventures fail to meet their objectives. What is surprising, however, is that the outsourcing success rate for first-time users of the strategy has not changed much since 1998. According to a survey conducted by the American Management Association in 1998, three-quarters of U.S. managers surveyed reported that outsourcing outcomes had failed to meet expectations.[1] Four years later, in a 2002 study conducted by DiamondCluster International, 78 percent of the companies surveyed admitted to ending at least one prior outsourcing relationship prematurely because it was not meeting expectations.[2] Although the reasons for dissatisfaction with outsourcing relationships are as varied and complex as outsourcing relationships themselves, there are several common reasons for failure cited in the studies.

Outsourcing failures are generally not strictly legal in nature, but careful consideration of the elements of a good outsourcing contract can help avoid many of the significant risk factors. In fact, a poorly drafted outsourcing contract is one of the most significant reasons cited by companies for failed outsourcing relationships.[3] Just as significantly, however, the careful negotiation and drafting of a good outsourcing contract will eliminate most of the other reasons for dissatisfaction with outsourcing relationships.[4]

This chapter examines the legal side of the outsourcing relationship, but it must always be remembered that the buyer–vendor relationship in successful BPO initiatives must have a foundation of interpersonal and interorganizational trust. The legal wordsmithing that is part and parcel of contract negotiations should be managed in a spirit that reflects the strategic nature of the relationship, while being thorough and precise in its terms so as to circumvent future problems. Contract development is an important phase of the BPO project life cycle. It is the first phase after a vendor has been selected, and it is the first opportunity for the buyer and vendor to begin to work together. The Executive Viewpoint highlights a few rules of thumb that should be followed in BPO contract development.

This chapter is segmented into two major parts: contract negotiations and contract terms. Although negotiations are an important part of contract development and a critical skill to develop, we spend only a brief time discussing important elements of a BPO negotiation. There are many great references on negotiating tactics and skills already on the bookshelves, and we do not want to compete with them in this brief chapter. We decided to spend more time discussing the terms that should be considered in a BPO agreement. Let us begin with a brief look at the essentials of negotiating BPO agreements.

NEGOTIATING BPO AGREEMENTS

Because of the complex and evolving nature of the outsourcing process, negotiation of BPO agreements requires a different mindset than that required in traditional commercial contract negotiation.[5] Outsourcing is by definition a collaborative effort, rather than a zero-sum game. Zero-sum negotiating means that each party is motivated to extract as much value as possible from the limited available resources, even to the detriment of the other party.[6] By contrast, in positive-sum negotiating, the parties are interested in creating more resources and value than currently exists and then dividing up the gains. The $64 word often associated with this type of negotiating is *synergy*.[7] A BPO negotiation should be conceived as closer in nature to negotiations with a joint venture partner than to negotiations with a vendor. Exhibit 6.1 provides insight into a few of the differences between the different types of negotiation settings.

From the BPO buyer's perspective, the process of selecting an outsourcing provider and negotiating the outsourcing contract is the first opportunity to evaluate the corporate culture and mindset of the vendor. Organizations that have decided to undertake a BPO initiative should use this opportunity to assess cultural fit with the BPO provider. There are many potential signals at this stage of the BPO relationship that could portend future problems. For example, if the vendor fails to recognize and take seriously this critical stage of the outsourcing relationship, that could be a red flag that the relationship may not develop as planned.

BPO buyers can use several strategies to determine the character of the firm they have selected as their vendor. For example, different negotiating strategies may be employed to distinguish a cooperative vendor from an

EXECUTIVE VIEWPOINT Rules of Thumb for Effective BPO Contracting

David S. Piper, attorney, Boyer & Ketchand, LLP, Houston, Texas

Developing an effective BPO contract has several basic rules of thumb. First, everyone involved in the contracting process should keep in mind the nature of the BPO relationship. The alignment of the long-term strategic interests of both the BPO buyer and vendor should be reflected in the terms of the contract. Second, it is important to be able to describe services and performance levels in precise language. The contract should include details about measuring service performance and steps to take to remedy performance shortfalls. Finally, it is important for the parties to plan for exit. This element of BPO contracts is often overlooked because it suggests that, at some point in the future, the relationship will end. However, handling exit provisions in the contract is a good way to make sure that when the relationship does end it ends amicably.

When it comes to common mistakes that companies make in developing an outsourcing contract, one is the failure to test performance metrics and measurement strategies. One firm that I recall outsourced its help desk process. Part of the agreement was that the quality of service would be measured using a help desk customer survey. The help desk vendor applied the quality survey to every single help desk inquiry, which greatly annoyed the BPO buyer's employees. To make matters worse, completion of the survey was required to close out the trouble ticket. As a result, help desk staff frequently called employees to implore them to answer the survey questions so they could close out the ticket. Overlooking the impact of the survey on the attitudes of employees led to a lot of criticism and needless griping in this case.

To help keep legal costs to a minimum in BPO contract development—and this may sound paradoxical—get the legal team involved early. Early involvement ensures that the team is well versed in the business process and understands appropriate service levels metrics. Firms should also get the legal team involved with the operational staff so they do not end up writing the contract in the abstract. The more familiar the team is with the actual business process, the better it will be able to draft effective service level standards.

EXHIBIT 6.1 Standard Vendor Negotiations versus BPO Negotiations

Negotiations with Vendor/Supplier	Negotiations with BPO Provider
Zero sum Adversarial Win-Lose Short-term Fixed terms	Positive sum Collaborative Win-Win Long-term Flexible terms

adversarial one. At the outset of the selection process, clients may attach a proposed form of the master outsourcing contract (without detailed exhibits such as scope of work, service level agreements, and pricing) to the RFP in order to evaluate which prospective vendors will accept the buyer's general terms and conditions. Vendors who are unwilling or reluctant to accept the buyer's general terms and conditions without significant negotiation can be readily identified and disqualified.

The significance of the collaborative effort is not limited to the buyer–vendor relationship, however. This cooperation is also required among the members of the buyer team. The contracting process requires that the buyer's lawyers and the personnel involved in the outsourced process work closely together. BPO buyers should be sensitive to personnel issues in this process. Employees whose jobs are being outsourced may not be cooperative or completely candid with attorneys working to bring the outsourcing initiative to fruition. In some cases, the use of outside consultants will be appropriate.

The distinction between negotiating outcomes is commonly referred to in general terms as win-lose, win-win, and lose-lose. In a zero-sum negotiation, the outcome is win-lose in that one party or the other gets its way, usually to the detriment of the other. In a standard buyer–vendor relationship, it is not uncommon for the winning negotiating team to be overheard bragging about "beating them down" on price. It is a mark of distinction to be the party that prevails in such a negotiation. The result of such a strategy may be lower prices, but the relationship may become adversarial rather than collaborative. Working with a BPO provider requires long-term collaboration to ensure that organizational learning and strategic advancement is occurring throughout the life of the project. An adversarial, win-lose negotiating strategy is unlikely to promote this type of relationship.

Instead, the ideal BPO negotiating strategy is one that is collaborative, based on a vision of a win-win outcome, and that seeks long-term, flexible contract terms. This will require compromise by both parties. At the same time, risks associated with compromise can be mitigated through creative incentive clauses and remedies in the event of nonperformance. Such contract innovations are part of the terms of a BPO contract.

TERMS OF THE BPO CONTRACT

We have stated that the BPO contract negotiations should be conducted in a positive-sum spirit, with an eye toward building a trusting, synergistic relationship. At the same time, it would be naive to assume that trust is a sufficient governing mechanism. In fact, drafting precise contract terms, including avenues for remedy in case performance falls short of expectations, can help preserve a relationship during difficult stretches.

The following sections outline terms that should be considered and included in the formal BPO contract. Although not an exhaustive set, the terms discussed are part of nearly every BPO contract and constitute the core of the working relationship. The terms discussed include the following:

- Scope of work
- Service level agreements
- Pricing
- Term of the contract
- Governance
- Intellectual property
- Industry-specific concerns
- Termination of the contract
- Transition
- Force majeure
- Dispute resolution

We discuss each of these contractual elements and, in many cases, highlight alternative strategies. Because the BPO contract is such a critical part of the success of the working relationship between buyer and vendor, it is recommended that third-party (legal) support be used in drafting, negotiating, and modifying the contract.

Scope of Work

The linchpin of the outsourcing contract is a description of the nature of the work being outsourced, often referred to as the "scope of work" or "statement of work." The BPO buyer's attorneys must work closely with the buying organization's personnel to become intimately familiar with the details of the outsourced processes in order to prepare a statement of work that is clear and complete. Provisions of a well-drafted outsourcing contract must also outline the change process as it pertains to the scope of work, whether such change is incremental because of technological developments or organic because of acquisitions or divestitures by the client.

The outsourcing contract should also specifically delineate the processes by which the work will be transitioned from client to vendor. In this respect, the transaction mirrors the purchase or sale of a business unit. Personnel, hard assets, and soft assets, such as intellectual property, vendor contracts, and license agreements, all may be transferred to the vendor.

Particular care must be taken in the personnel area. Employees with key institutional knowledge or other unique capabilities should be considered for retention. Well-qualified project managers must be retained to staff the buyer's governance team.

Attention must also be paid to the employment laws that regulate the BPO provider. For example, in the European Union (EU) in certain cases when a business unit is transferred, the new employer must offer the transferred employees the same wages and benefits that the employees have with their current employer. Staffing needs should be carefully considered because layoffs and reductions in force are often more complicated in foreign jurisdictions. Buyers and vendors should discuss and agree on the vendor's intentions regarding the use of subcontractors. Attention must also be paid to U.S. labor laws such as the Worker Adjustment and Retraining Notification Act (WARN).

In nearly every BPO relationship that involves international transactions, the parties to the contract must consider employment laws and regulations. Buyers and vendors alike can be held liable for violating or flouting employment laws, which vary widely from country to country. For example, the EU has enacted stiff worker protection laws that protect workers from loss of income if their employer should decide to outsource their jobs. The Applied Rights Directive was enacted nearly two decades ago and is designed to protect employees' jobs, pay, and conditions when organizations sold or outsourced parts of their business operations to other companies or contracting firms.

The United Kingdom (UK) has enacted similar legislation known as Transfer of Undertakings Protection of Employment (TUPE). Together, these regulations are potent protectors of employment rights and make it difficult for European firms to realize dramatic cost benefits from outsourcing. The Case Study highlights difficulties experienced by Compaq as it wrestled with TUPE regulations with an outsourcing client.

CASE STUDY

European Regulations Confusing to BPO Vendors

International regulations governing workers' rights are going to play a role in the future of BPO. In fact, it is likely that workers and politicians will seek new regulations as more and more jobs are uprooted and moved about the world.

Compaq and France's Atos Origin found themselves embroiled in an employment dispute stemming from employment protection laws that left 60 IT support staff members facing the prospect of job loss. The outsourcing service providers became embroiled in the dispute because it was not clear which firm was responsible for employing 30 former Atos support staff members in the United Kingdom and another 30 overseas, following a decision by Lucent to transfer an outsourcing contract from Atos to Compaq. The dispute arose over confusion about Europe's employment protection laws, known as the Applied Rights Directive, and Britain's Transfer of Undertakings Protection of Employment (TUPE) regulations. TUPE guarantees staff members employment under existing terms when their work is outsourced to a third party.

The dispute began when Lucent decided to end its outsourcing contract with Atos Origin and transfer the work solely to Compaq. Both suppliers had been contracted to provide desktop and network support services to Lucent in July 2000.

Under TUPE regulations, Atos staff in the United Kingdom, Netherlands, and Germany should automatically have transferred to Compaq, but Compaq blocked the move. Compaq e-mailed the Atos staff members affected, denying responsibility for their employment.

For its part, Compaq argued that TUPE rules do not apply because it plans to use a different operational model from Atos, service fewer users, and will provide services in fewer countries.

Employment lawyers say that the case highlights the confusion arising from conflicting TUPE case law and will place further pressure on the government to clarify the legislation.

Sources: Bill Goodwin, "Outsourcers Face Tribunals," *Computer Weekly* (September 12, 2002), p. 1; Bill Goodwin, "Dispute May Force Employers to Confront TUPE Muddle in Court," *Computer Weekly* (September 12, 2002), p. 18.

Service Level Agreements

In a service level agreement (SLA), a vendor agrees to achieve defined levels of performance. If the vendor fails to meet these defined objectives, the SLA provides the buyer with various rights and remedies. A carefully crafted set of SLAs aligns the interests of the vendor and buyer.[8] Poorly drafted SLAs almost ensure a failed outsourcing relationship.[9]

Unfortunately, SLAs are among the most difficult of outsourcing contract provisions. A well-drafted SLA requires an intimate understanding of business processes by the attorneys drafting the SLAs (SLAs should not be drafted by nonlawyers). The parties need to be able to document in great detail the requirements of each outsourced process and agree on the manner of measuring the service levels and the consequences for the failure to meet them.[10]

The foundation of the SLA is defining which service levels and key performance indicators (KPI) to measure. An SLA may be tied to anything that can be objectively quantified, but is usually a measure of such KPI as quality, speed, availability, reliability, capacity, timeliness, or customer satisfaction. For example, for a call center, service levels might include the average time to answer a call, the duration of the call, the percentage of issues satisfactorily resolved in the first call, and customer satisfaction. Service levels must be intimately tied to pricing in order to properly align the financial interests of the vendor and the business goals of the client. For example, pricing tied to the number of problems fixed may create a disincentive to stop the problems from happening in the first place. Quality is generally a better service level measure than quantity, especially in fixed-price scenarios.

Once appropriate service levels are agreed upon, terms must be used with precision. For example, what does it mean for a computer system to be "available"? If the buyer can access the system, but it performs sluggishly, is that system available? What if the system is unavailable to the buyer as a result of something beyond the vendor's control? Who bears the risk of a failed service level in that instance? Drilling down to issues such as these in the negotiation process will avoid needless disputes during the performance stage of the outsourcing life cycle.

Service levels may vary depending on hours of operation or other variables. Response times should take these factors into account, including differences in time zones. Agreement must be reached between the parties regarding how to measure service levels. Technologic capabilities may be a constraining factor, particularly with smaller clients and vendors. Softer measurements, such as customer satisfaction, may meet with resistance, both from the vendor and from the client's personnel who are now required to fill out satisfaction surveys as a result of the outsourcing process. If possible, the client should implement the service level measurements before outsourcing, both to obtain a baseline and to determine the adequacy of the measurement process.

The SLA should address who is responsible for measuring service levels and how often. Depending on the type of activity being measured, service levels can be measured by the vendor, the buyer, third parties, or some combination. The time period for which the service level is measured should be long enough to be meaningful, but not so long as to be cost prohibitive or unfair to the vendor. Of significance is the fact that pricing, in the form of credits or bonuses, may be tied to achieving or failing to achieve service levels, as well as events of default. Credits can be handled either through cash rebates to the buyer or credits against future amounts owed to the service provider. Reporting and availability of compliance data should be agreed upon.

One common mistake in setting service levels is to set a standard or average, but to neglect to define appropriate service levels for the out-of-compliance performance. For example, if the service level for a call center requires that 95 percent of all calls must be answered within a certain time period, the SLA should also address the minimum acceptable standard for the remaining 5 percent of the calls. SLAs should set target service levels and minimum service levels. Deviations from target service levels result in credits to the buyer or bonuses to the vendor, as appropriate. Failure to meet minimum service levels may result in termination of the outsourcing contract for cause.

Careful consideration should be given to the buyer's remedies resulting from failure to meet service levels. Beyond credits, termination of the outsourcing contract may be appropriate in the case of failure to meet minimum service levels, material deviations from target service levels, or failure to meet target service levels on a repeated basis.

As with scope of work and pricing, the BPO buyer and vendor alike need to anticipate that service levels will change over time, whether because of changes in customer requirements, technologic advances, regulatory requirements, or improvements in the service provider's processes. Because of the specificity required in SLAs, vendors and clients should fully discuss the change processes that will be agreed on. Both parties need to keep in mind that the touchstone for SLAs and change processes should be to align the interests of the service provider and the buyer as much as possible. Exhibit 6.2[11] is an example of an SLA.

Pricing

Pricing of outsourced services may be set in any number of ways, and combinations of the various pricing alternatives are common. Fixed fee, volume of transactions, and cost plus are some common examples of pricing alternatives used in BPO relationships. In evaluating the pricing of an outsourcing

EXHIBIT 6.2   Sample Text for Service Level Agreements

Scope and Definition:
Outsource contractor shall "own" continuation engineering for mature products, as agreed upon by the company and the outsource contractor. This will enable outsource contractor to design the product for a high volume assembly environment and with component parts sourced to take advantage of outsource contractor purchasing leverage. This is expected to drive significant cost reductions in future products.

Outsourcing Contractor Responsibilities:
- Release bill of material for new SKU number.
- Assume responsibility for initiating, executing and implementing engineering change orders in support of ongoing product enhancements.
- Perform cross-functional cost reduction and product improvement activities.
- Provide technical assistance to Company in effecting resolutions to product quality problems.
- Provide a cost reduction plan to Company. The plan should include feasibility report, design study, and analysis of specifications.
- Support product "end of life" activities to minimize scrap and obsolescence.
- Review and approve component-level first article inspection.

Company Responsibilities:
- Develop, maintain, and provide customer requirement specification.
- Approve key technology and engineering changes initiated by outsource contractor.
- Provide all specifications, artwork, and packaging of the products.
- Provide firmware support for outsource contractor–initiated and Company-approved engineering changes.

---

agreement, BPO buyers should be aware that certain costs relating to the management of the outsourcing relationship can never be eliminated. BPO costs were discussed at length in Chapter 4.

The choice of fee structure for a BPO contract should be motivated primarily by the outcomes that are to be attained. Buyers and vendors alike must think carefully about the fee structure of the contract because unexpected future events could lead to financially burdensome obligations. For example, a BPO contract may specify that the vendor receive compensation for every successful handling of a returned retail item. This may be a workable fee structure if the retailer controls its returns and has trained its customers to return goods only if they have the receipt. However, the fee structure would become unworkable if the retailer unilaterally decided to waive the receipt requirement. Under the changed policy, the BPO vendor may be overwhelmed with returned goods that it has no way of verifying.

Outsourcing arrangements can run from thousands to millions of dollars over the course of a multiyear agreement, depending on the size and complexity of the work. In general, contracts can be written on a fixed-price or variable-price basis. With fixed-price engagements, the vendor assumes the risk of absorbing cost variability. When set too low, fixed-price arrangements diminish the vendor's flexibility and motivation to respond to changing business objectives or emerging technologies. Although variable pricing allows for increased risk sharing, it may also create misunderstandings if and when costs exceed expectations, especially if scope and accountability are poorly defined.

Many BPO buyers opt for a "pay as you go" utility model for BPO services. This sounds good, in that companies pay only for as much capacity as they use, but how do you measure capacity? Not long ago, the utility fee model was based primarily on technology metrics, such as CPU cycles or storage consumption. More recently, firms have been using business metrics to determine fees. Canada Life, for example, pays IBM a small fee for each policy it sells in return for hosting its claims processing application. Digital River's fees are based on the amount of paraphernalia sold through the Major League Baseball Web site it built and hosts.[12] Exhibit 6.3 provides an overview of the various BPO contract pricing alternatives.

EXHIBIT 6.3 BPO Pricing Models

Cost Plus: This model entails the service provider to be paid the actual costs, plus a predetermined profit percentage. This model allows very little flexibility when business objectives and technology change during the duration of the outsourcing contract. Neither does it provide any incentive for the service provider to perform more efficiently.

Unit Pricing: This model assumes a predetermined rate established by the service provider for a particular level of service. The organization pays based on its usage.

Fixed Pricing: In this model, a fixed price for the service is established for the duration of the contract. Some organizations prefer this approach, as they know exactly what the service provider's price will be, even in the future. The challenge with this approach is that the organization must adequately define the scope of the process and design effective metrics before signing the contract. If not, the impact will be the service provider claiming a particular service or service level that is beyond the scope of the contract, making the buyer liable for additional charges.

Variable Pricing: This model involves the use of a fixed price at the low end of the service provider's service with variances based on higher service levels. The effectiveness of this model depends on specifically defining the scope of process and metrics.

EXHIBIT 6.3 Continued

Performance-Based Pricing: Providing incentives to motivate the service provider to perform at peak level is the main thrust of this model. For example, the organization could offer a bonus reward if a project is completed ahead of schedule or demand that the service provider pay a penalty if performance is below the satisfactory level stipulated in the contract. Performance-based model should be used to extract excellence in the delivery of the service provider.

Co-Sharing Risk/Reward: In this model, the organization and the service provider each have an amount of money at risk and each stands to gain a percentage of the profits if the service provider's performance is optimum and achieves the organization's business objectives. Outsourcing is not just about throwing everything away to the outsourcing partner to save costs. It can be a profitable relationship for both the outsourcing organization and the service provider if they were to work out the service level agreement and pricing model, as well as set the expectations from the beginning.

Term of the Contract

The term of the outsourcing contract is an important consideration, especially in view of the statistics suggesting that many companies terminate outsourcing arrangements before the end of the contract period. The negotiated term of the BPO contract should at minimum match the life cycle of the processes involved and changes in the business cycle. Setting the term should take into account the volatility of the outsourced service, including anticipated changes in scope, SLAs, and pricing. Setting the term should also be considered in the context of the client's right to terminate the contract for convenience and the direct and indirect costs associated with such termination, as discussed later.

Governance

As already discussed, an outsourcing relationship is a collaborative effort, and the outsourcing contract should be regarded as a living document in which it is anticipated that significant terms dealing with scope, SLAs, and pricing may change over the life of the contract. In light of these factors, governance of the relationship is critical. In essence, governance is the process of administering and monitoring the performance phase of the BPO Life Cycle to ensure that the interests of the service provider and the client remain in alignment and that the overall goals of the parties are met through the most efficient processes available. Stated more simply, governance involves assessing performance and managing change.

Depending on the size and complexity of the outsourcing relationship, governance may be implemented through single points of contact between the parties or through committees with multiple representatives of both parties. In the next chapter, we introduce the concept of the project management team to govern the operating phase of the BPO Life Cycle. The structure of the governance process is infinitely variable, but certain basic factors are fundamental to successful governance. Communication and reporting are essential elements of the governance process. The governance structure should address schedules of meetings and scope of authority, especially with respect to change processes involving scope of work, compliance with SLA standards, and the use of benchmarking to establish new SLA standards or pricing. Depending on the seniority of the personnel involved in the governance process, escalation of disputes arising from the governance process may be appropriate. Support of the governance process and personnel by vendor and client management is essential and should be established at the outset of the outsourcing relationship.

Intellectual Property

The transfer, use, disclosure, protection, and development of intellectual property are some of the most significant legal considerations of the outsourcing process. In the initial stages of considering an outsourcing initiative, companies should carefully consider the intellectual property ramifications of outsourcing.[13]

Intellectual property laws and enforcement vary considerably around the world. Many countries have laws protecting intellectual property and are signatories to the World Trade Organization's intellectual property rights provisions collectively known as the Trade-Related Aspects of Intellectual Property Rights (TRIPs). However, there is a mixed track record of local enforcement of intellectual property rights belonging to U.S. firms outsourcing offshore. Until the countries in which service providers are located establish a track record of protecting these intellectual property rights, BPO buyers who rely on these laws do so at their peril.[14]

Obviously, the most prudent course is to keep vital intellectual property within the United States. If an organization does transfer intellectual property offshore, however, it should rely heavily on self-help to protect its assets.[15] This begins with conducting thorough due diligence regarding potential vendors and their security and confidentiality procedures, as well as understanding the culture of the vendor's country toward the intellectual property of foreigners. It is no secret that certain countries have viewed the intellectual property of foreigners as communal property. There are indications that India would like to differentiate itself from these other countries as an outsource provider by providing strong legal protections for the intellectual property of

ETHICS & GOVERNANCE

IP Protection Standards Are Extraordinary in Some Offshore Vendors

One of the major worries of any organization considering outsourcing is protection of critical intellectual property. The packing up of coveted insights, customer information, or trade secrets into e-mail attachments bound for international destinations can be a source of sleepless nights.

Relax. Many observers of the outsourcing revolution have noted that the standards of information security and protection are actually HIGHER in some offshore locations than they are in the United States. For example, some Indian firms that provide tax preparation services have extensive security measures in place to protect the integrity of the information they process. Employees are prohibited from taking purses, briefcases, or notebooks into the processing facility. They must use lockers and are unable to print or otherwise save the information they are working on. In addition to measures with employees, many Indian firms also have superior physical, network, and communications security compared to U.S. firms.

While security and intellectual property protection must be of central concern to businesses considering BPO, rest assured that vendors are working overtime to ensure prospective clients can sleep at night. As the primary driver for BPO continues to shift from cost to strategic advantages, vendors around the world will compete on terms other than labor costs. And, they will be competing for higher value work that requires superior security measures.

Sources: Gary L. Boomer, "Indian Outsourcer's Standards Higher Than U.S. Firms," *Accounting Today* (September 22, 2003), pp. 24–26; Phillip Hunter, "Security Issues with Offshore Outsourcing," *Network Security* (August 2003), pp. 5–6.

foreigners. The Ethics and Governance insert cites evidence that Indian firms are superior in some respects to U.S. firms in their measures used to protect intellectual property.

Beyond due diligence, however, the outsourcing contract should specify measures to be taken by the service provider to protect the intellectual property of the client. These measures are not materially different than the measures that domestic companies should, but often do not, take with respect to their domestic operations: background checks on employees, restricting access to data on a need-to-know basis, monitoring retention rates of employees with access to key intellectual property, and use of confidentially, nondisclosure, and noncompete provisions with these employees. Putting these procedures in place is meaningless, however, unless the procedures are properly and consistently implemented and monitored through the governance process.

One way to increase the chances that these procedures will be properly and consistently implemented is to make sure that someone or some entity guarantees protection of intellectual property through the use of indemnification procedures. These indemnification procedures are more meaningful if the party providing the indemnity has assets within the United States that can be attached to fund any indemnification obligations. In addition to or perhaps in substitution for such indemnities, BPO buyers should investigate the availability and cost of insuring against the loss or theft of intellectual property.

Bankruptcy of service providers can create severe complications for buyers, even within the United States. BPO buyers should consider escrowing critical intellectual property to ensure access in case of bankruptcy or other financial or operational failures. Buyers should consider escrowing not just source code but also any and all intellectual property and other critical information related to the outsourced process, including the information necessary to contact and access personnel whose cooperation is necessary to exploit the full value of the intellectual property.

Another key issue concerns ownership rights to intellectual property created through the outsourcing relationship. Joint ownership of intellectual property such as patents, trademarks, and copyrights is a particularly complex issue. The outsourcing contract should specifically address who controls this intellectual property, including the prosecution of ownership claims to these types of property. Parties should also address the potential for licensing of this jointly developed intellectual property. Who has the right to license this property and to whom? Can it be licensed to competitors of the client?

Industry-Specific Concerns

Depending on the nature of the outsourced process, additional regulatory hurdles may need to be addressed. If the outsourced process involves health care information such as insurance claims processing, the outsourcing contract should address compliance with the Health Insurance Portability and Accountability Act (HIPAA). HIPAA requires that health care organizations establish procedures and systems to protect against unauthorized access to certain protected health information.[16] These procedures and systems include internal audit procedures, incident reporting procedures, data protection procedures, and termination procedures. Pursuant to HIPAA, the client must have the right to terminate the outsourcing contract if the service provider breaches any provision of HIPAA and fails to cure such breach.

If the client is a financial institution subject to the Gramm-Leach-Bliley Act (GLB), and the outsourced process involves financial information of customers, then the outsourcing contract should address compliance with GLB.[17] Under GLB, financial institutions must secure private customer data. They must implement a comprehensive, written information security program with administrative, technical, and physical safeguards for customer information. Once again, contractual provisions are just the beginning—implementation and governance must be addressed to ensure compliance.

Termination of the Contract

In light of the statistics concerning the number of firms that terminate outsourcing contracts prematurely, termination provisions are among the most valuable contractual provisions. The initial focus should be to anticipate the various circumstances under which BPO buyers might desire to terminate the outsourcing relationship. The contractual right to terminate a BPO relationship can be granted for two reasons: convenience and cause.

Because of the requirement for flexibility and change management in the outsourcing process, it is imperative that the buyer has the right to terminate for convenience (i.e., without cause). In most instances, service providers will be justified in requiring a termination fee in conjunction with termination for convenience. This is especially true in the early years of the outsourcing relationship, when the service provider may not have yet fully recouped any capital investments it made in conjunction with establishment of the outsourcing relationship. The amount of the termination fee should vary in relation to the anticipated financial position of the parties at the time of the termination.

Typically, service providers are not permitted to terminate for convenience because of the extreme cost, risk, and disruption resulting to the client. If the service provider insists on allowing termination for convenience, the termination fee should reflect these factors. Typically, service providers are only permitted to terminate for cause, usually meaning the failure of the buyer to pay amounts owed to the vendor.

The outsourcing contract should specifically define what permits termination for cause by the client. Termination for cause should include material breaches of the outsourcing contract, as well as continuing or repetitive nonmaterial breaches of the outsourcing contract. The parties should develop specific parameters with respect to the SLAs in this regard. Termination for cause should also address financial insolvency or insecurity of the service provider.

In cases of financial insolvency or insecurity, an ounce of prevention is worth a pound of cure. In order to adequately protect the interests of the client, the outsourcing contract should include various financial covenants and ratios, akin to those found in loan agreements, to provide objective standards for financial insecurity. These provisions should be supplemented with reporting requirements and auditing rights so that the client can monitor the financial health of the service provider. Financial insecurity may also be tied to precipitous declines in the stock price of a publicly owned vendor.

Termination for cause may also be tied to retention of key employees or overall turnover rates of the vendor's workforce. These are critical because they reflect on the organizational fitness of the vendor firm. High turnover levels or the inability to retain key managers and executives are proxy indicators that the firm has internal governance issues that may place the BPO buyer at unwanted risk.

Termination for cause should also include so-called cross-default provisions with respect to the vendor's contracts with other service providers (subcontractors) that may or may not be working on the buyer's outsourced process. If the service provider is in default under these contracts, it can constitute a default under the outsourcing contract. Depending on the degree of reliance by the vendor on subcontractors, termination for cause may also include default by either party under these subcontract arrangements or the financial insolvency or insecurity of the subcontractor.

Finally, termination for cause should also contemplate changes in control, both with respect to the vendor and the buyer. Changes of control of the vendor may result in the replacement of the management team in which the buyer placed its trust at the outset of the outsourcing relationship or may result in the vendor providing services to or even becoming a competitor of the buyer with attendant risks to the client's intellectual property. Changes of control with respect to the buyer may result in the divestiture of the processes being outsourced or otherwise obviate the need for outsourcing in the first instance. New management of the buyer may not be comfortable with outsourcing for any number of reasons. For these reasons, the vendor should also have the right to terminate the outsourcing contract as a result of changes in control at the top of the buyer organization.

Transition

If a BPO relationship falls apart and one or both parties decide to terminate the agreement, it may be necessary for the buyer to reabsorb the outsourced process or find another vendor. In either case, the transition of the outsourced process under these circumstances should be considered in the original contract.

The reasons that the original contract should include provisions for the transition of the outsourced process in the case of termination should be clear.

Consider all of the planning and implementation entailed in outsourcing a process from a buyer to a service provider. Now imagine how much more difficult that process might be when the original buyer is no longer in control of the process and its attendant assets and personnel. To add to the challenge, consider the fact that the transition may well be from an unhappy or incompetent vendor (and frequently, both). Thus the transition from a service provider to a second service provider, or the reintegration of the outsourced process back to the client, is exponentially more difficult than the original outsourcing process. Thus careful consideration should be given to how the transition may be effected, and detailed transition provisions included in the outsourcing contract. On the positive side, the elements of an effective transition plan are similar to those included in the original outsourcing process, just more complex.

A transition plan should include a commitment by the vendor to provide transition-planning assistance. This assistance should include inventories of hard and soft assets, copies of relevant data, detailed descriptions of procedures, and other information relevant to the outsourced process. The buyer should have the right to use this data and to disclose it to other potential service providers. The client should also have the right to purchase the assets and hire key personnel related to the outsourced process, as well as the right to assume key contracts.

The transition plan should address the need for parallel processing for some period of time while the process is migrating from the service provider to a new service provider or back to the client. There may be a need for continued use of shared assets, such as computer networks.

Just as aligning the interests of the service provider and the client is a key element of a successful outsourcing contract, aligning the interests of the service provider and the client during the transition period is significant. Usually, this takes the form of monetary incentives for a successfully implemented transition plan.

Force Majeure

Outsourcing contracts, like other commercial contracts, typically include force majeure clauses, which excuse the service provider from performance in the case of natural disasters such as fire- and weather-related catastrophes. In light of the geopolitical postures of many of the countries where BPO service providers are located, war and terrorism are also likely triggers of force majeure clauses. However, because of the significant function that outsourced processes often play in the client's business, a well-crafted outsourcing contract should contemplate more than just excusing the vendor from performance for the duration of the force majeure event. The outsourcing contract should link the triggering of a force majeure event with disaster recovery plans and business continuation plans. To the extent that a client cannot significantly minimize its risk in that regard, insurance should be addressed.

Dispute Resolution

As has been stressed throughout this discussion of outsourcing contracts, the outsourcing contract is a living document, which must have change management processes integrated within it. Change, however, inevitably invites disagreement, and the outsourcing contract should anticipate this eventuality. The dispute resolution process begins where corporate governance ends. When all of the elements of the corporate governance process have been engaged and the parties have failed to reach resolution of the dispute, the parties must seek resolution through legal processes.

These processes can have escalation procedures built in, just like the governance process. Dispute resolution may be initiated through informal nonbinding procedures such as mediation, although this is not a necessary step. Beyond these informal nonbinding procedures, however, the dispute resolution process will progress to either binding arbitration or litigation. If the parties decide to utilize the arbitration process, they must agree on the rules of arbitration. In international transactions, parties often use the rules and procedures promulgated by the International Chamber of Commerce's International Court of Arbitration.[18] In domestic transactions, parties often specify that arbitration will be conducted pursuant to the Commercial Arbitration Rules of the American Arbitration Association. In either case, questions of venue and choice of law must be addressed.

Venue is the place where the dispute is to be resolved. The parties should consider both questions of efficiency in terms of proximity to the persons and facilities proximate to the dispute and questions of neutrality. Choice-of-law provisions determine what laws will govern the interpretation of the outsourcing contract and rules of the dispute. Choice-of-law provisions are usually determined by the golden rule—he who has the gold rules.

CONCLUSION

Developing an effective contract is an important part of an effective BPO relationship. BPO buyers should not take this stage of the BPO Life Cycle lightly in an effort to reduce costs. Investment in a well-crafted contract, and in a legal team that has the strategic interests of both parties in mind, may well save time and expense in the future. As this chapter has noted, there are many common elements to a BPO contract. There are also many tough questions that a BPO buyer should ask itself before actually signing a contract. Exhibit 6.4 lists some of these questions.

EXHIBIT 6.4   Tough Questions BPO Buyers Should Ask Before Signing the Contract

- Does the contract clearly describe the results you need?
- Does the vendor warrant that it will deliver those results?
- What remedies are available to you if the results are not achieved?
- Does the contract contain all the vendor representatives you relied on?
- Does the contract show that the vendor has confidence in its ability to perform?
- What triggers your obligation to pay the vendor? Proven results? Or something relatively meaningless—like whenever the vendor says you must pay?
- If you later realize that the deal is not working, will you be able to explain to your senior management why you made this deal—and still be employed?
- Would disinterested third parties (read: jurors) be able to understand every aspect of the deal by looking at the contract?

Source: Joe Auer, "Who Gets the Risk? And Who Ducks It?" *Computerworld* (June 26, 2000), p. 78.

SUMMARY

- Seventy-five percent of managers report that outsourcing outcomes had failed to meet expectations.
- Careful consideration of the BPO contract can help avoid many of the significant risk factors associated with a BPO relationship.
- A BPO contract must be built on a foundation of trust between the buyer and vendor.
- Negotiating an outsourcing contract is a positive-sum process.
- Organizations that have decided to undertake a BPO initiative should use this opportunity to assess cultural fit with the BPO provider.
- The ideal BPO negotiating strategy is one that is collaborative, based on a vision of a win-win outcome, and that seeks long-term, flexible contract terms.
- Terms of a BPO contract should include scope of work, service level agreements, pricing, contract term, governance, intellectual property, industry-specific concerns, termination clauses, transition planning, force majeure, and dispute resolution.
- The BPO buyer's attorneys must work closely with the buying organization's personnel to become intimately familiar with the details of the outsourced processes in order to prepare a statement of work that is clear and complete.
- In a service level agreement (SLA), a vendor agrees to achieve defined levels of performance.
- Many companies cite the lack of adequate SLAs as a prime culprit in failed outsourcing relationships.

- The negotiated term of the BPO contract should at minimum match the life cycle of the processes involved and changes in the business cycle.
- Support of the governance process and personnel by vendor and client management is essential and should be established at the outset of the outsourcing relationship.
- In the initial stages of considering an outsourcing initiative, companies should carefully consider the intellectual property ramifications of outsourcing.
- The contractual right to terminate a BPO relationship can be granted for two reasons: convenience and cause.
- The transition from a service provider to a second service provider, or the reintegration of the outsourced process back to the client, is exponentially more difficult than the original outsourcing process.
- The dispute resolution process begins where corporate governance ends.
- Investment in a well-crafted contract, and in a legal team that has the strategic interests of both parties in mind, may well save time and expense in the future.

four

Executing an Outsourcing Project

This part is the most extensive of the book, exploring the challenges and management techniques associated with transitioning to and operating a BPO project. The final team in the BPO Life Cycle, the Project Management Team (PMT) is introduced. The PMT, similar to the other teams in the process, has cross-functional representation from within the buyer organization. It is also the first team to include members from the BPO vendor.

Chapter 7 provides insights into the variety of issues that may arise as the outsourced process transitions from the buyer to the vendor firm. The transition process will involve social and technical issues that must be managed to ensure that the transition runs smoothly. Internal human resource issues as well as technical data transfer and data sharing issues must be confronted and managed.

Chapter 8 examines the buyer–vendor relationship and provides insights into how this complex relationship can be managed effectively. More intense than a buyer–supplier relationship, the buyer–vendor relationship should focus on cross-enterprise collaboration that results in mutual strategic gains.

Chapter 9 considers the various organizational infrastructure issues that comprise the transition to an operating outsourcing project. The chapter examines both technical and social infrastructure issues.

Chapter 10 takes a serious look at the various risks that a business is newly exposed to as a result of a BPO project. These risks include financial and legal exposures, each of which has a variety of mitigation techniques. The mitigation techniques are discussed and explored, and case examples are provided.

CHAPTER 7

Managing the BPO Transition

It is not necessary to change. Survival is not mandatory.

—W. Edwards Deming, quality consultant and author

We have now entered the crucial transition phase of the BPO Life Cycle. BPO buyers have by now invested a lot of time and effort into determining what business processes to outsource, identifying and selecting a partner, and developing a detailed contract. The transition stage of the BPO Life Cycle is the stage in which risk management actions and strategies should be implemented. Risk management begins at home—with effective management of the changes that will be introduced to the organization undertaking the BPO initiative.

Managing internal change that results from the initiation of a BPO project actually begins sooner in the BPO Life Cycle. In previous chapters, we have repeatedly alluded to the internal management and leadership issues that are likely to arise as people deal with the looming prospect of a BPO project implementation. These managerial challenges must be confronted as the issues arise, and many of them call for change management techniques. Nonetheless, a full-blown internal change management strategy should not be initiated until the contract has been signed and the project launch date has been set. It would be a waste of resources and might unnecessarily stir up the internal staff to go into full change management mode before setting the BPO project launch date. With that starting point as a target, those responsible for change management can assess organizational needs and determine what tactics will be effective in promoting and ensuring a smooth BPO transition.

In this chapter, we discuss the change management process from a variety of perspectives. Change management has been the subject of thorough scholarly research, and it seems there are more change management consultants than points of light in the starry skies. We will try to make sense of the overwhelming change management literature, case studies, and principles of effective change management by singling out a few generically effective principles. Of course, any particular organization will have to assess the challenges it uniquely faces in conducting a BPO project, but there are some issues that any organization will face, including:

- Establishing a vision of the future state of the organization
- Securing leadership as well as management of the BPO transition
- Communicating with internal staff about the BPO transition
- Managing organization culture beyond the process affected by BPO
- Managing job loss and changeover to new management
- Establishing business continuity and new performance benchmarks

We begin by discussing the overarching project management plan, and introduce the final team—the project management team—to be used in managing the BPO Life Cycle. Next, we provide an overview of generally applicable change management principles where we look at each of the areas mentioned in the previous list in more detail. The overriding objective of this chapter is to help organizations undertaking a BPO initiative—whether on the buyer side or the vendor side—become alerted to the multiple change-induced organizational issues that are likely to arise and how they can be dealt with effectively. It would not be in anyone's interest to have a BPO initiative derailed or slowed down dramatically as a result of inattention to fundamental change management principles.

THE BPO PROJECT MANAGEMENT PLAN

The formal contract between BPO buyer and vendor has been signed and sealed. As discussed in Chapter 6, the BPO contract is a detailed document that includes service level agreements that specify the level of expected performance on defined organizational processes. These form the basis for developing metrics and for the system of rewards, penalties, and remedies that govern the buyer–vendor relationship.

At the same time, the BPO contract does not provide the flexibility and responsiveness required to manage an ongoing project. For that, we recommend development of a separate document that we call the project management plan. The project management plan should be alluded to in the BPO legal contract, but it is too fluid to be spelled out in detail in that governing document. The project management plan will need to adapt and change over time as the needs and competitive conditions of each firm change. The project management plan will include change provisions to enable adjustments over time. It will also include standard project management details such as goals and objectives, timelines, milestones, and key term working definitions. In essence, the project management plan provides a disciplined framework of execution to ensure that the BPO transition phase gives way to the operating phase.[1]

One of the main objectives of the project management plan is to establish and identify roles and role players from each organization—buyer and vendor. These roles and role players will be responsible for project outcomes and accountable to the BPO steering team.

Many firms vest the responsibility for the BPO project in a single individual, whom we have designated as the BPO champion. Others prefer to vest that responsibility in a project management team. The choice is not merely one of preference; there are several factors to consider in deciding between an individual or team approach to managing the BPO project.

Individual or Team?

Developing a formal project management plan requires that the buyer and vendor each assign a dedicated team or, at minimum, a dedicated internal BPO champion to design the plan, manage the project on an ongoing basis, and implement changes as needed.[2] Although this function adds short-term costs to the outsourcing project, it will usually prove to be less costly in the long run because issues can be anticipated, managed, and controlled before they become major problems. In general, project management costs should not exceed 7 percent of total project costs.[3]

Whether to use an individual or team approach to project management depends on several factors. For example, a far more intensive, team-based approach may be necessary to manage an offshore outsourcing relationship than an onshore one. Offshoring often brings a range of issues not generally encountered with an onshore relationship. Cultural differences, language differences, and time zone differences are just three of the variables that distinguish an offshore BPO project.[4] These are not minor distinctions, and they generally require additional resources to manage compared to an onshore project. Another major distinction in outsourcing projects is whether the buyer is managing a single or multiple vendors. Complications arise in managing multiple vendors. For example, it may be necessary to establish more than one BPO champion or project management team to deal with each vendor. This creates a further need to integrate the various project managers to make sure they are communicating and sharing best practices and lessons learned.[5]

However, a team-based approach can lead to problems of accountability if there are no one-to-one links between individuals and discrete project management responsibilities. That is, even when a team approach is used, individual team members should be assigned clear responsibilities for particular aspects of the project, and they should have clear reporting channels. Exhibit

7.1 highlights some of the issues to consider in making a decision to vest project management responsibility in a team or an individual.

A hybrid approach that may be used to alleviate the potential for the diffusion of accountability is to assign a BPO champion who has the responsibility of developing a project management team. With this approach, the BPO project management responsibility remains clearly with the BPO champion, who is held accountable for performance of the project. We recommend this approach, and we call the resulting team the project management team (PMT). This is the last of the various teams we have identified throughout the BPO Life Cycle and is illustrated in Exhibit 7.2.

As Exhibit 7.2 shows, the BPO steering team remains in ultimate control of the project. This team was constituted at the beginning of the BPO Life Cycle and retains its oversight role over the organization's BPO project.

The PMT should consist of individuals representing a range of organizational functions, including individuals from each firm. Just as with the BPO analysis team (BAT) and vendor selection team (VST), cross-functional representation on the PMT ensures a diverse skill set. This diverse skill set should range over financial, technical, and human resource skills. Issues that draw from each skill area are likely to arise during the transition and maintenance phases of the BPO Life Cycle.

The BPO champion is likely to be an individual who participated on the BAT, the VST, or both. This person will generally have high visibility within the organization and possess skills in communications, negotiations, and business reasoning. This person should have the additional capability to organize and manage a team. He or she should also be exceedingly familiar with the business case for BPO and be willing and able to articulate, discuss, or defend it within the organization whenever necessary.

Other roles that might be assigned to individuals on the PMT include facilitator, recorder, and liaison. The facilitator is primarily responsible for setting meetings and arranging meeting locations. The recorder is responsible for taking notes during the meeting and distributing minutes to each team member after each meeting. The liaison role is delegated to individuals who

EXHIBIT 7.1 Factors Relevant to Choosing between a Team or Individual BPO Relationship Manager

Individual	Team
Single BPO Provider	Multiple BPO providers
Cost reduction is primary goal	Strategic plan is primary goal
One process outsourced, with low probability of additional outsourcing	Multiple processes outsourced
Onshore BPO provider	Offshore a nearshore BPO provider

EXHIBIT 7.2 BPO Project Management Team in the Overall Project Team Structure

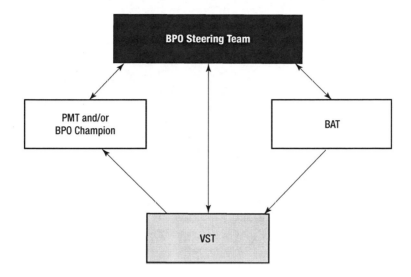

are responsible for maintaining contacts between the team and other organizational units, to ensure appropriate communications are occurring, and to detect and address issues before they turn into problems.

The PMT is responsible for implementing the change management strategy for the organization. Up to this point in the BPO Life Cycle, most of the skills required to manage the BPO project have focused on negotiations and analysis. The required skill set widens during the transition phase to include leadership, communication, and cross-cultural management. Let us turn next to the principles of effective BPO-related organizational change management.

GENERAL PRINCIPLES OF CHANGE MANAGEMENT

Effective change management in organizations has been studied and examined in great detail. No stone has been left unturned because scholars and organizational consultants recognize that this is a particularly needful (and lucrative) area in which to practice. Unfortunately for managers who have to sift through all of the articles, reports, books, and consultant schemes, it is not clear which of the approaches should be used to manage the changes produced by a BPO initiative. Take heart—in the end, the well-chosen actions taken to manage change are less important than their consistent and well-communicated application.[6]

Let us state that again: The well-chosen actions taken to manage the changes brought by BPO are less important than their consistent and well-communicated application. Of course, that does not mean to suggest that all managerial interventions are created equal. The consistent application of a poor technique will inevitably produce poor results. That is why we added the "well-chosen" caveat. The change management strategy adopted should be one that makes sense under the circumstances. It would be difficult for the project management team to explain and/or defend its change management tactics if it was obvious that they were inappropriate or plainly ineffective.

The most important insight that change management scholars and years of organizational experience have uncovered is that consistent application of a sensible strategy is necessary to produce effective results. Most would agree that any attempt to achieve "optimum" results is likely to lead to paralysis, as the search for the perfect technique to match current conditions would be inordinately time-consuming and fraught with endless debate. Rather, the predominant counsel today is to use a satisficing approach—one that will produce results that exceed certain prespecified and, hopefully, measurable parameters, but might not be the optimum solution.[7] Satisficing is a concept not used often enough among those who execute organizational change management tactics and strategies. It is a handy concept—handier than, say, synergy—that promotes action over inaction, results over paralysis, and consistency over trendy management theories. We recommend that the concept become a part of the PMT's lexicon and a pillar of efficient change management style.

In light of our recommendation that the consistent application of a well-chosen strategy rather than the strategy itself is the most important factor in effective BPO-induced change management, let us examine change management principles that qualify as well-chosen. Experience and scholarly research converge on a few guiding principles:

- Effective change management requires a compelling vision of the outcome of the change process.
- Effective change management requires visible leadership from top management of the organization.
- Effective change management requires extensive communication and opportunities for employee feedback.
- Effective change management requires the ability to deal with job loss and changeover.
- Effective change management requires an ability to maintain business continuity and benchmark performance.

In the following sections, each of these general principles is examined in greater detail and in light of their application within a BPO initiative.

Creating a Compelling Vision

It is easy for management to deride the value of vision to organizational achievement. After all, it is usually not the visionaries who are celebrated in song and story—it is the action figures we prefer. The visionaries are often considered to be soft, pensive, or overly cautious. And certainly, anyone could waste a lot of time in dreaming up a vision and trying to crystallize it in his or her mind.

Vision, so conceived, *is* a waste of time and has no place in the competitive global arena in which most organizations are striving to eke out advantages over rivals. Yet, a less exaggerated concept of vision does have an important role to play in the alignment of organizational goals and individual efforts. As has been amply demonstrated, clarity on the outcome of a difficult and challenging project helps people establish a sense of flow and ownership that can lead to high levels of performance under difficult circumstances.[8]

An effective organizational vision is not something that is pondered over and analyzed to infinite detail. It is nothing more than a tale—a story—of what the outcome of a project is expected to *look* and *feel* like to organizational members. It is up to the managers creating the vision to determine how much detail is required to tell a story that is compelling enough to drive high performance. For skeptical listeners, the story may need greater detail and more analogies to satisfy them. For already-converted listeners, less detail and more encouragement to step out and take action may be all that is required.

Corporate storytelling has become a high-value consulting specialization for some. Firms such as Hewlett-Packard, Nokia, and Rolls Royce recognize that overreliance on the alphabet soup acronyms of many change management programs leads to stupefying doubt and confusion. They have developed corporate stories to enliven the troops and align them on a common purpose.[9]

It is likely that many of the managers reading this book do not fancy themselves the storytelling type. A good corporate story does not need to have dramatic characters or daring action heroes. All that is required is a word-picture of the expected outcomes of the project and the likely impact for the people operating it. It strikes us that managers who lack such a vision are flailing about and succeed only by chance. Far better for personal success, as well as the success of the overall project and the organization, is to craft a working articulation (a story) of the outcomes of the project and then refine the story as required. Five basic elements must be present to make storytelling an effective technique for leading change, as shown in Exhibit 7.3.

These elements of effective organizational storytelling are straightforward enough to be practiced by nearly anyone in a project management role. Managing a BPO transition requires placing the project in the context of the bigger picture, including the likely future state of the organization and its people. Developing and articulating a truthful story about the organization's likely

EXHIBIT 7.3   Elements of Effective Organizational Storytelling

- **Effective stories are context specific.** Research indicates that linking an activity or project to a company's strategic challenges improves the effectiveness of the initiative.
- **Effective stories are level appropriate.** The storyteller should frame stories so that participants can see themselves in it and reflect on what they might do to resolve the challenges it poses.
- **Role models tell effective stories.** Storytellers must be both highly respected role models and highly accessible coaches.
- **Effective stories have drama.** The best stories focus on the storyteller's need to make tough choices, usually without perfect information or complete agreement among involved parties.
- **Effective stories have high learning value.** For a story to be effective it must stimulate learning, and for learning to have impact it must produce changes in behavior.

future state will not eliminate all change-induced problems. However, abdicating that responsibility will undoubtedly mean that the organization will experience a greater number and intensity of change management issues during the BPO transition.

Leadership and Management Roles

Standard definitions of leadership distinguish it from management by associating the former with something like vision and the latter with something like operations. This crude distinction does not always hold, of course, because managers are often called on to articulate a vision and leaders must occasionally roll up their sleeves and take action. Still, if we regard the distinction as one of degree rather than absolute, it is true enough. Leaders generally spend more time crafting and articulating vision than operating, and managers usually spend more time operating than crafting a vision.

With that said, it is possible to provide some useful recommendations into how leaders and managers differ in their respective roles during the transition and operating phases of a BPO project. The transition phase of the BPO Life Cycle is a true turning point in the BPO project—the organization is now implementing changes that heretofore had only been talked about. The rumors and fears that are often associated with the preoperational BPO phases have now given way to real changes in organizational workflow, personnel, policies, and procedures. Managers are needed to help guide these new ways of doing things into the organization's overall workflow. Leaders are needed to hold the organization together with steadfast vision and courage. Let us look at each role in a little more detail beginning with management.

It may help to envision the role of the manager during the transition phases of the BPO Life Cycle if we develop a scenario that reflects what might be occurring in the typical workplace. Exhibit 7.4 is a short story illustrating common employee reactions to organizational change. Most managers reading this will be familiar with these reactions.

The scenario in Exhibit 7.4 is a composite of thousands of similar situations that occur nearly every day with work changeovers in companies of nearly every size and complexity. That people resist change is one of the few things that can be counted on in the unpredictable world of business. Managers are faced with operational challenges, deadlines, and goals—yet they must motivate others in order to reach those goals. In BPO, it is occasionally necessary to motivate others to perform when their jobs are being eliminated and/or the threat of job elimination looms. Other impediments to a BPO implementation that have to be managed include the following:

- Effects on personnel not displaced by the BPO project, but who may fear being next in line
- Attitudes of personnel regarding the presence of outsiders in the organization
- Attempts by some to impede progress or a lack of willing participation in the changeover
- Fear of failure under the new workflow model

EXHIBIT 7.4 HighTech Software Outsources Its Help Desk

HighTech software, a $50 million custom software company, had a 30-person help desk that had grown from only two people when the company started four years ago. In fact, a friend of the founder initiated the help desk function. She was still managing the help desk when the decision to outsource the function was made. While she agreed with the economics of the decision, she was concerned about the employees. HighTech's executives assured her that they would be absorbed by the outsourcing company or offered reasonable severance packages.

When the BPO vendor was selected, it decided to shift the engine help desk function offshore to India, virtually ensuring that none of HighTech's existing staff would be retained. During the transition, the vendor found it very difficult to work with the staff to learn details about process flow, and the transitioning of data from HighTech to the vendor was taking more than three times longer than expected. The BPO vendor encountered what it described as "open hostility" in its efforts to acquire the information it needed to integrate workflows and processes with other HighTech departments. After nearly four months, the project was in jeopardy because HighTech's internal personnel were difficult to communicate with.

Individuals within the organization not displaced by the BPO project may harbor beliefs that it is only a matter of time before their jobs are outsourced. Many are aware of the outsourcing trend that has been in the news, and they may have witnessed the anguished faces of individuals within the organization whose jobs are being outsourced or eliminated. There is no managerial bromide that can be applied to eliminate the sense of loss people will feel if friends are displaced, nor any simple technique for motivating people to perform at high levels when they have been reminded so bluntly that the organization's social contract with workers is primarily based on economics.[10]

Managers must deal with the changes introduced into the organization by the BPO project with realism and determination. Sugarcoating an obvious organizational shift toward headcount reduction and cost containment through BPO will only add to the rumors and anxiety. During times of transformational organizational change, many managers mistakenly attempt to paint a rosy picture despite overwhelming evidence to the contrary. They do this out of a natural human aversion to being the bearer of bad news. They also do this on occasion based on denial; they do not want to believe that outsourcing might target their own jobs in the future.

Honest communication with everyone about the goals of the company, the likely outcomes of a BPO implementation, and the steps the organization is taking to help workers deal with the change is the best-practice technique for managers to follow. Yet, it is very difficult for many managers to practice this approach. Sometimes, they cannot be honest with employees because they simply do not know what is going to happen. That is a leadership issue, which we discuss in a moment. Even if the manager does not know the full implications of a BPO transition, it is better to communicate *that*—admitting to personal ignorance—than trying to provide false assurances.

Motivational experts can now agree that, when it comes to managing people at work, honesty really is (usually) the best policy. On issues regarding workplace changes, policies, and future expectations, there is simply no substitute for honesty. The next most important tactic for managing BPO-induced change is communication. A manager could practice honesty but at the same time be excessively Spartan in his or her communication patterns. In the throes of dramatic organizational change, people need to talk to one another. They need to talk because they need to understand. An individual manager may not be a great communicator, but great communication is not required. What is required is communication *quantity* leavened by *honesty*. Managers who have a tendency toward introversion are not excluded. If they are uncomfortable with speeches or group meetings, there are other communication channels at their disposal, including e-mails, memoranda, company newsletters, and employee portals. Managers should leverage multiple channels in communicating with employees about the changes they will be facing, the steps the organization is taking to help them during the change, and, most important, the rationale for the change. As the Case Study indicates, "the outsourcing culture rewards leaders who collaborate and communicate."

CASE STUDY

NYPH Managing the BPO Transition: Four Years Later

In November 1999, New York-Presbyterian Hospital (NYPH) announced a seven-year, $228-million IT outsourcing contract with First Consulting Group (FCG). The contract created a third entity, FCG Management Services, to perform the work—a step that included the hiring of more than 400 NYPH staff into the new unit.

NYPH wanted immediate benefits from the predictable costs, service levels, and outcomes offered by outsourcing. "The biggest issue a CIO faces after signing the contract is managing the performance objectives for the first six months," said Diane Daniele, Interim CIO for NYPH.

NYPH's office of the chief information officer (OCIO) designed a governance model to make IT a more effective investment tool by focusing on strategic planning and thinking, monitoring, governing partnerships, and change management. The OCIO is a champion of IT change at NYPH. "You must show people what the future looks like and restructure the business simultaneously," said Guy Scalzi, NYPH's former CIO and now the account manager for the New York outsource team.

The trench work of transition and change management continues each day at NYPH with core process improvement teams focused on everything from leadership training to wiring closet inspections. Sharing leadership roles with the OCIO speeds up integration.

Change in how people communicate is another benefit of outsourcing. Scalzi put high-potential managers into the applications areas and told them to break down the runtime performance barriers and open up the client communication channels. The outsourcing culture rewards leaders who collaborate and communicate and does not reward the information blockers, Daniele says.

Although they were initially skeptical about the outsourcing agreement's impact on service and loss of control, physicians, too, have experienced positive changes.

Source: Adapted from Bob Smith, "Outsourcing on a Grand Scale," *Health Management Technology* (July 2000), pp. 18–20.

As the BPO transition unfolds, managers will encounter some individuals who will attempt to obstruct the BPO project. Obstruction can occur in two ways: overt and covert. Overt obstruction is fairly easy to deal with. Overt obstructionists are vocal, identifying themselves as being opposed to the BPO project. They can be dealt with directly using common disciplinary and motivational tactics. It is the covert obstructionists who are the most insidious. They oppose change but work quietly in their obstructionist efforts. This can include direct sabotage, but covert obstructionists are usually more cunning. They impede progress on a change effort by omission, rather than commission. They withhold key information or data that they know would aid the transition process. They do not offer helpful information unless directly asked. They appear to be contributing and happy when they are in fact happy only in their subversion.

Managers can deal with covert obstructionists, but only after they have rooted them out. They are unlikely to identify themselves, masking their inner desire to undermine the BPO project—and maybe the manager. They can be uncovered, but only with help from those who are working on the BPO transition phase. Managers must actively query others to determine if there has been any unnecessary foot-dragging or apparent lack of motivation to assist in the BPO transition. This type of querying should be handled in a matter-of-fact rather than an accusatory manner. It is important in the effort to expose covert obstructionists that managers do not impugn those who are, in fact, working diligently to help the process along.

Covert obstructionists are identified through behavior patterns rather than direct acts or verbalizations. As the manager queries various individuals involved in the BPO transition about how easily they are finding it to get the information they need and where the bottlenecks seem to be, covert obstruction will reveal itself. It will be revealed in a recurrent pattern of tardiness or sloppiness in deliverables. Covert obstructionists will deliver what they are asked, but it will usually be less than professional grade and often delayed.

Covert obstructionists must be confronted to be controlled. Of course, they will usually deny their obstructionism, claming that they have delivered all they have been asked or that they are working on delivering all they have been asked. In the worst cases, the covert obstructionists may actually believe their own story. Covert obstructionists must be managed directly. The manager must be involved with detailing the expected deliverables and time frame, which must then also be linked to the covert obstructionist's regular performance review process. The best way to deal with covert obstructionists is to out them and then provide them with clear and unambiguous expectations of future performance. Of course, the manager must follow up on these expectations, including the use of disciplinary tactics if objectives are not being met.

Leadership throughout the BPO transition must be visible and accessible. BPO transition leaders (as opposed to managers) are expected to have a firm grasp of the BPO business case and an ability to articulate it as needed. Furthermore, BPO leaders should have a *granular* grasp of the BPO business case, which we define as an ability to link it to organizational units and the individuals who work in those units. Above all, leaders must be able to provide people with answers to the inevitable question "what's in it for me?"

Companies that undertake BPO projects are most often those that already have experience with transformational change. In that regard, many within these organizations have personal experience with restructuring initiatives and may have developed some level of maturity, if not outright boredom, with managing change of that magnitude. In organizations like this, leaders are called on to inject new enthusiasm into the organizational *zeitgeist*. Expressions of better possible futures for the company and its employees are the preferred strategy. Occasionally, leaders are prone to shield themselves from negative reactions by asserting that the decision to use a BPO approach is a matter of organizational survival in a highly competitive economy—the decision was beyond anyone's control. Although that may be true, it has the ring of cowardice about it. Far better for the leader to proclaim the BPO strategy as a carefully laid plan that stands to generate compelling advantages for the organization and its employees. Leaders simply cannot shrink from the need to articulate a vision during times of transformational change.[11] Change is difficult and often requires that people tolerate pain in the short term. This is made easier by leaders who are able to help people paint a mental picture of a future that will be better and more satisfying than the present.[12]

Communicating with Employees

Effective communication with employees is vital to the BPO transition process. A lack of communication from managers to employees does not mean a lack of communication within the organization. Organizational space abhors a communication vacuum. If the space is not filled with deliberate, optimistic, and directive messages from leadership, it will be filled by rumors, gossip, and speculation from the employees. People need to understand their environment and will settle for half-baked speculative explanations if no better alternatives are available.

Effective employee communications begin with a simple notion: honesty. Honesty is the best policy not only because it is ethically correct, but also because half-truths and lies will ultimately destroy morale and productivity. At the same time, blunt honesty is rarely a useful strategy. When asked about the results of a person's weight loss efforts, the savvy respondent gives the aspiring weight loser an answer that does not offend, rather than the bluntly honest one. This is called common sense.

In organizational life, it also does not do any good to answer questions with blunt honesty. Tact and sophistication can reduce the impact of a bluntly honest message. Organizations seeking to undertake a BPO initiative will often be entertaining the prospect of headcount reduction. As one might expect, communicating that reality to employees may be detrimental to productivity. At the same time, equivocating about the potential for job loss or outright denial of the possibility would be disingenuous, and that would be obvious even to those less talented at reading social cues.

The key to effective communication, then, is not simply honesty, but rather sophisticated honesty. By that we mean managers must communicate accurately and competently with employees about the extent and implications of the BPO initiative. Accuracy pertains to the truthfulness of the message. There should be no question about the value of this quality. Competence pertains to the level of detail that is provided in a message to a given party. Employees at different levels of the organization will need and benefit from different levels of detail about the initiative.

At a minimum, managers should communicate with all employees about what the BPO initiative means to them personally and what the organization intends to do to help them through the transition.[13] Every impact message delivered by management should be accompanied by a "here's what we're going to do about it" message. This may even include the level of outplacement support that is going to be provided to employees who stand to lose their jobs as a result of the BPO initiative.

Managing Culture Beyond the Outsourced Process

Beyond the organizational units immediately affected by the BPO project are employees who are friends, relatives, and acquaintances of those affected. BPO project managers must not overlook the ripple effects that are created by outsourcing and the threat that others might feel from witnessing the introduction of BPO into neighboring work units. In addition to the heightened sense of insecurity that may arise, there will be concerns about workflow issues and day-to-day business continuity. Organizational units that work closely with the outsourced function may be concerned about the capability of the vendor to achieve the same level of productivity. Other concerns that may arise are as follows:

- Will we have to work extra hard to make the BPO transition work?
- Will my job change as a result of the introduction of new work processes?

- Who will be receiving my work output, and will he or she be able to understand it?
- Will I be able to adapt to the vendor and its people?
- How will the organization's customers react to changes in personnel and/or procedures?

Earlier in this chapter we talked about the importance of developing a vision—an organizational story—to articulate the anticipated future state of the organization. In managing the BPO transition as it affects units beyond the outsourced activity, the story has immense value. A consistent story will help quell the rumor mill and alleviate confusion and misunderstanding.

At the same time, it will be vital for managers throughout the organization to be able to demonstrate buy-in to the BPO project and refrain from public naysaying if they do not fully support the initiative. Thus the top leadership of the organization must develop support for the BPO project across organizational boundaries, vertical and horizontal. At a minimum, the management team must be united in its public support of the BPO initiative. At best, everyone should be aligned to support the initiative and be mobilized to lend a hand whenever and wherever needed.

Managing Job Loss and Changeover

Managing job loss and changeover is assuredly among the most difficult challenges that managers face, no matter what the cause of the upheaval. It is no secret that most rank-and-file employees in the organization who are likely to be displaced by a BPO initiative are living paycheck to paycheck. The looming prospect of job displacement as a result of the organization's decision to outsource is not likely to be met with shouts of joy. Whether the anticipated job displacement includes termination or shifting responsibilities, the reaction is predictable: Some will rush for the exit, others will cower and hope for the best, others will fight, and some will simply deny reality. Each of these reactions to the prospect of outsourcing must be managed and, the good news is, each of these can be managed.

A thorough analysis of the costs of a BPO project will include projected job losses and job shifts, and the cost of outplacement and/or retraining services. Many firms opt for a ruthless strategy during reduction-in-force (RIF) initiatives, but others have found tremendous value in using a more humane approach. Whatever approach is chosen, a detailed RIF plan is essential to minimize rancor, control the culture, and reduce exposure to liability.[14]

A detailed RIF plan will consider a wide range of factors when identifying the individuals who will be terminated and the procedures to be used to undertake the terminations. An RIF plan should consider each individual's skills and abilities and determinations of their relative contributions to the firm. It would be unwise to simply use an across-the-board RIF strategy if there are promising up-and-comers who would be terminated in the process. The organization does not want to lose potential future stars to the cost-cutting measures that are part of the BPO project. An RIF plan is typically developed by the management team in an off-site and secure setting. The list of individuals targeted for termination should be carefully guarded. Managers should receive thorough training on the procedures that will be used with the terminated employees. The Ethics and Governance insert provides a few guidelines on how to develop an RIF plan that minimizes exposure to liability.

The RIF plan should consider the options available to reduce the impact of the displacement for employees. For example, early retirement programs may be an option for senior employees. Voluntary buyouts of employment agreements may be used in cases where a contract is in force. Many organizations attempt to obtain a release of potential claims from workers terminated as a result of an RIF. This will require some form of consideration from the organization, usually severance pay. Other forms of consideration for a release include a reference letter or payment of insurance premiums for a defined period.[15] Some firms have been able to shift employees from direct employment to contract labor, using them on an as-needed basis. Such an arrangement often works very well both for the organization and for the displaced worker.

ETHICS & GOVERNANCE

Elements of a Defensible RIF Plan

Employers should follow these essential steps when carrying out a reduction in force (RIF):

- Decide what criteria will be used to select those for termination (e.g., geography, seniority, line of work, merit ranking).
- Make sure the criteria are followed.
- Be certain that the RIF criteria conform to company policy.
- Have at least one level of review of termination decisions.
- Perform a "disparate impact" review of those chosen for termination to make sure there is no discrimination, even unintentional.
- Document the entire process.

Source: Fair Employment Practices Guidelines, January 15, 2003 (Aspen Publishers).

The RIF plan should also include provisions for assisting displaced employees in their desire to gain new employment. Some firms set up career and psychological counseling services to assist employees through the initial shock. Many also establish job centers—usually away from the corporate campus—to help employees find new jobs. The job centers provide support in résumé writing, interviewing skills, and job listings. They may also provide employees with other short-term services such as daycare for parents who cannot afford it without a job, seminars on job hunting, and even training programs to help people achieve new skills for a changed job market.

Business Continuity and Benchmarking

The final consideration in managing the BPO transition is to ensure business continuity throughout the process. It is to be expected that performance indicators for the outsourced process are likely to be down or flat during the early stages of the transition. It might also occur that processes tightly linked to the outsourced process will also experience performance difficulties during this phase. Despite the expected performance dips, managers should have detailed performance benchmarks that provide a means of judging the extent of the effect and whether intervention is required.

Business continuity during transformational change is difficult, often requiring long hours and skill-stretching behavior. Managers who find frequent employee meetings and communication an annoyance will be challenged to stretch their skills in these areas. The organization as a whole may need to work carefully with local media representatives, who may have spotted a human-interest story amidst the outsourcing-induced RIF. Public relations and corporate communications, two units that may have been sleepily releasing good-news items on a regular basis, may now be called on to assertively address challenging questions about global job shifts and free trade.

Business continuity requires that the organization manage the internal disruptions to workflow by establishing acceptable limits on variation in normal performance. Six Sigma goals may need to be relaxed slightly during the transition phase to account for the learning curve that will need to be traversed. Yet, the organization does not want merely any result to count as acceptable. Reasonable, transition-phase-only benchmarks should be adopted and carefully monitored. Managers should be ready to intervene only when performance falls below the benchmark value, and they should be equally vigilant to stay the course and allow employees to learn and improve the new system through the transition. The latter is a difficult but necessary management tactic. Too-early intervention will short-circuit the learning process. Performance levels should rise as the transition unfolds, and new performance peaks are more likely to be sustained if managers practice the discipline of allowing the mistakes and learning process to run its course.

CONCLUSION

The transition phase of the BPO Life Cycle is filled with traps and potholes for unwary managers. These can be avoided through thoughtful application of some of the change management principles we discussed in this chapter. BPO has the potential to be an important and potent technique for allowing firms to reestablish their focus on core competencies and reestablish an entrepreneurial spirit in the organization. Leaner, highly focused organizations can adapt more quickly to changing competitive conditions and create greater value for customers through innovation and constant improvement. The economic forces in favor of BPO speak loudly for it to continue to be used across industry and market segments.

Organizations that recognize the competitive value of BPO should be careful not to rush into the BPO Life Cycle lest it overwhelm internal coping capacity. As stated in Chapter 1, BPO is a socio-technical phenomenon, requiring that managers pay as much attention to the social aspects of the BPO transition as the technical ones. Although the technical aspects are usually regarded as essential and acceptable, the social aspects of change are too often derided as being caused by immature employee attitudes and behaviors. Managers must strive to recognize each aspect of the change process as equally important to the overall success of the BPO project. This chapter dealt primarily with the social aspects of the internal change process. In Chapter 9, we look at managing the technical infrastructure during the BPO transition and operating phases.

SUMMARY

- Managing internal change begins early in the BPO Life Cycle, but a formal change management program should not be initiated until the project launch date has been set.
- Managing the BPO transition phase requires vision, leadership as well as management, effective communications, managing organizational culture, managing job loss and/or changeover, and establishing business continuity and performance benchmarks.
- The project management plan is the operating plan for the transition and maintenance phases of the BPO project.
- Each side, buyer and vendor, should appoint a BPO champion to serve on the BPO project management team (PMT).
- The PMT should include individuals with diverse skill sets, including financial, technical, and interpersonal.

- The well-chosen actions taken to manage the changes brought about by BPO are less important than their consistent and well-communicated application.
- The most important insight that change management scholars have uncovered is that consistent application of a strategy is necessary to produce effective results.
- The predominant counsel in change management today is to use a satisficing approach—one that produces results that exceed certain pre-specified and, hopefully, measurable parameters, but might not be the optimum solution.
- An effective organizational vision is not analyzed to infinite detail. It is nothing more than a tale—a story—of what the outcome of a project is expected to look and feel like to organizational members.
- Managers are needed to help guide new ways of doing things into the organization's overall workflow. Leaders are needed to hold the organization together with steadfast vision and courage.
- Overt obstructionists are vocal, identifying themselves as opposed to the BPO initiative.
- Covert obstructionists are more insidious; they oppose change, but work quietly in their obstructionist efforts.
- Organizational space abhors a communication vacuum. If the space is not filled with deliberate, optimistic, and directive messages from leadership, it will be filled by rumors, gossip, and speculation from the employees.
- Top leadership of the organization must develop support for the BPO project across organizational boundaries, vertical and horizontal.
- A detailed reduction-in-force (RIF) plan can help manage the likely reactions to BPO-induced job loss and/or changeover.

CHAPTER 8

Managing the Buyer–Vendor Relationship

*Every kind of peaceful cooperation among people is primarily
based on mutual trust and only secondarily on institutions such as
courts of justice and police.*

—Albert Einstein, scientist and professor

M anaging the BPO relationship successfully is a challenge for buyers and vendors alike. Notwithstanding the potential benefits of outsourcing, which have been articulated at length in the previous chapters, the complex nature of an outsourcing agreement lends itself to a variety of challenging relationship management issues. Although relationship management is a key component of any successful outsourcing project, it is the most often neglected one. Companies considering BPO must be aware that the traditional tactics for managing relationships between buyers and suppliers are inadequate for managing a BPO relationship.[1] Although it is true that outsourcing is a service procured by a company in accordance with its needs and usually in compliance with its established procurement process, the dynamics and nuances of an outsourcing partnership go beyond that normally found in a typical buyer–supplier relationship. For that reason, it is imperative that BPO buyers recognize the need for a formal approach to BPO relationship management.

The foundation of a BPO relationship is laid when a company begins to communicate its intention to outsource. Successful management of the outsourcing relationship depends on how the requirements are defined, the objectives described, the vendor chosen, and the contract written. Additionally, the people selected to manage the relationship are key because managing BPO relationships requires a variety of skills, including the following: [2]

- *Negotiation skills.* There will often be give and take in a BPO relationship. Thus, it is important that the project management team be skilled in negotiating points of view and in presenting them in an acceptable manner to the vendor.
- *Communication skills.* Outsourcing project management teams are the glue between a company's business needs and the vendor's services. Effective communication skills are necessary to prevent simple problems from becoming complex ones.
- *Business skills.* It is important to continually understand the changing business needs and align the services from the vendor with the BPO buyer's business objectives.

The senior management of the BPO buyer must necessarily be involved in periodically monitoring the BPO relationship and in ensuring that it stays on track. Senior management plays a critical role in communicating the reasons for and results of outsourcing across the company. Some firms, such as FMC Corporation, have created the position of outsourcing relationship manager, as the Case Study indicates.

Ultimately, the barometer of a good relationship is the ability of both parties to respect each other's roles and responsibilities and to operate within the confines of a mature, communicative, and trusting project management plan. It is worth the time and investment on the part of both the BPO buyer and vendor to institute such a formal plan to continuously monitor various aspects of the BPO relationship and take immediate corrective measures whenever it goes awry. As the quotation from Albert Einstein at the start of this chapter indicates, the legal framework of a BPO project is inadequate to extract the great benefits that it potentially can deliver. To achieve those benefits, both parties must also have a trusting relationship built on a stable framework of communication, information sharing, and mutual understanding.

In this chapter, we examine the essentials of an effective BPO relationship based on a formal project management plan. The relationship management principles discussed are applicable to most BPO projects across all industry segments. Where added complexities arise from the nature of the industry or the BPO type (i.e., onshore versus offshore), we attempt to highlight them and suggest possible ways of managing the additional challenges. However, every BPO relationship is unique and there is clearly no generic approach to relationship management. BPO buyers and vendors alike should use the principles we articulate as guidelines for effective action, not as prescriptions to impose under any circumstances.

This chapter also examines generic principles of a successful BPO relationship and some common mistakes firms make in managing BPO relationships. The principles and issues discussed in this chapter are linked to the

CASE STUDY

FMC's Outsourcing Relationship Manager Position

It is near the end of the workday on July 3, a few hours before the long Fourth of July weekend, and Jill Fosmire is fully engaged in her most serious crisis since taking her job nine months ago.

FMC Corp., a $2-billion, Philadelphia-based chemical company, outsources its global wide-area network and telecommunications to Plano, Texas–based Electronic Data Systems Corp. (EDS), which relies on the communications networks of now-bankrupt WorldCom Inc. Her biggest question is, will WorldCom's communications systems fail? If so, what then? Fosmire asks EDS for a contingency plan, and her own team sketches out alternatives.

In this newly created position of manager of IT outsourcing and contracts, Fosmire's job is to handle outsourcing crises such as these, as well as daily communication with service providers. A 20-year IT and business veteran, she is part marriage counselor, part quality-control maven, part salesperson, and exactly what FMC needs to keep its four IT outsourcing relationships focused on business results.

Outsourcing relationship manager positions are on the rise as outsourcing agreements become more complex and business environments more unpredictable. This has created a serious need for seasoned negotiators on the enterprise side who have a combination of IT experience, business savvy, sales ability, problem-solving skills, and a tight relationship with executives.

Source: Excerpted from Stacy Collett, "Wanted: Outsourcing Relationship Managers," *Computerworld* (August 12, 2002), p. 35.

operating phase of the BPO Life Cycle. It is during this phase, after the contract has been signed and the BPO project has begun, that each party begins to reveal more of itself to the other. Tense situations can arise based on unexpected difficulties and sensitivities. We discuss six ingredients that are mandatory for a successful BPO relationship and seven common errors organizations make to derail a BPO relationship. We begin with a discussion of fundamental characteristics of all BPO relationships.

FUNDAMENTAL CHARACTERISTICS OF THE BPO PROJECT

Four fundamental characteristics will give shape to any BPO relationship, regardless of industry or BPO type:[3]

1. The depth of the relationship
2. The scope of the relationship
3. The choice of assets to use
4. The choice of business culture to adopt and exploit

The depth of the BPO relationship depends on the criticality of the out-sourced business process. The closer the outsourced process is to the core business process of the BPO buyer, the greater the depth required in the BPO relationship. Based on the importance of the outsourced functions and how these functions would change or evolve, the resulting relationships can be as follows:

- *Arm's length*, and primarily cost or service level agreement (SLA) driven
- *Cooperative*, necessitating intense dialogue between the parties
- *An extension of the buyer's organization*, with a number of dependencies and commitments between the parties for each other's success

As a rule of thumb, the deeper the BPO relationship, the more tightly coupled and potentially synergistic are the buyer and vendor firms. From an operational perspective, tight coupling refers to the extent and frequency of information and resource sharing between the two firms. Deep relationships require tight coupling because the outsourced process is usually proximate to the buyer's core competence and is highly fault intolerant. Information must flow freely in both directions to ensure that the outsourced process is being executed to specifications and to ensure that any variations are kept within tolerable performance limits.

A deep BPO relationship requires that the parties develop a project management plan that specifies regular interorganizational communication and information sharing in a transparent manner. This should include provisions for routine contacts as well as emergency meetings and communication channels. A BPO relationship that is not considered to be deep will not require as-frequent communications. The project management team (PMT) will need to determine what is appropriate based on its shared expectations and beliefs about this characteristic of the relationship.

The scope of a BPO relationship depends on whether the buyer works with separate BPO providers for various outsourced functions or develops a relationship with one or only a limited number of providers. Working with multiple vendors for a wide variety of business functions will necessitate a proportionately larger PMT or perhaps multiple PMTs. There are advantages to working with multiple vendors, as well as disadvantages.

Single-service providers often have developed levels of specialization and expertise that enable them to deliver world-class levels of service. The downside of working with single-service vendors is that each outsourced process requires getting to know and manage each new vendor. Managing multiple vendors presents a multitude of challenges for the BPO buyer and adds to the overall costs of outsourcing.

Multiple-service vendors provide enhanced opportunities for strategic gains based on level of familiarity with the buyer. The more processes, information, and knowledge shared between BPO buyer and vendor, the greater will be the potential for insights into overall business processes and strategy. New ideas and ways of operating can and should be derived from a working relationship of this type. The downside of working with a single or limited number of vendors is that there is greater risk to the business. This risk is mitigated by the level of familiarity and comfort that would necessarily precede any decision to continue to shift processes to the multiple-services vendor. It would be foolhardy to continue to shift processes to a vendor if the buyer lacked confidence in the vendor's ability to perform.

The project management plan may necessitate multiple internal BPO champions and PMTs if a multiple vendor strategy is used. In this instance, the steering team will need to integrate the various internal teams to enable cross-functional knowledge sharing. This integration role is in addition to the standard oversight role that the steering team must perform regardless of the number of BPO relationships.

Companies that opt for a single or limited number of vendors may be able to assign each to a single champion or PMT. In that case, the steering team's role is primarily oversight.

Because outsourcing usually involves handing over the control and maintenance of certain processes to a third party, the issue arises of whose assets will be used to execute the deal, including people, physical infrastructure, and technical assets. There is no simple answer to the "whose assets?" question, but the answer is made easier by focusing on business-specific issues. For example, germane to this question is the relative ease with which the buyer or vendor can obtain and manage the needed assets. Another relevant factor to consider is which firm is better able to invest in asset development, both for scale and innovation purposes.

The choice of which organization's culture and operating style to choose should be entirely pragmatic. There is no need to take political stands, nor should one party or the other insist on adopting one or the other culture based on personal familiarity and comfort. The latter issue will be particularly important in offshore BPO where cultural issues, from length of workday to disparate treatment of gender or socioeconomic class, are most likely to arise. Of course, no BPO buyer or vendor should violate laws or their own ethical standards when working with an offshore (or onshore, for that matter) partner. At the same time, there will be occasions when insisting on imposing one's own culture and way of working will be counterproductive.

The watchword to keep in mind when choosing which firm's culture to leverage for the BPO project is *pragmatic*: Which culture will be most likely to lead to a successful project? This question is not easy to answer, but sev-

EXHIBIT 8.1   Weighted Culture Selection Framework

Cultural Consideration	Weight
Individuals working with the outsourced process are primarily from buyer or vendor.	.05
Culture that is closer to that of buyer's clients.	.10
Culture that is most likely to assimilate the other without major difficulty.	.15
Culture that is most likely to be able to adapt to the buyer's competitive challenges.	.20
Culture that will provide long-term stability.	.50

eral key considerations can be weighed and evaluated. Exhibit 8.1 illustrates how a firm can answer the "whose culture?" question.

BPO buyers should work closely with their vendors to address the "whose culture?" issue. This is not a time to shrink from the hard and possibly awkward questions that must be asked. A solid BPO relationship must deal frankly with cultural differences and must focus on the common goal— effective performance of the business process. Of course, a BPO buyer must always be concerned about the consequences at home from its vendor selection. Historically, a primary issue of contention has revolved around unacceptable foreign labor laws. However, as the Ethics and Governance insert

---

ETHICS AND GOVERNANCE

Political Debate Heating Up

There is little doubt anymore that companies can reduce costs through outsourcing. However, the vast number of jobs moving offshore in recent years has now caught the attention of politicians, who are indicating their concern to constituents. One manifestation of that concern is proposed legislation to make offshore outsourcing more difficult. Rep. Rosa DeLauro, for example, has proposed a bill to limit L-1 visas. Companies often use these visas to bring in foreign workers temporarily for training. Her bill would cap the number of L-1 visas at 35,000 (it currently has no cap) and would prohibit their use by companies that have laid off U.S. employees within the prior six months. Other legislation surely is on the way.

Sources: Mary Hayes, "Politics: Lawmakers Jump into the IT Jobs Debate," *InformationWeek* (July 28, 2003), p. 38; "Uproar Grows on Moving Jobs Overseas," *Houston Chronicle* (January 22, 2004), p. 3B.

indicates, the issue has now heated up politically around the issue of moving jobs outside the United States.

BPO RELATIONSHIP SUCCESS FACTORS

In the previous chapter, we outlined the project management structure that should be used during the transition and maintenance phases of the BPO Life Cycle. The project management plan can be changed and altered over the life of the BPO project. At the same time, changes to the plan should only be done in a systematic and carefully considered manner. The PMT should include members from both the buyer and vendor organizations. These individuals must learn to adapt to and trust each other, while balancing the needs of their respective organizations. This balancing act is difficult, but not impossible.

The project management plan established between the BPO buyer and vendor is intimately related to the contract between the parties, but is not confined to the contract alone. The project management plan includes elements of interpersonal and interorganizational interaction that simply cannot be specified in a contract. For example, in order for strategic benefits to be realized through BPO, each party must develop trust in the other to understand and seek to advance each other's core business competencies. This means that companies must reach beyond the deliverables, timetables, penalties, and remedies specified in the contract and SLAs. Each party must strive to understand the competitive conditions under which the other must operate, excel, and remain profitable. This requires that each party dedicate sufficient time and resources to the relationship to build trust. It is difficult to conceive how the requirement to build trust could be specified in a contract. In fact, the very idea that it would be spelled out in legal terms seems to contradict the meaning of the term.

Trust is essential if the partners to the BPO relationship are to realize gains that go beyond those articulated in the contract. A trusting relationship may lead to interorganizational transactions and to new, unexpected revenue opportunities that may not be included in the scope of the original contract. In fact, a dynamic BPO relationship will constantly be seeking ways to extend and deepen the working relationship for mutual strategic gains. Exhibit 8.2 highlights some basic ingredients of a trusting BPO relationship.

Unlike the traditional buyer–supplier relationship, the BPO relationship must be meticulously planned and managed from day one with strategic intent. That is, the project management plan established by the parties should be designed to manage the BPO project and achieve its basic goals, while seeking strategic gains for both buyer and vendor.

It is commonly accepted that the tactics to effectively manage outsourcing relationships vary as widely as the relationships themselves. For example,

EXHIBIT 8.2   Ingredients of a Trusting BPO Relationship

- Shared vision and expectations
- Consistency of actions
- Predictability of responses
- Respectful of confidentiality issues
- Long-term, mature, and enduring
- Aligned interests and goals
- Mutual respect and understanding
- Proactive and intense communication
- Integrated systems and processes
- Encouraging and participative
- Sharing of risks and rewards
- Operating as extended organizations

the strategies for managing a BPO project that focuses on IT functions differ from those that would be used to manage a BPO project focusing on HR functions. At the same time, there is overlap and general lessons to be learned from any BPO initiative that apply regardless of the target function. We have examined hundreds of BPO cases and reviewed voluminous articles in both the popular and academic literature to seek patterns among the wide variety of successful BPO relationships. Although each relationship is unique and has nuances that cannot be generalized, several ingredients of a successful relationship have appeared often enough to be considered mandatory. Based on a basic foundation of trust, we have identified six other essential ingredients of a successful BPO buyer–vendor relationship:

1. *The BPO buyer must understand and respect the vendor's need to make a profit.* The BPO relationship cannot be driven by cost reduction above all other considerations. In order for the vendor to continue to be motivated to provide high-quality services, there must be profit in the relationship.
2. *The contract should have provisions for SLA recalibration.* As business conditions change, the original SLAs may be out of line with industry practice and need to be recalibrated.
3. *The buyer's responsibilities should be clearly articulated.* Many BPO contracts clearly articulate the vendor's responsibilities, ignoring or minimizing those of the buyer.
4. *The BPO project management plan should include provisions for changing the PMT structure or members.* Although changes in PMT structure and membership should not be cavalier, allowances should be made for member attrition and rotation.
5. *The PMT should use systematic problem identification and resolution techniques.* Rather than waiting for problems to arise in the relationship,

the PMT should use a systematic and proactive approach. Of course, such an approach must be based on interorganizational trust and honesty.

6. *The PMT should develop interpersonal relationship norms.* Such norms should arise from within the group and should govern the manner in which PMT members relate to one another.

Profits and the BPO Relationship

A reasonable profit margin for the outsourcing vendor is essential to the long-term success of an outsourcing relationship. In an outsourcing relationship, neither party should aspire to an unrealistic business advantage.[4] Outsourcing is designed to deliver financial benefits to the BPO buyer, to be sure. It must be kept in mind, however, that the vendor is also a business and must maintain a profitable operation to survive and excel. The profit and reward that goes along with outstanding work motivates the provider to commit resources, ensure quality and service levels, identify new opportunities, address the client's business issues in a timely and proactive manner, and innovate. Outsourcing relationships that are focused exclusively on cost reduction often result in situations in which the vendor ends up delivering minimum levels of service to justify the continuation of the contract. This can be avoided, and both parties can reap benefits, if the buyer expects a fair profit for the vendor and encourages reinvestment of profits in extension of the vendor's core competencies. This will enable the vendor to commit additional high-level services to the buyer.

Recalibration of Terms

SLA recalibration clauses are effective tools for reassessing and adjusting contract terms.[5] Incorporating and exercising a benchmarking clause in the contractual framework of a BPO relationship provides an opportunity to baseline service levels, repair a strained relationship, and adjust terms to new business or service conditions. By identifying and quantifying the specific elements of service delivery that need to be recalibrated from time to time, the parties can stay motivated by virtue of the tenor of the contract. The project management plan should incorporate any contractual clauses regarding changes to SLAs and should execute changes as required. This is not as easy as it sounds, of course. Each change will require negotiations and a thorough review of the implications. The PMT should handle all changes according to its operating principles, which may include voting guidelines and issue resolution protocols. For example, in the case of a deadlock, it may be necessary to escalate the issue to the Steering Team for final resolution.

Buyer's Responsibilities

The BPO buyer's responsibilities to manage the outsourcing partner are one of the most neglected areas of outsourcing relationship governance. Companies tend to minimize the internal management resources required to effectively manage a provider. BPO buyers either devote too few resources to managing the vendor relationship or supervisory resources deployed in charge of the relationship lack the skills, training, and inclination to make the relationship succeed. Relationship management becomes especially difficult if the buyer views outsourcing primarily as an opportunity to reduce costs and cut headcount. The general tendency to draw PMT members only from the affected process can also be problematic. Although people from the process area may be technically qualified, they may lack the other skills needed to effectively manage the outsourcing process. Attention must be paid to the nontechnical skills of individuals on the PMT, as discussed previously.

Changes in the Project Management Team

In a strained BPO relationship, the existence of ill will on one or both sides often presents a major hurdle to a successful resurrection of the relationship. In some cases, it may be useful to replace team members who have become hostile to the BPO project or who have developed personal animosities.

The PMT may also want to turn over members, other than the BPO champion, from time to time. This can help reduce the potential for interpersonal conflicts to develop into lingering problems. This approach may also bring in fresh perspectives and improve the possibilities of revitalizing the relationship.

Systematic Problem Identification and Resolution

Several tools are available to the PMT to constantly monitor and assess the results of the BPO project. The metrics specified in the SLAs are the starting point for assessing the project's effectiveness. Beyond that, the team should regularly scout the external environment to determine whether strategic advantages are also accruing to the partners as a result of their BPO-based working relationship.

Many BPO partnerships have adopted the balanced scorecard approach in order to evaluate performance and facilitate discussion on value creation opportunities. By using added value as one of the scorecard perspectives, the model provides the vendor with an opportunity to identify value provided over the course of the contractual term and to define the linkages between business needs and services delivered.

If an outsourcing relationship is damaged or strained, another strategy is for the PMT to use a Top Ten Issues approach. Using this approach, the PMT identifies at each meeting the Top Ten Issues confronting the project. Subsequent meetings track the progress on the issues and, hopefully, drive them down the list and out of the top ten. This approach requires a substantial amount of due diligence to establish that the concerns are objective and can be unambiguously documented. Once both sides agree on the nature and extent of the ten issues, they are given time to develop and implement acceptable solutions to each one. The PMT's responsibility is to establish monitoring mechanisms to ensure that the buyer's or vendor's actions agreed to for each of the issues are actually implemented. In either case, the task requires a high level of senior management commitment to implement the metrics, mechanisms, and processes necessary to ensure that both sides are meeting expectations.

Develop Interpersonal Relationships

Tools and techniques will help in monitoring the relationship and the level of performance on the outsourced process, but there is no avoiding the necessity for buyer and vendor to develop trusting interpersonal relationships. Exhibit 8.3 provides a few recommendations to help organizations develop effective interpersonal relationships with their BPO partner.

Most of the standard principles of interpersonal relationship development apply to BPO relationships. Offshore BPO relationships will be challenging in that on-site meetings may require international travel. Today, international meetings can be handled using a form of teleconferencing. Teleconferencing technology should be leveraged to help reduce costs associated with managing the offshore BPO project. However, each party should visit the other's premises at least once per year to keep the interpersonal feelings alive and to renew personal and business bonds.

The most important factor in the interpersonal arena is the establishment of acceptable norms that govern the relationship between the parties. The norms of behavior in a healthy BPO relationship are based on three dimensions:[6]

1. *Flexibility.* Which defines a bilateral expectation of the willingness to make adaptations as circumstances change.

EXHIBIT 8.3 Tips for Developing Effective Interpersonal BPO Relationships

- Develop an approach for the relationship as allies.
- Regard attendance at the regularly scheduled PMT meetings as a top priority.
- Be tolerant of cultural differences as they apply to issues of power and authority.
- Arrange seating during PMT meetings in a manner that avoids furthering an "us versus them" mentality.
- Seek "win-win" in negotiations over SLA term changes or contract extensions.
- Develop an understanding of and appreciation for the other party's business and competitive arena.
- Hold meetings at each other's premises on a rotating basis, allowing each to serve as the "host."

2. *Information exchange.* Which defines a bilateral expectation that buyer and vendor will proactively provide information useful to each other.
3. *Solidarity.* Which defines a bilateral expectation that a high value is placed on the relationship. It prescribes behaviors directed specifically toward relationship maintenance.

As the individuals assigned to the PMT interact and develop a sense of comfort with one another, norms of behavior will develop, although it may take a while for that to happen. One of the biggest mistakes in managing teams is to intervene with prescribed norms, circumventing the natural group team norming process. Enabling the PMT to meet often during the early stages facilitates the norming process. The PMT should attempt to codify some of its norms into its project management plan, being cognizant that the norms may need to be changed and rewritten from time to time as the team matures.

RELATIONSHIP RISK FACTORS

Although a mature and seamless relationship would most likely enhance the benefits of outsourcing, failure in the BPO relationship can lead to negative and potentially irreparable consequences. The business literature is rife with stories about BPO relationships gone bad, and there will be many more in the coming years. As the BPO revolution picks up steam, no doubt many new vendor firms entering the market will make claims about capabilities and capacities they do not possess. Unwary BPO buyers will get burned, and large amounts of money will go to waste.

It is impossible to control the way the BPO market will evolve, but organizations can control with whom they partner and how that relationship evolves. There is ample experience among BPO buyer and vendor firms alike to highlight some of the more common pitfalls of failed BPO relationships. Seven common pitfalls have been identified as follows:

1. Lack of appropriate buyer control
2. Cultural differences
3. Inflexibility in BPO agreements
4. Inadequate SLA specifications and/or metrics
5. Inadequate governance
6. Lack of goal alignment
7. Lack of integration

Lack of Appropriate Buyer Control

Organizations that undertake an outsourcing initiative must recognize that outsourcing is not the same as abdication. When an activity is outsourced, the buyer should dedicate a manager (BPO Champion) or team (PMT) to interact with the vendor. This relationship will work best when both sides seek to provide value-added service to the operations and strategy of each other. However, a buyer that tries to maintain complete control over the outsourced process will undermine the leverage the vendor can employ to deliver satisfactory services.

The danger in an outsourcing relationship lies in the inability of the buyer to develop an appropriate level of relationship control. An appropriate control level is one that allows the vendor the freedom to provide the services for which it was contracted without ceding the ability to prevent small problems from becoming large ones. This is a delicate balancing act that will undoubtedly need to be adjusted over time. For example, at the beginning of the relationship, the vendor is focused on performing at a high level and pleasing the new client. At this point, the buyer may not need as much control as later in the relationship when the enthusiasm wanes and performing on the contract becomes routine. Problems are most likely to arise when the vendor unconsciously shifts to viewing performance on the buyer's contract as routine and reduces its level of internal oversight. A proactive relationship management approach will anticipate these fluctuations in vendor diligence and will establish metrics and reporting regimes to counteract these variations.

Cultural Differences

Differences in culture and work styles between the client and the BPO provider can result in severe misunderstanding and mistrust. Organizational culture is defined as the operating principles and norms that are embodied in an organization's policies, decisions, and actions.[7] Problems can arise when a BPO buyer initiates a project with a vendor whose culture and operating style are vastly different. Such differences can and often are bridged. What matters is whether the two firms recognize the cultural differences and take proactive steps to deal with them.

Differences between buyer and vendor cultures are exacerbated if one or both parties is unable to listen to and understand the other. BPO buyers should be especially sensitive during the vendor selection process to how well the various bidders listen to their needs and whether they ask the penetrating questions that reveal their awareness of the potential for problems arising from cultural differences. A vendor that does not listen well or ask the right questions during the selection phase should probably be eliminated from consideration.

Of course, it is impossible to uncover all cultural differences during the vendor selection phase; some will only become manifest during the operating phase. The project management framework should include inducements for each side to identify and detect problems that are a direct result of cultural differences.

Inflexibility in BPO Agreements

It is necessary that BPO agreements be designed to provide for adequate flexibility in order to withstand both the dynamics of the business environment and the pressures that are inherent in such a contractual agreement. Typically, BPO contract agreements are crafted on certain key assumptions pertaining to technologies, business conditions, personnel, and other relevant issues. But these assumptions are likely to change with time. No matter how detailed the contract or favorable the terms, BPO agreements cannot anticipate all of the changes that occur in a dynamic, global business environment. This inability to anticipate changes tends to ensure that one, if not both, of the parties will become disenchanted with the relationship over time. Long-term contracts that lack flexibility significantly increase the likelihood of dissatisfaction between the parties and can adversely affect the relationship.

Once the contract is in force, there is a great temptation for both parties to suboptimize the relationship and attempt to better their lot—often at the expense of the other party. The best way to reduce this temptation is to craft a contract for a long-term relationship with short-term SLAs that can be adjusted to meet changing conditions. The long-term provisions in the contract spell out the spirit and intent of the parties. The short-term SLAs can be adjusted to include changing metrics and measurement instruments, as well as changing strategic goals of one or both parties.

Inadequate SLA Specifications

SLA specifications and metrics measure the provider's performance during the operating phase of the BPO Life Cycle. They must be clearly defined and effectively designed into the contract because this is what allows the buyer a comfort level in turning over control of its business processes to the vendor. The metrics associated with SLAs indicate whether the company is receiving the services it is paying for.

Many organizations have learned that the business process they have been performing for years is exceedingly difficult to describe in precise written terms. Yet, clear specification of the manner in which a process must be performed is critical to ensure effective vendor performance. Too often, firms turn over a business process to a vendor and expect them to deliver services that conform to expectations, without providing a clear statement of those expectations.

The task of specifying a process in detail is difficult. It requires discussions with people involved in the process, mapping the process, and specifying acceptable service levels and remedies. Most organizations will find that, no matter how careful they are in specifying expectations for vendor performance on a given process, there will always be a few details that slip through the cracks. In addition, vendors are not in perfect control of their employees, many of whom may decide unilaterally that the specifications they receive can be ignored. They will simply do things their own way because they do not agree with the specifications or believe they have a better idea. Carefully structured SLAs and rigorously applied metrics will ensure that none of these potential corrupters of vendor performance levels result in adverse consequences.

Inadequate Governance

Informal, unstructured, and/or inadequate attention given to relationship governance issues often leads to relationship difficulties. There is adequate contractual attention given to compliance to service levels, but attention is rarely given to governance and achieving relationship maturity levels. We described the concept of a project management team (PMT) in Chapter 7. It is important to note that this team performs both judiciary and legislative roles in the oversight and implementation of the executive document—the contract. In its judicial role, the PMT specifies how often the parties will share information and measure performance. It will also specify what will be done in the event of nonperformance.

In its legislative role, the project management team will develop and deliberate changes to the project management plan. This ongoing process should be conducted in the spirit of the contract, which serves as the constitution to the judicial and legislative roles of the PMT.

Lack of Goal Alignment

An outsourcing relationship is bound to fail in a situation where the parties do not align goals, objectives, and interests. As separate economic entities, the parties are not naturally aligned. In fact, there are market incentives for one or both parties to suboptimize on the contract, as mentioned previously. Goal alignment means that both parties take action, including investment of time and financial resources, toward the goals they articulate to one another. Merely stating goals is not enough. Both firms must demonstrate commitment to those goals through actions.

Many BPO relationships fail when one or the other party perceives that the other is not acting on its articulated goals—or is not acting in a manner consistent with its goals. This can be observed through a lack of investment in new technologies or innovations that might further the stated goals or a lack of interest in pursuing joint development projects. When one party feels the other is not living up to its stated goals, resentment and other negative emotions can arise. If left untreated, these negative emotions can rot the spirit of a healthy and enduring relationship, leading both parties to develop mistrust for one another. A strong project management plan will require each party not only to articulate its organizational goals and objectives, but also to demonstrate how it is pursuing them. Regularly updating each other on goal attainment and aspirations for the future is a strong antidote to fear and mistrust that can arise from uncertainty about the other party's commitment to the BPO relationship.

Lack of Integration

The development of an effective BPO relationship is not only a process or infrastructure issue but also requires cultural replication, and sharing of vision and values. The integration of IT will carry unique challenges, especially if the process is to be outsourced offshore. At the same time, anyone who has ever initiated a major software installation or hardware changeover will readily cite integration as a major challenge. From that perspective, the IT integration issues associated with a BPO project are not unique. Even more, most vendors are prepared for the data and information integration challenges based on their experience with other clients and their desire for economic survival. BPO buyers should leverage the market pressures that force integration responsibilities and costs primarily onto vendors. Additionally, third-party firms that specialize in getting disparate databases to talk to one another can be hired to assist in the process. Again, the buyer should seek to shift the integration cost burden to the vendor.

Integrating cultures, work styles, and policies and procedures is a less specific science and will pose difficult challenges for BPO buyer and vendor alike. We have already discussed the need for the PMT to consider questions of "whose culture?" and "whose assets?" in the BPO transition and operating phases. These are pragmatic questions, but the process of transitioning from one cultural style to another requires change management tactics. These are covered in greater detail in Chapter 7. Here, we mention only that this area is frequently overlooked in the administration of a BPO project. Overlooking the cultural transition, as well as the policy and procedure transition issues, is a leading cause of BPO project failure. Application of the internal change management tactics discussed in Chapter 7 will help avoid these potentially fatal problems.

CONCLUSION

Because of the comprehensive nature of any potential BPO project, the buyer–vendor relationship can only be mastered through continuous focus on the business benefits anticipated by both sides. Buyers and vendors need to employ a competent and empowered BPO champion and/or a full-fledged project management team, particularly in the operating phase of the BPO Life Cycle. Along with the transition of the process from an internally delivered service to an externally delivered service, the relationship must be implemented as roles and responsibilities of the parties become exposed and refined. Contracts must be built on the realization of the business goals, with SLAs that measure the critical success factors of the outsourced business process. The entire relationship must be viewed as a business asset that is worthy of investment over time. Not only will the SLAs evolve, but the relationship will also evolve as market conditions change and as strategies for delivery of outsourcing services respond to dynamic business conditions.

With outsourcing having the potential to add significant competitive advantage to companies through quantifiable business and strategic value, it is imperative that buyer–vendor relationships are aligned seamlessly in an integrated manner. If the BPO buyer does not have internal capabilities to design and execute an effective project management plan, assistance should be sought from external consulting agencies to help craft a project management model that would best meet the outsourcing objectives.

SUMMARY

- Companies considering BPO must be aware that the traditional tactics for managing relationships between buyers and suppliers are inadequate for managing a BPO relationship.
- Management of a BPO relationship requires negotiation, communication, and business skills.
- The project management plan will include elements of interpersonal and interorganizational interaction that simply cannot be specified in a contract.
- Trust is essential if the partners to the BPO relationship are to realize gains that go beyond those articulated in the contract.
- The BPO relationship must be managed from day one with strategic intent.
- Instead of specifying the project management plan in the formal contract, a separate plan should be drafted and shared between the organizations.
- The BPO champion will generally have high visibility within the organization and possess the essential business skills. He or she should also be familiar with the business case for BPO and be willing to discuss it within the organization whenever necessary.
- The four fundamental characteristics of a BPO relationship are (1) depth of the relationship, (2) scope of the relationship, (3) choice of assets to use, and (4) choice of business culture to adopt.

- BPO buyers should recognize the vendor's need to make a profit and include that in the calculation of project costs.
- BPO success factors include (1) the need for the vendor to make a profit, (2) contractual provisions for SLA recalibration, (3) clear specification of the BPO buyer's responsibility, (4) provisions for changes in PMT structure or members, (5) use of methodical techniques for problem identification and resolution, and (6) development of strong interpersonal relationship between team members.
- Common sources of problems in a BPO relationship include (1) lack of buyer control of the outsourcing relationship, (2) cultural differences between buyer and vendor, (3) inflexibility in BPO agreements, (4) inadequate SLA specifications and/or metrics, (5) inadequate governance, (6) lack of goal alignment, and (7) lack of integration.

CHAPTER 9

Infrastructure Considerations and Challenges

Computers make it easier to do a lot of things, but most of the things they make it easier to do don't need to be done.

—Andy Rooney, CBS News

Working with an outsourcing vendor involves the integration of a variety of formerly distinct systems, both technical and social. In previous chapters, we considered the social aspects of project and relationship management, including the difficulties associated with intermingling organizational cultures and managing organizational change. This chapter focuses primarily on technical infrastructure issues that arise after the BPO project has been launched and operations have begun. These issues range over hardware, software, knowledge, security, and training and support. We touched on some of these issues in Chapter 4, where we outlined the total cost management approach that is a part of the BPO opportunity analysis.

In this chapter, we do not focus on the *cost* elements of the infrastructure considerations. Instead, we focus on the *management* issues that will arise and questions that need to be asked and answered during the transition and operating phases of the BPO Life Cycle. Readers who are using this book as a guide to a BPO project may want to revisit their cost estimates as a result of the more detailed discussion of the technical issues contained in this chapter.

Fundamentally, the goal of infrastructure integration is to embed and reinforce the collaborative nature of the relationship between buyer and vendor. Before the interlinking of their respective systems, the two companies have interacted only on a surface level. Up to this point, there have been no process changes on either side and no threats to business continuity. The integration of buyer and vendor infrastructures represents a true turning point in the BPO relationship—the partners are now becoming familiar with one another. The transition phase is characterized by sharing systems, data, and knowledge. Each party now has additional risk exposure. The buyer is concerned about data and systems integrity. The vendor is concerned with meeting the contract terms that were established by the sales team. Cross-enterprise collaboration to improve performance must be the overriding objective for each organization.

In this chapter, we examine a variety of infrastructure issues that must be managed during the transition and operating phases of the BPO Life Cycle. Although these issues are exceedingly interdependent, we have divided them for clarity into the following sections:

- Hardware infrastructure
- Software infrastructure
- Knowledge infrastructure
- Training and support infrastructure

A truly effective BPO project will elevate itself beyond the service level agreements (SLAs) established in the contract.[1] The project management plan discussed in Chapter 7 highlights the basic operating rules, and procedures for modifying them, that are freely agreed to by each side. Establishing a collaborative mindset that seeks to leverage economies of scale and each party's core business strengths can lead to amazing and unexpected results. However, if the entire BPO relationship is governed solely by the SLAs, the relationship will be more traditional in nature, focusing on service delivery, monitoring, and meting out rewards and penalties. To achieve breakthrough results from the BPO project, the infrastructure needs to support that potential. Throughout this chapter, we address infrastructure issues from the perspective of creating the potential for breakthrough performance through cross-enterprise collaboration.[2]

HARDWARE INFRASTRUCTURE

The first issue to consider with respect to the hardware infrastructure underlying the BPO project is whose systems to use. Because providing high levels of service in the specific business process is the vendor's core competence, their hardware capabilities usually outstrip those of the buyer. Despite this common circumstance, the decision to use the vendor's hardware system should not be based on technology maturity alone. Buyer and vendor must also consider other factors when determining whether to shift processes to the vendor's hardware.

Among the considerations that affect this decision is the intent of the BPO agreement. Firms that outsource primarily to save costs should leverage the vendor's systems, eliminating depreciating assets from the balance sheet and converting them to monthly pretax expenses. However, BPO buyers seeking to develop strategic advantages through the BPO project may elect to leverage and/or build their own hardware systems utilizing the vendor's knowledge and experience to design the necessary systems. This ensures that any competitive advantages realized through hardware advances will be retained within the buyer organization in the event that the contract with the BPO vendor is terminated or not renewed.

The extent of the BPO buyer's interest in developing and retaining new capacities in the outsourced process is a major determinant of whose hardware to use in the BPO project. Another consideration that affects this decision is the potential to develop synergies with other business units as a result of building internal hardware maturity and capacity for the BPO project. While scaling systems to meet the demands of the enhanced business process, the BPO buyer creates capacities that may be applicable to other units within the organization. These additional capacities are often unexpected and can result in improved performance across the organization. Relying on the vendor's hardware means forgoing development of internal capacities and the possibility of unexpected process improvements in other business units. Of course, this risk can be mitigated through a deep, collaborative buyer–vendor relationship that seeks to leverage hardware advances for process improvements no matter where the hardware resides or who has title to it.[3]

A final consideration when assessing whose hardware to use to manage the BPO process is location. When a BPO buyer decides to use the vendor's hardware, that hardware is often located off the buyer's site. This is usually not a problem if the vendor is local or onshore in the United States. Problems may arise, however, when the vendor is offshore. As the BPO revolution continues, offshore locations may include increasingly remote regions of the world. BPO buyers must confirm the vendor's ability to obtain technical support and spare parts to maintain their systems and minimize downtime. Systems that are state-of-the-art but that have been damaged by an earthquake, political uprising, or other unexpected event are not much use if they cannot be repaired and placed back online in a hurry.

Regardless of whose hardware systems are used, the infrastructure compatibility between both organizations must be reviewed and managed. This is a critical step because both organizations will be relying on the combined system to provide transparency. One distinction that is important for BPO project managers to appreciate is that between a system's infrastructure and its architecture. Infrastructure refers to the system's hardware components and their functionalities. The hardware infrastructure hosts a variety of applications that rely on the components of the infrastructure and management procedures (i.e., software distribution, backup, recovery, and capacity planning) to provide reliable and efficient services.

A system's architecture refers to the configuration of the components—the way they are structured and the way they interact with one another. In other words, an infrastructure model provides a description of hardware resources and their individual functions, whereas the architecture describes their interrelationships and the services that can be delivered. For example, a system's infrastructure may include e-mail servers and network cabling. Their arrangement into a specific architecture enables delivering e-mail services to specific groups of employees.

When considering the hardware needed for a BPO project, the project management team (PMT) must be cognizant of both infrastructure and architecture issues. Because BPO projects will require resource sharing regardless of where the bulk of the components reside, a complete audit of the available resources and their current configuration should be conducted. The IT resource audit enables the PMT to do the following:

- Avoid needless duplication of systems and services.
- Pinpoint any gaps in infrastructure capability.
- Ensure infrastructure/business alignment.
- Ensure adequate scope of IT components to accommodate service enhancements.
- Assess security issues associated with data and knowledge sharing over networks.
- Reengineer processes that are obviously inefficient or anachronistic.

Exhibit 9.1 highlights some key infrastructure and architecture questions that a BPO buyer should pose to vendors.

EXHIBIT 9.1   Key Questions for Infrastructure Management

- What operating system, Web server, commerce server, database management system, payment system, and proxy server does the vendor use?
- What are the service level arrangements, in terms of availability, performance, and security?
- How scalable is the BPO infrastructure? What are the scalability constraints?
- What is the aggregate bandwidth at the site locations?
- Is there any load-balancing scheme in the site?
- What type of redundancy is available at the site (i.e., server redundancy, uninterrupted power service, RAID disks, and multiple Internet backbone providers)?

The system architecture designed for the BPO initiative will most often be based on the vendor's systems. At the same time, it is important to note that many BPO projects uncover inefficiencies in noncore processes and systems that are linked to the business process slated for outsourcing. The PMT should be trained to identify such inefficiencies as candidates for reengineering. Many outsourcing contracts allow for buyer–vendor cooperation to reengineer processes that are coupled to the outsourced process. Such cross-enterprise collaboration on reengineering buyer-side processes and systems is a vital component of transformational BPO.[4] Each reengineering initiative can be managed independently or as part of the PMT's charter. As the buyer systems interact with the more efficient vendor services, opportunities for reengineering will undoubtedly emerge. The PMT wants to stay vigilant for such opportunities, striving to ensure that buyer-side systems do not become the chief bottlenecks in constantly improving process flows.

SOFTWARE INFRASTRUCTURE

Software compatibility is often a difficult issue *within* an organization. Compatibility issues are amplified in a BPO relationship when attempting to bring buyer and vendor applications into alignment. Database issues will confront nearly every BPO relationship, as data sharing is the backbone of most BPO projects. This book is not intended to be a treatise on how to get disparate databases to talk to one another, but BPO project managers should be alert to the difficulties often encountered when two systems attempt to connect at the database level.

Organizations that use BPO to *improve* their service levels—as opposed to seeking mere cost savings—are those most likely to encounter difficulties because their internal systems are likely to lag behind the latest technology upgrades. The BPO vendor, however, has chosen to focus on the specific business process as its core business competence and is likely to be current in its software infrastructure, including its database systems. The greater the gap between buyer and vendor software maturity, the greater will be the challenges in database integration and data sharing. It is reasonable, if not expected, that the burden will be on the vendor to manage database integration, but the cost is likely to be borne, at least in part, by the buyer.

In addition to the initial data integration challenges—which focus on getting the buyer and vendor systems to communicate with one another—another important challenge concerns data and information distribution and publishing. During the operating phase of the BPO Life Cycle, the vendor is performing service-related transactions that generate new business data and information. That information needs to be distributed to relevant databases and published to relevant screens for others in both the buyer and vendor organizations to use. Thorough analysis of data flows is required to ensure, at a minimum, that the people who need the information generated by the outsourced transactions continue to receive it—and receive it in a familiar format and at the right time.[5]

In addition, the BPO buyer must be conscious of the potential hidden value in transaction information that is not destined for immediate additional processing and that is stored in a data warehouse. *Data mining* is the term that is used to refer to the process of analyzing an organization's collected data that has not been immediately routed for additional processing. These data are stored in the data warehouse and often contain insights into customers and competitors that would otherwise have gone unnoticed.[6] The BPO buyer should ensure that the vendor captures and stores all transactional data that can later be mined for strategic insights.

Once the two systems have established database connectivity, their respective software applications must be able to communicate. This can pose a problem if there are a large number of applications because many of them will not recognize one another. If the two software systems are unable to communicate, then an independent piece of software—called middleware—may be necessary.

Middleware is software that enables two noncompatible applications to communicate, acting as a data translator between the applications. If executable commands are needed, the logic scripts can be written and executed off the middleware platform, while delivering data via what is known as ODBC drivers to existing back-office databases. ODBC stands for open database connectivity, which is a standard database access method developed by Microsoft. The goal of ODBC is to make it possible to access any data from any application, regardless of which database management system (DBMS) is handling the data. ODBC manages this by inserting a middle layer, called a database driver, between an application and the DBMS. The purpose of this layer is to translate the application's data queries into commands that the DBMS understands.

This is as much technical information as we intend to discuss on the issue of software compatibility. Suffice it to say that a BPO buyer's technical support staff may point to the necessity of a middleware package to facilitate software integration with the vendor. This adds costs, of course, but the goal is to create as much interorganizational transparency as is required to perform services at the highest levels—and to support transactional data capture, storage, and mining.

In addition to the details of software and database compatibility, the BPO buyer must be concerned about the method that will be used to connect its systems with those of the vendor. One alternative is to have a single or multiple servers connecting with the vendor's system via a wide area network (WAN), or sending the necessary information via electronic flat file.

One effective method that many BPO projects adopt is the use of active server pages on an application server. Under this approach, the application server allows the BPO partners to see and use familiar screens to conduct their jobs. The application servers usually utilize ODBC drivers to map into the back-office databases, enabling both companies to interact with real-time data.

In some cases, the BPO vendor's services may be so tightly integrated into the buyer's back office that the vendor requires full access to data systems. If full access is required, a common technique to facilitate that is through a global virtual private network (VPN). VPNs have become popular over the last several years, and third-party companies offer support services at reasonable prices.[7]

If the BPO vendor is providing the buyer with services that do not require access to the buyer's computer system, it is recommended that a file transfer method be used. This can be as simple as the vendor sending a weekly e-mail outlining all activity, sending a flat file, or setting up a basic electronic data interchange (EDI) translator. With today's technology, two companies around the world can fairly easily select a reliable and secure method of exchanging data.

Another issue that must be managed is the licensing agreement that governs usage of the BPO buyer's software. Purchasing a software license, in most cases, does not legally authorize the buyer to use the software in every given networking scenario. For example, when a third party joins a network, the software company may require a client access license (CAL) for each additional party that accesses the system.

KNOWLEDGE INFRASTRUCTURE

We have already discussed the data and information infrastructure that is an important part of any BPO relationship. Competitive businesses are data driven, and in many cases a large part of their overall value is derived from the industry and market data they have collected, stored, and analyzed. A company's knowledge infrastructure is even more important because knowledge refers to the practical application of the analyzed data and information.

The knowledge infrastructure of the BPO buyer refers to several components, some of which are directly affected by the BPO relationship. Knowledge is defined as "analyzed and applied information that helps the organization compete and grow." Data and information are generated by raw transactions; knowledge is generated by analysis and reflection on aggregated transactions. Organizational knowledge comes from a variety of sources. One common source is analytic software that seeks patterns in transactional data and reports these patterns to human users, as we discussed in Chapter 1. For example, the balanced scorecard approach used by many companies today conveys aggregated and analyzed transactional information to the desktops of users who can apply that knowledge to their work. Sales managers who receive daily reports that aggregate real-time sales data will know when to crack the whip and when it is acceptable to relax a bit.

BPO buyers and vendors should ensure that the output provided by the buyer's analytic software systems before the BPO project is not corrupted or changed without intent. The systems used by the buyer before the BPO project may need to be upgraded or replaced, but such upgrades should not be made without a full understanding of who is using the generated knowledge and how it is being used. Knowledge output from an analytic software application may be distributed to multiple databases. If a new analytic package is introduced, each output database should be identified to ensure minimal disruption of internal workflows. Too often a reengineering process in one business unit results in an unexpected loss of essential data in another unit. BPO project managers must always be mindful of the interdependence of data flows within an organization and between an organization and its various stakeholders. For example, many organizations routinely share data with suppliers and customers to create efficiencies and, in the case of customers, to increase perceived value and switching costs. The integrity of these data flows must be maintained.

Although analytic software is a common source of organizational knowledge, it often goes unrecognized that another common source is wetware. *Wetware* is the term used to refer to the analytic resource between the ears of organizational employees (i.e., their brains).[8] Far too often, organization leaders neglect to recognize the knowledge-generating capacity of their human resources. It is easy to maintain the perspective of people as knowledge repositories, but their key role as knowledge generators is too often underappreciated.

Outsourcing a business process means that the organization will not be exposed to the raw data that used to be transformed into knowledge by people within the organization. For example, as a result of outsourcing the firm may no longer employ front-line employees who used to recognize data patterns and call attention to outliers, anomalies, and opportunities.

The outsourcing vendor can generate the knowledge that used to be generated by internal staff if appropriate incentives are established. Internal staff were motivated to recognize and react to data patterns based on their commitment to the organization's strategic objectives, their interest in receiving greater compensation, and their desire to simplify their jobs. These incentives may not exist for the offshore agent, who may not even be aware of nor deeply care about the industry or market of the BPO buyer.

To ensure that this valuable source of organizational knowledge is not lost in the operating phase of the BPO Life Cycle, the buyer and vendor should establish incentives for front-line agents (vendor employees) to seek and report data patterns that may result in process improvements. One way to address this issue is by specifying incentive terms in the BPO contract. However, the establishment of knowledge-generation incentives may be too granular for the BPO contract and may be better established in the project management plan. This provides greater flexibility to both parties to determine where the likely points of mission-critical knowledge generation are within the workflow and how to properly arrange incentives for individuals at those critical points.[9] The Case Study illustrates how British automobile manufac-

CASE STUDY

LDV Integrates Its Systems with Gedas to Improve Performance

LDV started out as a division of British Leyland. When the U.K. manufacturing giant closed its doors, many industry observers believed that LDV, which builds commercial vehicles, would soon follow suit. But LDV was saved by a management buyout and today employs more than 1,000 people at its Birmingham factory.

LDV has extensive expertise in the automotive market, but its niche also presents management with significant challenges. "We specialize in custom-designed vehicles, and rely heavily on our supply chain applications, which run on IBM mainframes," stated Chris Linfoot, LDV's IT director. "The problem is that those mainframes were designed to be used by Leyland, which had a far larger IT staff than we can afford."

For five years LDV had outsourced the maintenance of its mainframes to IBM, but Linfoot felt the company was not getting enough benefits from the arrangement. When the contract ended, Linfoot switched the outsourcing deal to Gedas, the information services arm of Volkswagen.

The outsourcing contract has allowed LDV to focus on what it does best—manufacturing vans and other commercial vehicles—while still benefiting from the mainframe applications.

LDV has already benefited from Gedas's expertise in automobile manufacturing. For example, Gedas has helped develop new processes that will eliminate the need for batch processing and enable the factory to operate 24 hours a day. "The result is that we are now on the verge of a major growth spurt which will see volume quadruple," says Linfoot. "Outsourcing one part of our business to a company which understands it so much better than a traditional service provider is a key part of that process."

Sources: Adapted from Sally Whittle, "Who Can You Trust to Take Care of Business?" *Computer Weekly* (October 21, 2003), pp. 48–49.

turer LDV switched its IT outsourcing vendor and gained valuable new insights into its manufacturing processes.

An additional consideration in the knowledge infrastructure of a BPO project is cross-enterprise knowledge management. In many cases, BPO buyers share mission-critical information with their BPO vendor—information that is not only important for organizational processes but that also may be of high interest to competitors. The criticality of this information creates two worries: maintaining information integrity and maintaining information security.

Maintaining information integrity means that the information shared between buyer and vendor organizations does not get corrupted or reconfigured. Data corruption would result in inappropriate conclusions and errant actions as a result of analysis of altered—and possibly false—data. Data reconfiguration refers to the potential that raw data has been altered in some way that makes it unreadable and simply unable to be converted into usable knowledge. Altered display screens are an example of data reconfiguration. Often, a BPO vendor uses proprietary data displays for internal use. These displays, if published to the BPO buyer as replacements for familiar screens, may render the data useless to the end user although the integrity of the data has been carefully maintained. Displaying data in a new and unfamiliar user interface can befuddle—or at least frustrate—even the most adaptable users.

When entering into an outsourcing partnership, the two organizations, in effect, become one. In order for the outsourcing project to produce results that meet and exceed expectations, there must be transparency between both entities. However, when two computer systems situated in separate locations begin interfacing, security becomes a major issue. BPO buyers must ensure that the vendor will adhere to the buyer's security policies and that all work done adheres to up-to-date security procedures. Exhibit 9.2 provides some questions that the BPO buyer can use to assess the vendor's commitment to and capability to maintain information security.

In many cases, BPO buyer and vendor communicate with one another via the Internet. When entering into a new BPO relationship, both organizations

EXHIBIT 9.2 Security Issues for the BPO Vendor

- What is its security policy?
- What are its data backup and disaster-recovery procedures?
- How is its data safeguarded from that of other customers?
- How is its data safeguarded from the vendor's own employees?
- How is it insured with regard to security breaches?

should review their Internet security policies. When developing an Internet security policy, BPO buyers should keep the following points in mind:

- Limit access. Many security breaches come from within an organization; thus, the fewer people with access to the inner workings of the system, the better.
- Establish granting privileges. A rigorous procedure should be in place for granting and revoking rights of access, and granting privileges should be recorded and made available to both client and BPO partner.
- Streamline hardware and software between the two organizations because a complex system is more open to attack.
- Develop a password policy, and do not allow users to choose simple or obvious passwords.
- Have procedures for data backup and disaster recovery in place before going live.
- Have procedures for responding to security breaches in place, and determine actions to be taken.
- Have your security policy audited by an external professional organization, and have them on call in case a major breach occurs.

Although system backups may seem like a common task for the average IT department, the backup process becomes very important when executing a BPO project. There are going to be times during the process redesign phase when both groups will overlook an important procedure, data interface issue, or technology support opportunity. There are so many factors to be managed during a BPO project that there will be times when the backup system is critical. The three most important factors involved in backup systems are as follows:

1. Scheduling backups
2. Tape rotation
3. Tape restoration

When conducting a tape backup, the administrator must determine the type of backup he or she is going to conduct:

- *Full.* Copies all files in a selected volume and/or directories, clearing the archive bit for each file.
- *Differential.* Copies all files changed since the last backup and does not clear the archive bits.
- *Incremental.* Copies all files changed or added since the last full or incremental backup, clearing the archive bit for each.

EXHIBIT 9.3   Sample Tape Backup Schedule

Daily Tapes	Weekly Tapes	Monthly Tapes
Monday-Even	Friday-First	January
Monday-Odd	Friday-Second	February
Tuesday-Even	Friday-Third	March
Tuesday-Odd	Friday-Fourth	April
Wednesday-Even	Friday-Fifth	May
Wednesday-Odd		June
Thursday-Even		July
Thursday-Odd		August
		September
		October
		November
		December

The BPO project managers should mix and match backup methods on successive days. Differential and incremental sessions have the advantage of speed because they do not work on all files and may be suitable on a daily basis. But the most complete method is a full backup that may be run weekly or on a bi-weekly basis.

It is also possible that the BPO buyer already has an adequate tape rotation strategy. Exhibit 9.3 presents a rotation strategy that has been found to be sufficient for most BPO projects.

The daily tapes are used over a two-week period. For example, on Monday the seventh day of the month, the Monday–Odd tape is used. On Monday the 14th day of the month, the Monday–Even tape is used. On the first Friday of the month, the Friday–First tape is used; on the second Friday of the month, the Friday–Second tape is used, and so on.

The two parties should select a regular date on which to conduct the monthly backup (e.g., the 15th of each month). If the system includes an accounting, order entry, or some other type of application that executes a month-end close, the partners may want to select either the day before or the day after that close occurs to conduct the backup. The parties may also want to keep a few blank tapes around for emergency occasions.

Tape restoration goes hand in hand with tape backups. However, many companies do not have policies for tape restoration. Before developing a tape restoration procedure, the PMT should ask a few basic questions:

- What should be backed up each day?
- How many tapes should be used?

EXHIBIT 9.4   Tape Restoration Guidelines

- Before starting the BPO project, test all tape backup options. Run large backups and try restoring random files.
- Rotate backup media.
- Do not exceed the tape life. Check how many times the manufacturer suggests reuse.
- Purchase high-quality backup tapes.
- Check backup logs daily.
- Always conduct a verification pass when data is backed up.

- Is just doing a backup enough?
- Where should the tapes be stored?

These important questions provide a starting point for managing data restoration. Even if the BPO project never needs to restore a single byte of data, it is better to be prepared. Exhibit 9.4 provides a few additional tape restoration suggestions.

TRAINING AND SUPPORT INFRASTRUCTURE

Most of the problems employees will experience during a BPO project will not be related to the hardware or software infrastructure associated with BPO. They will more likely be related to failures in understanding new workflows, work procedures, and work responsibilities. From the apocryphal user who cannot find the "Any" key ("Press any key to continue") to the individual struggling to find data that, without warning, now appears under a new field name, there are always problems with human adaptation to new systems. When the buyer and vendor system architectures come together in a BPO project, there will be workflow and responsibility changes. To avoid some of the problems that arise from process-related changes, and to ensure a smooth transition to the new system, training should be provided to everyone—even those who are adamant that they do not need to be trained.

One hurdle that many BPO project managers face with respect to training employees and getting them to be more self-sufficient is obtaining support from midlevel managers, because the middle manager is trying to learn the new processes while maintaining the unit's productivity. This juggling act can be challenging in the throes of a major BPO-based business transformation.

Perhaps the most compelling argument in favor of a thorough training infrastructure to support the BPO transition is that employee training has been shown to be an important differentiator between BPO projects that succeed and those that fail.[10] When training is neglected, the chance that buyer-side employees will be surprised and/or disappointed with new procedures and workflows increases. BPO project managers will have a small window of opportunity during the transition phase to win converts to the new routines and work patterns.

In Chapter 7, we referred to two different types of obstructionists who may block or sabotage the BPO project. Some of these people can be won over via a vigorous training and support regimen. Asking people to participate and take on a leadership role in some aspect of the BPO transition is an excellent way to counter their obstruction. For example, delegating responsibility for training others on the new procedures, along with appropriate levels of accountability for the success of the transition, is an effective project management tactic. It is nearly impossible for someone to be involved in training others without developing enthusiasm for and interest in the training topic. Public performance, even if not necessarily freely chosen, leads to a phenomenon known as "social facilitation."[11] People—even those who have a tendency toward obstructionism—simply perform at a higher level when they are in a social setting. BPO project managers can co-opt potential obstructers by getting them involved in the training and support offered to employees in the BPO transition phase.

The content of employee training offered during the BPO transition should include a detailed and thorough review of new work procedures, responsibilities, and expectations. Exhibit 9.5 provides general guidelines to consider in developing the BPO-related training and support regimen.

Design of the training should be modular, with each module independently constructed and each focusing on a specific aspect of the new standard operating procedures. Modularization of the training enables managers and employees to determine who needs to attend which training modules. It also enables greater training depth in each module. If training is not modularized, it often is either too detailed for some users who already understand a process or not detailed enough for those who are unfamiliar with or new to the process. Modularization allows training designers to deliver both depth and

---

EXHIBIT 9.5 Considerations for the BPO-Related Training Program

- Develop a clear set of standard operational procedures (SOPs).
- The training program should revolve around the SOPs.
- Conduct multiple training sessions:
  1. Train in a group setting.
  2. Train while working alongside the employees during their workday.
  3. When answering questions, always refer back to the SOP.
  4. Final training should be completed after 60 days (refresher).
- Do not take training lightly.

scope, while ensuring that employees have opportunities to select the training sessions (or for managers to appoint them to training sessions) from which they can truly benefit. No one enjoys sitting through a training session that relays information he or she has already well understood. Carefully developed two- to four-hour training modules help avoid training overkill, while providing adequate coverage of the knowledge gaps.

A common error that hampers BPO projects is a failure to train vendor-side employees, probably because of the erroneous assumption that the vendor is expert in the business process and therefore does not have a need for training. This is true in some cases—especially those that involve an onshore outsourcing relationship—but it is prudent to review training needs of the BPO vendor.[12] Some types of vendor-side training that are being provided to accelerate the transition to the BPO operating phase include the following:

- Cultural adaptation training to help buyer and vendor employees adapt to one another
- Language training, including voice and accent modification training, to reduce communication barriers
- Training on laws and customs of the BPO buyer
- Training on culture and lifestyles of the BPO buyer's customers[13]
- Training on differing management and leadership styles of the BPO buyer

In addition, training should be designed to integrate the cultures of the BPO buyer and vendor. This may include some training offered at each location so that key employees are able to experience the culture and work habits of their BPO partner firm. In some cases, BPO buyer and vendor employees work side-by-side for a period of time in a form of on-the-job training that facilitates cross-enterprise understanding.[14]

Merging two diverse organizations and their various infrastructures, as discussed in this chapter, is daunting. The BPO transition phase is the most difficult of the life cycle and the one where future operating patterns, routines, and procedures are established and frozen into place. In the best of all possible worlds, the procedures established lead to a highly efficient interorganizational system that runs trouble-free for years. Of course, we do not live in the best possible world, and problems arise in even the most carefully crafted systems. To deal with ongoing challenges to system integrity caused by breakdowns or other factors, a systematic support system, troubleshooting approach, and record-keeping strategy should be established.

The support system established for the BPO transition and operating phases must be adequate to meet the needs of the buyer and vendor organizations alike. Each will face unique challenges based on exposure to new operating procedures, in addition to the challenges associated with the merging of two independent work cultures. The support system established to manage the technical issues that arise should be modeled on the common help desk approach used by many IT departments. The only consideration unique to a BPO project is which firm will manage the help desk function. The vendor should inherit most of the responsibility for troubleshooting and supporting the outsourced process. This should be part of the contract and should have its own SLAs. However, because the BPO vendor is usually geographically distant from the buyer—maybe overseas—the buyer should have on-site support personnel who may be on the vendor payroll but accountable to a buyer-side manager.

CONCLUSION

The process of integrating BPO buyer and vendor infrastructures is the beginning of the operating phase of the BPO project. What had been a courtship has now become a working relationship, with all the difficulties associated with the knowledge that a commitment has been made and easy escape routes have been closed. The BPO partners must now confront problems and challenges from a collaborative perspective and learn to work through them systematically. Patience is a key virtue during infrastructure integration, as unexpected problems rear their heads and create bouts of confusion and anxiety. A clear vision of the anticipated advantages of a fully functioning BPO project will help everyone deal with the setbacks and continue to work toward a fully transparent cross-enterprise infrastructure.

The role of the project management team (PMT) during the integration phase is primarily one of outcomes management. Much of the integration work will be done beyond the direct supervision of the PMT. A focus on outcomes, including conformance to SLAs, time tables, and quality standards, will help keep the integration process on track and key leaders informed.

SUMMARY

- Fundamentally, the goal of infrastructure integration is to embed and reinforce the collaborative nature of the relationship between buyer and vendor.
- The first issue to consider with respect to the hardware infrastructure underlying the BPO project is whose systems to use.
- Firms that outsource primarily to save costs should leverage the vendor's systems.
- BPO buyers seeking to develop strategic advantages through the BPO project may elect to leverage and/or build their own hardware systems.
- BPO buyers must confirm the vendor's ability to obtain technical support and spare parts to maintain their systems and minimize downtime.

- As the buyer systems interact with the more efficient vendor services, opportunities for reengineering will undoubtedly emerge.
- The greater the gap between buyer and vendor on software maturity, the greater will be the challenges in data exchange.
- Thorough analysis of data flows is required to ensure that the people who need the information generated by the transactions continue to receive it.
- If full access is required, a common technique to facilitate that is through a virtual private network (VPN).
- BPO buyers and vendors should ensure that the output provided by the buyer's analytic software systems before the BPO project is not corrupted or changed without intent.
- BPO project managers must always be mindful of the interdependence of data flows within an organization and between an organization and its various stakeholders.
- In order for the outsourcing project to produce results that meet and exceed expectations, there must be transparency between both entities.
- Most of the problems employees will experience during a BPO project are related to failures in understanding new workflows, work procedures, and work responsibilities.
- Asking people to participate and take on a leadership role in some aspect of the BPO transition is an excellent way to counter their obstruction.
- Design of training should be modular, with each module independently constructed and each focusing on a specific aspect of the new standard operating procedures.

CHAPTER 10

Business Risks and Mitigation Strategies

Take calculated risks. That is quite different from being rash.

—George S. Patton, U.S. Army General

Because it is the catalyst of such significant changes for the organization, there are also business risks associated with a BPO initiative. The pioneering firms that led the current wave of interest in outsourcing were Global 1000–sized companies that have the capacity to absorb occasional business mistakes, even relatively large ones. When IBM outsources a sizable portion of its programming needs to India, it is a risk, but not as big a risk as when a small enterprise stakes the future of its business on the programming abilities of a little-known group of Bangalore-based programmers. As the sizes of the outsourcing projects increase in proportion to the size of the BPO buyer, business risk also increases proportionately. In order for BPO to become a source of competitive advantage for small- and medium-sized enterprises (SMEs), proven techniques for managing and mitigating risks must be developed.

Fortunately, the BPO pioneers not only have reaped tremendous advantages from BPO, but they have also progressed along the learning curve, suffering many painful lessons along the way. No doubt, not every BPO horror story has yet been written, but many have been, and the lessons learned can help the next generation of BPO buyers avoid writing the sequel.

In this chapter, we explore the most common BPO risk factors and consider effective management techniques for mitigating those risks. We will particularly be looking at risk factors from the perspective of those that are most important to SMEs that are seeking to gain their fair share of the advantages offered by BPO. Lacking the capital and other resources to absorb the impact of major strategic decision errors, SME executives and managers must be especially vigilant about risk avoidance and mitigation. The risks that we consider in this chapter include the following:

- Human capital risks
- Project risks
- Intellectual property risks
- Legal risks
- Vendor organizational risks
- Value risks
- Force majeure risks

From the beginning of this book, we have been emphasizing that BPO is a socio-technical phenomenon. The convergence of the six major BPO drivers that we have identified was not anticipated nor planned by any government or international agency. Managers and executives currently employed in organizations seeking to outsource business processes cannot rely on their business school education or their experience to help them deal with BPO opportunities and challenges. Not many have led business transformation opportunities that comprise the many facets of BPO—technical *and* social. The following discussion partially fills that educational and experiential gap, but there is far more to be learned about each risk area than we can cover here. BPO managers should actively seek to engage in ongoing education and learning about BPO even during the execution of a real-time project. The risk of writing this book now is that BPO is evolving rapidly, and new and important lessons will be learned in the time between turning in this manuscript and actual publication. Our risk is to be irrelevant before the book goes to press. Our risk mitigation strategy is to remind you to seek resources beyond this book to mitigate risks associated with an operating or planned BPO project in your organization.

Within the organization, risk management of the BPO project is primarily the responsibility of the project management team (PMT). The PMT should develop a thorough risk management plan within the overall project plan. The risk management plan will address each of the areas cited earlier, including details about risk mitigation, roles, and responsibilities. Let us begin by exploring the human capital risks associated with a BPO project.

HUMAN CAPITAL RISKS

In Chapter 7, we discussed the challenges associated with managing the organizational changes that go hand in hand with a BPO project. Change management is a human resource issue, involving a well-understood pattern of overcoming resistance, instituting changes, and reestablishing standard operating procedures. Some change management consultants have expressed this as unfreezing–moving–refreezing the organization.[1]

In this section we are not addressing the risks associated with change management; rather, we focus on the technical risks involved with the thorny issues of equal employment, immigration, and foreign trade regulations. Each of these topics touches the BPO project on the margins and must be understood and managed.

Onshore outsourcing usually has minimal human capital risks because it is strongly in the domestic BPO *vendor's* interest to understand and comply with all U.S. employment laws and regulations. Furthermore, the vendor is highly motivated to assist clients with any labor issues they may face as a result of engaging vendors in an outsourcing relationship. The human capital issues most likely to arise in an onshore outsourcing project are those associated with equal employment opportunity regulations. For example, BPO buyers must be especially careful when outsourcing results in reductions in force (RIF). Such reductions must be handled in a manner that is transparently related to business interests and has not selectively targeted a protected class of individuals. This risk can be managed by establishing formal RIF policies and procedures as outlined in Chapter 7. The Case Study insert highlights a case where an employee RIF was handled in an indelicate manner.

Other human capital risks associated with onshore outsourcing concern those that stem from collective bargaining and labor relations laws and regulations. For example, the U.S. Supreme Court has established basic guidelines governing whether and when subcontracting should be deemed a mandatory subject of bargaining under the National Labor Relations Act (NLRA). Beginning in the early 1980s, the National Labor Relations Board (NLRB) issued several decisions that created additional uncertainty when evaluating the bargaining status of outsourcing or subcontracting decisions. The NLRB's lack of clarity on the obligations of employers to the collective bargaining process is unlikely to be resolved any time soon. To reduce risk, companies should consult with labor attorneys as part of the BPO opportunity analysis to determine the likely disposition of their preferred strategy and its implications for possible liability exposure.[2]

BPO buyers that use an offshore outsourcing vendor can benefit from an absence of many of the employment liabilities that are present in the United States. Many foreign countries do not have laws governing employee matters such as those in the United States, including workplace discrimination, sexual harassment, or privacy.

At the same time, companies must understand the labor laws that govern their outsourcing vendor. India, for example, has a radically different system of employment law than the United States. "At will" employment, which allows employers in the United States to easily terminate or lay off employees, does not exist there. Under a much more restrictive concept called

CASE STUDY

WatchMark Corporation: How *Not* to Manage an RIF

As a 48-year-old senior engineer at WatchMark Corp., a Bellevue, Washington, software company, Myra Bronstein had spent three years searching for bugs in the company's software. She knew that things were not going well; she had been asked to log 12- to 18-hour shifts frequently, her boss reiterating that the company's success depended on her "hard work and efforts." So when she received an e-mail in March 2003 instructing her to come to a meeting in the boardroom the next day, she began to worry.

Bronstein logged on to a Yahoo users' group for WatchMark employees. There, in a post written by "Saddam Hussein," was an ominous note stating: "For all the quality assurance engineers reading this, your jobs are gone." At that very moment, it said, their replacements were on their way from India.

The next morning, a Friday, Bronstein and some 60 others were told that they were being terminated. Some left immediately; others, like Bronstein, were asked to stay on for several weeks to train the new folks. "Our severance and unemployment were contingent on training the replacements," she says. And so the next week, Bronstein walked into a room to find her old coworkers on one side and the new group from India on the other. "It was like a sock hop where everyone is lined up against the wall blinking at each other," she says. In an attempt to lighten the mood, her boss said she would like to introduce the old staff to the new staff, while the VP of engineering chimed in with familiar words. "We're depending on you to help this company succeed," he said.

Sources: Jennifer Reingold, Jena McGregor, Fiona Haley, Michael Prospero, and Carleen Hawn, "Into Thin Air," *FastCompany* (April 2004), pp. 76–82; John Cook, "Debate Over Outsourcing Heats Up, Ignited by Election-Year Politics," *Seattle Post-Intelligencer* (February 12, 2004).

"termination indemnity," employers must follow a lengthy notification process before letting Indian employees go. They must also indemnify employees for some of the wages they would have earned if they had remained under their employment. Failure to follow the appropriate process can result in fines for an employer operating in India. Additionally, employers cannot enter into contracts under which individual workers sign away such rights. Similar employment laws restricting an employer's right to terminate workers exist in many countries that are hotbeds of outsourcing.

The more restrictive labor laws in foreign countries can limit the flexibility that BPO buyers are seeking. For example, a BPO project management team may recognize the need to reorganize a vendor's process to improve it.

In some countries, it can be difficult for a company to restructure or change its operation strategies. Even moving an employee to a new work site could be a challenge in the foreign vendor's regulatory environment. The ability to restructure the organization—which is taken for granted in the United States—can be more difficult and riskier in many foreign countries.[3]

The most important risk mitigation strategy regarding human capital is to vigorously scrutinize vendor labor practices during the selection phase. The BPO buyer can avoid future headaches by seeking vendors whose human resource practices and policies resemble their own. Beyond that, it is important to also assess the professionalism of the vendor in its HR procedures and policies. This concept is difficult to define with precision, but some earmarks are provided in Exhibit 10.1.

HR risks associated with offshore outsourcing also encompass the potential implications of practices acceptable in the foreign jurisdiction but unacceptable to consumers in the United States. The most common example of this is the so-called sweat-shop labor practices that have damaged the image of firms such as Nike and Wal-Mart. Working with foreign companies whose HR practices are patently offensive to U.S. consumer sensitivities does pose the risk of potential backlash if those practices are exposed. The BPO buyer, although not directly responsible for the offensive practices, is nonetheless considered to be an enabler because it has a contract with the vendor. To mitigate this risk, it is imperative that BPO buyers regularly assess the HR practices of the vendor. Better still, the buyer can protect itself by specifying minimally acceptable labor standards in the BPO contract. The contract should also specify metrics that will enable the buyer to hold the vendor accountable to those standards.

Another human capital risk centers on pending legislation in the United States to limit the ability of foreign workers to service U.S. clients on guest

---

EXHIBIT 10.1   Earmarks of Professionalism in Vendor HR Practices

- The vendor has a turnover ratio below local averages and that approaches U.S. professional firm rates.
- The vendor has a clean work environment that includes professional markers such as individual work areas, private conference facilities, a reception area, security, and employees wearing business attire.
- The vendor has employee policy handbooks, and employees understand their rights and responsibilities.
- The vendor has an up-to-date organizational chart, and most of the positions are filled.
- The vendor has employee grievance procedures and evidence that grievances have been raised and effectively addressed (be wary of the vendor that claims it has never had a grievance).

worker visas. In addition, state legislatures in at least five states are considering laws banning outsourcing of government services contracts to foreign vendors. These bills pose risks to organizations seeking to use offshore vendors because costs are involved in reabsorbing processes that had been outsourced.

PROJECT RISKS

Project risks are defined as the potential that the BPO initiative may not provide the cost savings, strategic advantages, or productivity improvements anticipated. The reasons for this potential risk are too numerous to list. Unexpected incompatibilities between software infrastructures could prove intractable and lead to delays, cost overruns, and lost business. The cultures of the two companies may pose unyielding challenges that become more trouble than they are worth. Changes in U.S. or foreign labor laws could upend the cost equations that had been the primary reason for the offshore outsourcing.

To mitigate project risks, the BPO buyer should first assess its readiness to undertake the outsourcing project before making the leap. This includes assessing the organization's ability to adapt to change, the presence of an internal BPO champion, and the time that is available to make the transition and ramp the project to full operational mode. Organizations that have a poor track record in managing large-scale change are at a higher risk of project failure than those that have a record of successful change management. An organization's record of success in this area is indicative of its organizational culture and is likely to be consistent in the BPO initiative. The presence of an internal BPO champion, especially one with broad influence within the organization, can reduce project risk. The internal BPO champion can be relied on to work long hours and lay awake nights thinking about solutions to project problems when other members of the PMT are sleeping well.

The time available to transition a process from buyer to vendor can also affect the risk profile of the project. In general, the less time available for the transition, the higher the risk. It is often not practical to move all of a process to an offshore BPO vendor at once. Buyers should increase the time available to implement a BPO transition, building on successes along the way. A technique that can be used to mitigate risks associated with project timing is to develop a reasonable value horizon. The term *value horizon* refers to the amount of value the organization expects to receive from the BPO project in a specific amount of time. For example, an organization that expects to reduce costs by 25 percent within three months may not be able to realize that value horizon because of project implementation costs. However, a 25 percent cost savings within two years may be achievable and would set the appropriate value expectations.

The PMT often ignores the risks associated with unrealistic expectations on the part of the BPO buyer's executive team. Project expectations must be managed from a variety of perspectives: up, down, horizontal, and external.[4] Upward expectations management refers to the procedures the PMT follows to ensure that the organization's executive team (and the BPO project steering team) is informed about project risks, their potential costs, and mitigation strategies. Downward expectations management refers to the challenge of managing employee expectations as the project unfolds. The PMT must also manage the expectations of managers in nonoutsourced functions and those of customers, suppliers, and other stakeholders external to the organization who have a need to know.

Managing senior leadership expectations is critical to the BPO project. Too-high expectations among senior managers can lead to overly critical feedback and potential plug pulling on a project that cannot meet excessively lofty expectations.[5] Elevated and maybe even unreasonable expectations among senior management should be expected with the current level of media attention and hype that surrounds outsourcing. The PMT must ensure that senior managers are aware of the many challenges a BPO project faces and manage expectations accordingly.[6] Some have called this process "managing up."[7]

There are many effective techniques for managing up. Of course, this can be a delicate process because managing expectations up the chain of command may also often require that senior leaders be educated on technical or other issues.[8] To manage the expectations of senior leaders, the PMT should develop a project plan that articulates not only the problems and challenges likely to be encountered, but also those that have a lower probability of occurring. A good technique for communicating risk and managing expectations is to develop a BPO risk-probability matrix. The matrix will include as many *reasonable* risks as the PMT can envision, including those that are classifiable as worst-case risks. The BPO risk-probability matrix will also include the mitigation tactics that are either in place or that would be mobilized in the event that the risk became real. Exhibit 10.2 provides an example of a BPO risk-probability matrix.

The BPO risk-probability matrix should be widely circulated and updated as needed. This document will serve as the starting point for understanding the wide range of potential risks associated with the project and their potential costs. In Exhibit 10.2, costs are expressed as a percentage of total project costs. It is important to note that the cost figures expressed in the BPO risk-probability matrix are *in addition to* those already agreed to in the BPO contract—in other words, they are meant to specify potential cost overruns.

Another effective technique for managing the expectations of the executive team is to include one or more senior leaders on the PMT. This individual will serve in the liaison role and maintain communications between the PMT and the executive team. The liaison will be *responsible* for regularly

EXHIBIT 10.2   Sample BPO Risk-Probability Matrix

Risk	Probability	Cost	Mitigation Tactics
Implementation will take longer than expected	95%	10%	Bonus plan, penalties
One or more key staff will resign	60–70%	2%	Retention program, training
Hardware/software inadequate for project	30–40%	5–8%	Vendor agreement to absorb costs
Customers will be dissatisfied or lost	10–15%	5%	Customer training, monitoring
Legal issues in foreign country	2–5%	10–15%	Top U.S. legal team support
Mission-critical data will be lost or damaged	1%	NA	QC program, mirror backup
War breaks out in vendor country	<1%	50%	Mirror backup in U.S.

communicating BPO project results to the executive team and for feedback to the PMT. Importantly, the senior leader assigned to the liaison role on the PMT will be *accountable* to both the PMT and the executive team. This dual accountability should make the senior leader a true member of the PMT and will ensure that the role is taken seriously and adds value to the expectations management task.

Managing horizontally means ensuring that managers of functions not being outsourced are informed and aware of potential risks. We have spoken before of the potential for a BPO project to have cross-functional impact on organizational processes and workflow. Regardless of the process outsourced, it is likely that the output of that process is utilized by others within the organization. Changes to that output, whether in quality, quantity, or timing, can affect the ability of internal functional units to maintain their standard operating procedures. Managing expectations horizontally means minimizing workflow surprises and bringing managers from the nonoutsourced functions into the workflow redesign process. It would be disastrous to simply launch a BPO project without first determining in detail the effects of process output changes on units that depend on that output. Managers who are surprised by changes in data quality, quantity, or timing will defend the integrity of their work units and may become obstructionists to the BPO project.

Customers, suppliers, and others external to the organization may also have a vested interest in the BPO project. Customer reactions to BPO have been precipitated by several different factors. Some customers are concerned about BPO from a political perspective—they are worried about outsourcing jobs to offshore workers, for example. Dell responded to such political pressures when it pulled some of its technical support work in-house after outsourcing most of it to India.[9] Organizations need to consider BPO as a political issue that may affect customer perceptions. Communications with customers who are concerned about outsourcing jobs should include a recitation of the benefits they are likely to receive as a result of the outsourcing project. It may also include a statement about the domestic jobs that the company has created and the number of new opportunities that may be generated as a result of moving some of the lower value-adding jobs to foreign labor markets.

Suppliers should be managed in much the same way as the PMT manages the expectations of internal managers whose functions are linked via workflow to the outsourced process. Suppliers linked to the outsourced process should also be included in workflow redesign so they are aware of changes and who to contact in the case of disruptions or inefficiencies.

Managing expectations is not difficult, but this process is often overlooked because it involves proactive decision making and confronting problems before they arise. Engaging everyone—internally and externally—whose responsibilities, livelihood, or performance capabilities may be affected by the BPO project is the goal of the PMT. The PMT must communicate with these individuals (and groups, in some cases) to manage their expectations and to increase the amount of slack available in the event that some things go wrong (and they almost always will). If the goodwill of these stakeholders is won early in the process, and expectations are appropriately managed along the way, the PMT will have more latitude and time to fix problems that arise. Failure to properly manage expectations means that some will be out to kill the project at the first signs of trouble.

INTELLECTUAL PROPERTY RISKS

Most businesses have a significant amount of sensitive information, including trade secrets, business plans, and proprietary business knowledge. Safeguarding critical business information is a concern, even in the United States. Threats to information security, such as theft by company insiders, former employees, and computer hackers, abound. Offshore outsourcing presents different and in some cases more potent threats than the domestic variety. Legal standards and business practices governing whether and how sensitive information should be guarded vary around the world.

Some industry groups, such as banks and financial services firms, have developed stringent guidelines for organizations to follow to secure their proprietary information. The Bank Industry Technology Secretariat (BITS), for example, released security guidelines as an addendum to an existing framework for managing business relationships with IT service providers. The BITS goal is to help financial services firms streamline the outsourcing evaluation process and better manage the risks of handing over control of key corporate systems to vendors.[10] The BITS IT Service Providers Working Group developed the BITS Framework for Managing Technology Risk for IT Service Provider Relationships (Framework) in 2001. Although the original Framework provides an industry approach to outsourcing, additional regulatory and industry pressures and issues have emerged.

To address these changes, the Working Group updated the Framework with further considerations for disaster recovery, security audits and assessments, vendor management, and cross-border considerations. The Framework is intended to be used as part of, and in supplement to, the financial services company's due diligence process associated with defining, assessing, establishing, supporting, and managing a business relationship for outsourced IT services.

The U.S. Federal Trade Commission (FTC) has developed so-called Safeguard Rules to govern the security of customer information as it is used and managed by domestic firms. These rules implement the provisions of the Gramm-Leach-Bliley Act that requires the FTC to establish standards of information security for financial institutions. Penalties for failure to comply with FTC rules are up to $11,000 per violation (which may be assessed daily) and exposure to lawsuits claiming any harm to customers as a result of non-compliance.[11]

The Health Insurance Portability and Accountability Act (HIPAA) has led to a host of security risk management concerns for health care institutions that outsource processes that require electronic transmission of patient information. Passed in 1996, HIPAA is designed to protect confidential health care information through improved security standards and federal privacy legislation. It defines requirements for storing patient information before, during, and after electronic transmission. It also identifies compliance guidelines for critical business tasks such as risk analysis, awareness training, audit trail, disaster recovery plans, and information access control and encryption. There are 18 information security standards in three areas that must be met to ensure compliance with the HIPAA Security Rule. The three areas are as follows:

1. *Administrative safeguards.* Documented policies and procedures for day-to-day operations; managing the conduct of employees with electronic protected health information (EPHI); and managing the selection, development, and use of security controls.

EXHIBIT 10.3　Outsourcer and Client Information Security Responsibilities

MSP	Client
Installs and maintains data security software.	Defines business needs and identifies data security issues.
Writes and maintains data center data security policies and procedures.	Writes and maintains internal data security policies and procedures.
Quality ensures client's logon ID structure and access rules.	Defines structure for logon IDs and access rules.
Establishes logon IDs and access rules according to agreed-on specifications.	Approves logon IDs and access rules as implemented.
Provides data for violation reports.	Updates logon IDs.
Supports client liaison to internal users and customers as needed.	Investigates and resolves violation reports.
Supports client training through technology transfer; may deliver training on contract basis.	Acts as liaison between outsourcer and internal users and customers.
Upholds service level agreements and enforces policies and procedures to protect all clients.	
Implements regulatory compliance procedures in a timely fashion.	

2. *Physical safeguards.* Security measures meant to protect an organization's electronic information systems, as well as related buildings and equipment, from natural hazards, environmental hazards, and unauthorized intrusion.
3. *Technical safeguards.* Security measures that specify how to use technology to protect EPHI, particularly controlling access to it.

The most effective information security risk management strategy is to adopt and comply with best practices and standards. Tort law in the United States includes four possible means by which a firm may be found liable for information security lapses: duty, negligence, damage, and cause. Duty refers to whether the organization has a responsibility to safeguard information. That duty is not in doubt in today's security-conscious environment. Negligence refers to an outright breach of the duty to safeguard information. It asks: "Is there evidence that the organization did not fulfill its duty of care?" Damage refers to whether there is harm to someone (the plaintiff) as a result of negligence. Cause refers to the question of whether the negligence led to or was the primary cause of the damage.

To manage the information security risk, BPO vendor organizations should adopt and be able to prove compliance with global best practices and standards. Many firms turn to managed-security providers (MSPs) to assist them in managing this risk. Good MSPs provide valuable analysis and reporting of threat events, supplementing the efforts of in-house security personnel. They do this by sifting through vast amounts of data with the goal of uncovering, identifying, and prioritizing security vulnerabilities that must be addressed.[12] The best MSPs provide BPO buyers with the following:

- The ability to compare and correlate multiple monitoring points and to distinguish between false positives and actual threats
- Skilled experts on duty around the clock to assess and react to each threat in real time
- The ability to combine existing technology with expert analysis to look for anomalous behavior
- The ability to develop custom monitoring for specific networks or systems, including the development of an "attack signature" for each new vulnerability threat.

Using a third party to manage information security helps relieve the organization of information security concerns, but it does not remove liability if there is a security breach.[13] Liability cannot be transferred to a third party, unless the buyer invests in appropriate insurance policies. Exhibit 10.3 provides separate lists of responsibilities for MSPs and clients in maintaining information security.[14]

A good source of security risk management guidelines, policies, and best practices is the SANS Institute Web site at *www.sans.org*. The SANS (SysAdmin, Audit, Network, Security) Institute was established in 1989 as a cooperative research and education organization.

LEGAL RISKS

Legal risks associated with offshore outsourcing are legion, and their threat is made worse by the relative lack of legal precedent. For example, there currently are no clear legal rules governing the extent to which remedies can be extracted from a BPO vendor in the case of a security breach or other gross malfeasance. Countries differ in their laws for foreign firms seeking damages from private enterprises.

Chapter 6 discusses details of the BPO contract and the legal relationship between BPO buyer and vendor. This governing document provides a framework for the buyer–vendor relationship. Today, many law firms and consultancies specialize in assisting BPO buyers in developing contract terms that are favorable and enforceable. Of course, each contract must foster and promote the BPO relationship. In an offshore BPO project, the BPO buyer may have to concede some governing jurisdiction to the vendor's home country. That is, it may not be possible to draft contracts with offshore vendors that demand all legal conflicts be decided in the buyer's preferred jurisdiction. Some give and take may be required on different contract elements, with some potential areas of conflict to be decided in a domestic forum, some in a forum preferred by the vendor, and others in an international forum such as the International Arbitration Association. BPO buyers should mix and match forums to ensure that matters of potentially greatest impact to competitive ability are decided in their preferred forum. This can be achieved if there is a willingness to concede matters of less importance to be decided elsewhere.

One technique that has been effective for avoiding legal disputes is to split outsourcing contracts depending on different deliverables and service level agreements (SLAs). For example, many firms outsource software development as well as IT management to third-party vendors. A BPO buyer would be wise to split the software development contract from the IT services contract. IT management services are generally governed by SLAs that require regular fee payments. However, software development fees should be payable at development milestones—with a substantial portion of the fee withheld until final acceptance of the final code.[15] Splitting the contract so that standard service provisions are kept distinct from software development reduces the risk of financing development of code that does not perform as expected.

Firms should also be careful to separate continuous service or transaction-related terms from those that concern development of some type of output, such as software or knowledge that is the property of the BPO buyer. The transaction-related services are usually covered in the SLAs and are paid on a regular basis. Development contracts should be treated separately. It is reasonable for the BPO buyer to withhold a substantial portion of the development contract fees until the final product has been delivered and tested.

VENDOR ORGANIZATIONAL RISKS

The risks associated with the BPO vendor's organization are perhaps the most difficult to accept because they are not easy to control. This risk is also enhanced when the vendor is offshore. The risks associated with the vendor organization can range from business practices to authenticity of certification and reference claims.

Vendor business practices can vary greatly around the world. Practices that are clearly prohibited or considered highly questionable in the United States can be routine in the vendor's home country. The problems of bribes, kickbacks, or money exchanged under the table have affected U.S. businesses abroad in a wide range of industries. The U.S. Foreign Corrupt Practices Act of 1977 is designed to discourage domestic companies from participating in practices abroad that are proscribed at home. Most BPO vendor companies were founded after the 1977 Act was passed and are generally managed by individuals who are sensitive to the need to conform to its strictures. Market-based governance mechanisms also compel vendors to conform to U.S. standards. Still, the potential for abuses is present, and the frequency of abuse may increase in the Wild West atmosphere that is shaping up overseas as increasingly more vendors seek to strike it rich in BPO gold.

Another risk concerns the potential for vendors to overstate their competencies and to exaggerate the business and technical certifications they possess and the clients they serve. This risk can be mitigated through comprehensive due diligence that insists on objective proof of certifications and permission to talk to representatives from the vendor's client list. Vendors that refuse to share certification evidence or balk at client referrals should be treated with caution.

Vendor organizational risk also includes its HR practices. Many manufacturers that chose to outsource to foreign companies turned a blind eye to labor practices long banned in the United States. Child labor, excessively long hours, and outright sexual and other forms of harassment or discrimination are not uncommon in some foreign labor markets. Firms choosing to outsource business processes should consider the labor practices of the vendor and determine whether the risk of participating in domestically reviled practices abroad can damage domestic reputation and goodwill.

VALUE RISKS

Whether the rationale is cost savings or business transformation, an outsourcing project is undertaken to create value for the BPO buyer. With the myriad uncertainties inherent in any complex BPO deal, extracting anticipated value can be a challenge. This risk can be mitigated through several techniques, most of which center on managing the projected outcomes. For example, if the outsourcing deal is expected to save the BPO buyer $1 million during the first year, the PMT should manage to that figure. Adding additional people or hiring consulting firms may be a temptation as project difficulties mount. This temptation can be resisted if the PMT is committed to hitting the cost savings targets established for the project.

Another technique for mitigating project value risks is to empower the PMT to constantly seek opportunities to leverage the competencies that develop between the buyer and vendor firms. This tactic, often referred to as "pressing the value model," will expand the reach of vendor competencies and those jointly developed through the BPO relationship. For example, firms that outsource payroll may find that additional advantages can be gained by turning over other back-office functions to the same vendor. When the PMT presses the value model, it seeks to identify other noncore processes that may be suitable for outsourcing under an existing buyer–vendor relationship umbrella.[16]

Value risks are inherent in any project as people strive to work together to achieve future organizational states. Working with international vendors presents higher-value risks than working with domestic vendors in that the extent of potential value is often overstated by the foreign vendor and can take longer than expected to achieve. Mitigation of these risks centers on the effectiveness of SLA negotiation, implementation, and management. The project management plan can also be an important tool for mitigating value risk because it specifies tasks and responsible parties that can be held accountable on a one-to-one basis. Critical process flows should not be allowed to linger out of compliance for long periods without explanation and plans for remedy. The PMT should have provisions in place for emergency meetings in the event that value goals are not being reached.

FORCE MAJEURE RISKS

Force majeure risks are the most difficult to quantify and specify. What is the likelihood of a war? A hurricane? An earthquake? No one really knows. Yet these risks can be estimated with some measure of objectivity, and an appropriate mitigation strategy can be developed and enacted.

Geopolitical realities around the world today have brought the threat of war to nearly every doorstep. At the same time, reasonable assessments of the probability of war affecting a BPO vendor can be made. Business Monitor International provides extensive coverage of the political, economic, and military risks that exist for countries around the world. Their Web site at *www.businessmonitor.com* provides a starting place for assessing the war risk associated with the home country of the BPO vendor. Another great source of country-specific information is the U.S. Department of State Web site. This site at *www.state.gov* has extensive information for travelers and business people to determine the risks associated with regions around the globe. The PMT can manage its own exposure to liability by utilizing objective information sources in the development of its force majeure risk management plan.

The potential for political unrest exists in many countries that are desirable outlets for outsourcing, such as India and the Philippines. Firms outsourcing to foreign countries should plan for the possibility of war and the impact such a conflict would have on their business. Contingency plans should account for a worst-case scenario that would address issues such as the following:

■ What would you do if the country were attacked?
■ How would you perform the outsourced functions?

- How would you protect your facility and its contents and your intellectual property?
- Where would you relocate your business?

The recent outbreak of severe acute respiratory syndrome (SARS) affected several companies that outsourced functions, especially those based in China. But the effects of SARS were felt in the United States, too. Companies that had employees working in China when the SARS outbreak occurred had to move those employees back to the United States or have them quarantined. In addition, companies in the United States that received packages from China were concerned about opening them in case the disease could spread. The SARS outbreak illustrates the importance of planning for unusual and unexpected events. Companies need to understand the flow of their business and how each function or operation could be affected by an unusual event.

If they have not already, companies that outsource overseas need to develop disaster recovery and business continuity plans. Such plans force companies to examine possible risks, and they are crucial if the outsourcing firm wants to purchase insurance to cover property, liability, or business interruption exposures. Also, it is a good idea to have a backup in place in case anything goes wrong with infrastructure, business partners, or distribution channels. In addition to a backup, BPO buyers should consider drawing up a contract with the company responsible for securing the outsourcing. The terms of the contract and the shifting of the risk can be governed by that document. Exhibit 10.4 provides some standard language that can be used to designate vendor responsibilities with respect to disaster recovery planning.

EXHIBIT 10.4 Sample Language for Disaster Recovery

Scope and Definition: The outsourcer shall develop and implement a plan for the prevention and mitigation of business interruptions due to natural and other causes. The outsourcer shall make all reasonable efforts to prevent and recover from such events to ensure the continuity of business operations.

Outsourcer Responsibilities: Make all reasonable efforts to ensure the continuity of operations through implementation of a disaster recovery and business continuity plan. And develop a more detailed and comprehensive plan to ensure business continuity in the event of natural or other events that may cause service, supply chain, delivery, or performance interruptions.

The plan must address these activities that are necessary to resume operations at the optimal level at an alternative location within X number of days of a catastrophic event.

Source: "Touch These Bases Before You Sign to Outsource Your IT," *Contractor's Business Management Report* (November 2003), pp. 4–5.

CONCLUSION

Outsourcing does not mean eliminating business risk; it simply means that some of the risk is transferred to the BPO vendor. BPO buyers should consider whether they could go back to their old systems if all else failed. The fallback plan may be more expensive than the development, but it could save the business if it all goes wrong.[17]

To be effective, an outsourcing deal requires that each partner has considerable benefits to be gained, and that means sharing both risks and rewards. To make that work, the BPO deal must fund the necessary investment and motivate each partner's commitment by aligning goals. Although the financial structure of conventional outsourcing arrangements typically includes bonuses and penalties based on the achievement of minimum service levels by the vendor, business transformation outsourcing deals focus instead on upside targets. They align incentives around enterprise-level outcomes such as market share and return on equity.[18]

When thinking about using outsourcing, the BPO buyer must also consider the risks it brings to a potential BPO relationship. The BPO provider's readiness to undertake a BPO project is a major determinant of risks to project success. A good starting point to a risk management strategy is for the potential buyer to develop a risk profile of itself. Issues to consider in a risk profile include outsourcing maturity, financial stability, operational capabilities, market goodwill, and access to credit.

Managing risks associated with outsourcing are not unlike managing the risks associated with any other business project. Firms must establish their goals before undertaking the project and then manage to those goals. They must also be aware of the internal and vendor-related human resource and change management issues that will arise as a result of launching a BPO project. Each of the various risk factors discussed in this chapter can be managed, but constant attention is required to ensure both that problems are addressed before they become unmanageable and that project value is constantly pressed to extract maximal benefit for buyer and vendor alike.

SUMMARY

- ▓ The pioneering firms that led the current wave of interest in outsourcing were Global 1000–sized companies that have the capacity to absorb occasional business mistakes, even relatively large ones.
- ▓ Managers and executives currently on the job in organizations seeking to outsource business processes cannot rely on their business school education or their experience to help them deal with the current opportunities and challenges.

- There are human resource risks with both onshore and offshore BPO initiatives. Onshore risks center on reduction-in-force (RIF) policies and procedures. Offshore risks center on HR policies and procedures that differ from those in the United States.
- Project risks are defined as the potential that the BPO initiative may not provide the cost savings, strategic advantages, or productivity improvements anticipated.
- To mitigate project risks, the BPO buyer should first assess its readiness to undertake the outsourcing project before making the leap. This includes assessing the organization's ability to adapt to change, the presence of an internal BPO champion, and the time available to make the transition and ramp the project to full operational mode.
- There are many standards now in existence pertaining to information security and privacy. BPO buyers can mitigate intellectual property risks by ensuring that the vendors they choose adhere to global best practices on information security.
- Legal risks center on the relative lack of precedent in rulings pertaining to offshore labor and BPO contract disputes. These can be mitigated through the BPO contract, which should specify dispute resolution protocol and forums.
- Vendor organizational risks refer to the business practices of the vendor and their compatibility with those of the buyer and its key stakeholders.
- Value risks refer to the potential for the BPO project to run into critical difficulties or challenges before full value is realized.
- Force majeure risks are those so-called acts of nature that are beyond the control of the project management team. These are best dealt with through effective disaster and business continuity planning, in addition to appropriate language regarding force majeure events and responsibilities in the governing contract.

five

The Future of BPO

This part explores the future of BPO and some of the consequences it will have on economics, politics, work, and education. No one can say with certainty what the future will hold for global outsourcing. Certainly, there is the potential for legislative barricades to be erected. Worse, global terror could make all nations rethink the value of unfettered free trade and return to protectionist and nationalist policies.

In Chapter 11, we take the view that free trade is a global revolution that is likely to continue unabated over the coming decades and that its effects will be felt in many different ways. The opportunities for intrepid entrepreneurs to disrupt their industry by using highly scalable and talented global labor pools are unprecedented. We predict an investment and new venture creation boom centered on global outsourcing to be a modifier to the threat of jobs going overseas. Jobs will be created to take advantage of that labor. We end on the hopeful note that a rising standard of living available through outsourcing will help create a more prosperous future for people all around the world.

CHAPTER 11

Future Potential for BPO

*America is the most innovative country on earth. It won't stay
that way if we run away from the reality of the global economy.*

—Carly Fiorina, CEO, Hewlett-Packard

This book has been difficult to write because the pace of change in BPO continues to accelerate. The BPO issue heated up in the second half of 2003 and throughout the first half of 2004, becoming a central topic in the political campaigns of the presidential candidates. An explosion of media attention focused on the number and types of jobs that were being sent offshore. People on both sides of the issue have made compelling arguments for free trade and protectionism, respectively. Although the jobs issue is important and the reality of worker displacement must not be ignored, it is highly unlikely that outsourcing is going to go away. Similar pain was felt and protectionist arguments were raised during the era when manufacturing jobs were hopscotching to cheaper labor regions around the world. Today, outsourced manufacturing is no longer an issue that raises a lot of political wind. A similar trajectory of issue emergence, growth, and maturity is likely to be followed by the outsourcing of business processes.

We do not have a crystal ball to consult to determine how outsourcing will emerge and grow in the coming years, but we believe the most useful approach to take in this chapter is to examine the future of BPO on the assumption that it will continue to proliferate. Our challenge, then, is to extrapolate some of the trends in BPO, examine global education and labor patterns, and analyze the predictions and projections of leading consultants and analysts to develop a picture of the future prospects of BPO. We recognize the dangers inherent in making predictions about the future of any business trend. Many who have attempted this before us now lie on the increasingly large scrap heap of business punditry. To avoid that fate, we will be conservative in our musings about the future of BPO. We save our most daring predictions for a brief final section, assuming that readers will recognize the tentativeness of our remarks there and will not hold us entirely accountable if they fail to materialize.

We begin this chapter with a look at the future of business in a world that is increasingly comfortable with global labor cost arbitrage. Related to this issue are the regulations and policies enacted on a worldwide scale that are likely to govern BPO. We will examine the state of international policies and make some predictions about their likely trajectory. We will also examine the effects of BPO on organizational strategy and competitiveness, on the global workforce, and on the role of education in the shifting patterns of labor import and export. Finally, we will conclude with a few less restrained predictions about the future of BPO, focusing on what we believe to be the most interesting opportunities it may afford and the darkest threats it engenders.

GLOBAL BUSINESS ENVIRONMENT

Outsourcing, and most notably offshoring, has leapt into the consciousness of Americans, producing both entrepreneurial zeal and protectionist backlash. Dire predictions of the demise of U.S. global competitiveness are balanced by enthusiastic invocations of Schumpeter's "creative destruction" theory and the proven ability of the U.S. economy to recover from whatever shocks might come its way. The *Wall Street Journal*'s Daniel Henninger calls "the global migration of human labor" the "most powerful force on the globe today."[1] The *New York Times*' Thomas Friedman has adopted outsourcing as a personal *cause célèbre*, authoring more than a month's worth of weekly columns defending and endorsing the offshore outsourcing phenomenon.[2] Meanwhile, over at CNN, avuncular Lou Dobbs has seemingly dedicated his entire "MoneyLine" program to warning Americans against the evils of offshore outsourcing.[3]

Politically, outsourcing is shaping up to be an important election year issue. It is difficult to predict how state and federal regulators are going to respond to increasing demands for action. The AFL-CIO, as might be predicted, is strongly in favor of preventing the movement of jobs to offshore labor markets. To counter the labor union's lobbying efforts, business and industry trade groups have formed the Coalition for Economic Growth and American Jobs. This pro-outsourcing lobby consists of more than 200 trade groups, including the U.S. Chamber of Commerce, the Business Roundtable, the American Banker's Association, the National Association of Manufacturers, the Information Technology Association of America, and a host of individual companies.[4]

As of mid-Spring 2004, dozens of bills ostensibly designed to "protect U.S. jobs" had been introduced into state legislatures and Congress. One bill, introduced by Senate Minority Leader Tom Daschle, would require workers at telephone call centers to disclose their physical location at the beginning of each call. The logic of the bill is that American consumers would then be able to make an informed choice about whether they wanted to continue the call, or hang up and dial again until they reached a call center worker who would be sitting in front of a computer workstation at a preferred physical location. The irony of waiting long minutes for a technician only to be dismayed by the physical location of the person who finally picks up on the other end of the line is apparently lost on the bill's backers. One company that has preempted any such bills is E-Loan, which allows users to select the physical location of their home equity loan request processor merely by clicking an appropriate button on its Web page.[5]

STRATEGY AND COMPETITIVENESS

Experience has amply demonstrated that the early stages of most business revolutions are periods of great innovation, great progress, and great pain. The total quality management (TQM) movement in the United States, for example, was characterized by long-overdue advances in manufacturing processes. Ford Motor Company adopted the "Quality is Job 1" mantra in the early 1980s after superior-quality products from foreign automakers had already seriously eroded its domestic and international market share. The NBC news program "Quality or Else" and the subsequent book of the same title lit a fire under American managers and business school educators, ushering in sweeping changes in business processes and educational curricula. W. Edwards Deming was the dominant figure of the decade, sermonizing to managers across the land on the virtues of TQM until his last days. Many companies made major advances by implementing TQM in their operations—often because their processes were in need of major improvements. Others were less fortunate. Many TQM programs introduced into companies languished and festered, precious resources were squandered, and employee morale was compromised.

The early days of TQM were marked by a good deal of experimentation, and the popular business literature was filled with case studies of companies that did things right and gained advantages and those that did not do things right and wound up disappointed. In the long run, the TQM revolution resulted in lasting changes to organizations and is the forerunner to today's better-known managerial strategies, such as Six Sigma. People do not talk about TQM as much as they used to because it has become an expected part of doing business. The personal computer was a remarkable business revolution in its day, but no one pays attention to a business today because it uses a PC—more remarkable would be the firm without one. The same has occurred with TQM and the quality movement in general: It is a necessary part of business, and a business that lacks quality will stand out—usually in a negative way.

BPO is likely to cover the same business innovation trajectory as that experienced by TQM, the PC revolution, and other business innovations. We have already stated that early pioneers have made many of the big mistakes with BPO, and there is much to be learned from their examples. Firms such as GE, IBM, Microsoft, and other giants were the early adopters of BPO, and they agonized through the learning curve. That they were largely successful in their outsourcing initiatives is one of the main reasons that BPO has become a common part of the daily lexicon. In his March 21, 2004 syndicated column, noted language watcher William Safire acknowledged that the term *outsourcing* is here to stay.[6]

BPO will slowly become accepted across the globe and will eventually lose its ability to provide competitive advantage. As the TQM movement burst on the scene, early adopters were able to gain advantages over laggards. Eventually, that advantage was eroded as increasingly more firms adopted the TQM approach. Something similar is bound to occur with BPO, but it may take years for that to happen. Over the next five to ten years, U.S. firms should seek to take advantage of the fact that Indian and Chinese higher education systems are churning out five times as many engineers as U.S. institutions. Large and even industry-disrupting advantages can be gained by leveraging this inexpensive and high-quality labor pool. During the early days of TQM, failure to leap on the bandwagon and adopt quality measures within the organization led to steady losses in market share. A similar effect could occur for failure to adopt BPO.

In the long run, TQM was a market-share–driven business innovation. The cost savings and efficiencies gained by quality management practices eventually found their way to the consumer. Today's early adopters of BPO can retain much of the cost savings for themselves because many of their competitors have not adopted outsourcing and have no other compelling inclinations to lower prices to consumers. However, it will not be long before this increased net margin luxury disappears and the savings gained from BPO are reflected in the prices charged to consumers. Early adopters get to reap the windfall. Late adopters will only level the playing field.

BPO AND POLITICS

The election year of 2004 is shaping up to be one of many issues, with jobs and their apparent flight to offshore labor markets one of the central ones. Both major political parties have staked out positions on the issue in a manner that is in line with their overall economic platforms. Democrats stand in favor of some type of regulation, although most are staunchly opposed to anything that smacks of overt protectionism. Republicans defend free trade and hail the unimpeded flow of goods and services around the world. They favor allowing the short-term pain to subside before leaping to any policy decisions with respect to outsourcing.

The Republican perspective on outsourcing was summarized by noted economist N. Gregory Mankiw. Speaking in his role as Chairman of President Bush's Council of Economic Advisers, he noted that outsourcing is a positive thing for the U.S. economy. Of course, in the midst of some painful displacement of workers who paid a lot of money for educational credentials, the remarks rang rather hollow and created a small tempest for Mankiw. He quickly backtracked, stating that his remarks were poorly worded. Nonetheless, it does reflect the basic conservative position that outsourcing is a component of their free-trade platform plank and unlikely to be modified. Shortly after Mankiw's comments, Secretary of State Colin Powell visited a group of young workers in India and assured them that the United States was not going to enact policies that would jeopardize their newly lavish lifestyles.[7]

For their part, liberal politicians have also supported free trade over the past decade. In fact, the North American Free Trade Agreement (NAFTA) was supported by and ratified under the first term of the Clinton administration. Still, as a matter of political leverage, there is room for inconsistency on the free-trade issue, and the growing anxiety over job security by middle- and upper-middle-class workers is a potential voting bloc worth waffling over. In fact, a December 2003 Zogby poll noted that 25 percent of Americans earning at least $75,000 were worried about job security. That is the largest percentage in any income bracket.[8]

BPO AND GLOBAL ECONOMICS

From an economic perspective, outsourcing service jobs to offshore labor markets makes obvious sense. Of the approximately $1.45 to $1.47 of value derived from every dollar spent offshore, U.S. firms receive $1.12 to $1.14, while foreign firms receive only $0.33 of the value.[9] Furthermore, if income taxes paid by H1-B visa holders, and software and service imports by India are considered, outsourcing provides an aggregate benefit to the U.S. economy of $16.8 billion.[10]

The global economy has suffered potent shocks over the past decade: the collapse of the Japanese, Mexican, and Russian economies; the unbelievable rise and fall of the Internet economy in the United States; and the rise of terrorism that threatens nearly everyone. These global shocks are usually met with great uncertainty and hand wringing by tycoons, politicians, and blue-collar workers alike. BPO has been elevated to levels of everyday consciousness that is usually reserved for more exciting business trends. Given the pressing concern about economic recovery in the post-bubble era, and given the amplification of small issues during an election year, anxiousness about job loss from offshore outsourcing is heightened.

Despite the obvious overemphasis on the impact of outsourcing, there are clear economic implications of the trend that need to be examined and understood. Business leaders must take stock of outsourcing from the perspective of strategy—seeking to understand how they can leverage outsourcing for their own purposes in line with the movement of the global economy.

The most significant concept that can be applied to BPO from an economic perspective is David Ricardo's theory of comparative advantage. Every economics student learns Ricardo's macroeconomic theory, which states that sovereign nations should compete in the global economy on the basis of advantages that stem from their natural resources or geographic location. For example, Saudi Arabia could conceivably compete in the global economy by attempting to make and sell automobiles. From the perspective of comparative advantage, however, it would not be in the Saudis' interest to do so. Although it is entirely possible for the nation to be an efficient source of automobiles, it is far more advantageous for them to be the source of the world's crude oil. Saudi Arabia happens to have been blessed by the fates to be located atop one of the largest oil reserves in the world. Comparative advantage simply states that a nation should pursue those economic interests in which it has an advantage compared to its competitors.

To bring the concept into greater clarity, Milton Friedman used the example of the high-paid attorney and the administrative assistant. While it is entirely possible that the attorney would be a more efficient administrative assistant, it is neither to the attorney's nor the company's comparative advantage to divert him or her from legal to administrative duties. Better to have a less efficient administrative assistant continue in that role and allow the attorney to pursue higher-value interests.[11]

Comparative advantage has nearly imperceptibly shifted from a theory of leveraging natural resources to one of leveraging the intellectual and human resources of a nation. The service and information economies of our time place high value on the ability to manipulate symbols. A decade ago, former U.S. Labor Secretary Robert Reich wrote a book titled *The Work of Nations*. In that somewhat prescient work, Reich identified the new class of knowledge workers emerging in America and called them "symbolic analysts." According to Reich, symbolic analysts are those individuals who spend the bulk of their workday in front of computer terminals crafting original material, analyzing data, and sending and receiving electronic messages. The level of expertise required for these individuals to perform their duties is comparatively rare, placing them among the higher strata of the U.S. socioeconomic classes.

When Reich wrote during the early 1990s, the United States was hardly threatened by international competitors for symbolic analyst roles. In fact,

Reich was fairly comfortable that America would continue to lead the world in that regard. His book was written in part to assuage the doomsayers who felt threatened by the pace of American manufacturing shifts to foreign providers. Reich reasoned—rightly at the time—that the U.S. higher education system would enable the nation to stake out a long-term lead in symbolic analyst roles, employing the world's labor only in the grimier, more menial tasks of physical labor.

The great shift that has occurred since Reich's book is the upgrading of the higher education systems around the world to match their superior K–12 systems, which had been the subject of some concern for years. Americans have long known that the K–12 system in the United States produces graduates that are comparatively weak by international standards. Concern about the United States lagging far behind European and Asian counterparts on K–12 educational attainment had been offset in part by our vastly superior higher education system. That edge remains, but the gap has closed markedly and likely will disappear in a very short time.

The United States no longer enjoys a dramatic comparative advantage in the critical role of symbolic analyst. Around the world, eager young people are seeking to improve their economic status by applying the technical and analytic skills that are at world-class standards. They will transform their nations by creating the critical middle class that has been missing. The consumerism mindset that is necessary to drive an economy to greater levels of growth is taken for granted in the United States, where the middle class has enjoyed nearly 70 years of unabated consumerism. Not so in the Asian and Latin American countries that are the hotbeds of offshore outsourcing. The rising middle class that is being created through offshore outsourcing will demand products that fit their middle-class lifestyle, many of which are offered by U.S. companies. It is likely that global demand for higher-value goods and services associated with middle-class lifestyles will increase rapidly in the coming years. This global economic shift has a positive-feedback potential that could eventually raise all participating nations to higher living standards.

BPO AND GLOBAL WORKERS

We have been through this situation before. Outsourcing jobs to low-cost, usually foreign, labor markets is a familiar strategy in manufacturing. When the U.S. automobile industry turned to outsourcing to reduce the costs of producing an automobile, a great hue and cry went up to reverse the trend. However, on further analysis, it became clear to economists and social analysts that outsourcing some labor to offshore destinations actually helped *preserve* American jobs. As MIT economist Lester Thurow put it at the time, "Either half the car is produced in Detroit and the other half in Mexico; or the whole car is produced in Japan. By attempting to use legislative measures to tilt the balance in favor of Detroit over Mexico, one would in fact be tilting the balance in favor of Japan."[12]

The effect of outsourcing on the professional service workers in America will undoubtedly produce short-term pain for many thousands. In response, and especially in this election year, legislators and politicians will attempt to appeal to those displaced by outsourcing by introducing new laws and regulations that will have long-term consequences for jobs. One possible response on the worker side is an increasing push to unionize service workers. Currently, most professional services workers are not unionized. There has been some movement toward unionizing workers in the software industry, represented by organizations such as the IBM Employees' Union. If an increasing number of service workers join unions in an effort to curtail the movement of jobs offshore, their numbers could have influential political effects.

The commonly held belief that BPO leads to net job loss in America has been challenged by economic research. The value of U.S. service exports in computer programming, telecommunications, banking, engineering, and management consulting exceeded $130 billion in 2003, up more than 6 percent from the previous year. In the meantime, imports of such services were in excess of $77 billion for 2003, up more than 10 percent from 2002. Thus the United States posted a net surplus in these service areas for 2003, a rarity among its current account balances.

Using government accounting standards, when a U.S. company opens a technical-support center overseas that handles inquiries from the United States, that is considered an import of services to the United States. However, when a U.S. service provider does work for a foreign company, that is considered an export of services. These numbers suggest that any efforts by the federal government to restrict the flow of service imports could backfire and lead to reciprocal restrictions on U.S. service exports. Given that the U.S. current account deficit overall hit $541 billion in 2003—a record high—it is not likely that legislation leading to curtailment of the one area of surplus is going to have an easy ride through the political system.

In addition to hiring high-level U.S. white-collar service workers, foreign companies have also increased their direct investment in U.S. firms. In 2003, foreign direct investment in U.S. companies hit a record $82 billion—nearly double that of 2002.[13]

In addition to the net service-industry current accounts surplus, which largely reflects the activities of large enterprises, small- to medium-sized firms are also creating jobs in the United States by using foreign labor. For example, Claimpower, Inc., a Fairlawn, New Jersey–based medical claims processing firm, was able to expand its domestic market share through the use of low-cost foreign labor. The business, formerly run only by the founder and his wife, now has the capacity to expand nationally. This will require hiring local managers and sales representatives to develop business opportunities, which will then be processed in India.[14]

Entrepreneurs who see outsourcing as an opportunity to cost-effectively grow their firms will be able to scale their new ventures at a pace never before possible. We predict that entrepreneurs and venture capitalists will recognize the disruptive potential of outsourcing over traditional modes of conducting business in a wide variety of industries. Firms that are based on analyzing data as a service are going to be competing on an uneven playing field unless they find a way to leverage the booming global labor market.

BPO AND EDUCATION

As pointed out in Chapter 1, educational attainment is one of the primary drivers of the global outsourcing trend. For years it has been common knowledge that foreign K–12 education is superior to that offered in the United States. High school graduates in European and Asian countries notoriously outperformed their U.S. counterparts on basic knowledge tests, especially those covering universal topics such as science, mathematics, literature, and world history.

U.S. education analysts have long lamented the gap between U.S. high schoolers and their international peers, but they could always bask in the superiority of American higher education. No longer. Higher education around the world has caught up with the United States in terms of quality of education and intensity of ongoing research programs. Once a major drawing card for scholars from around the world, U.S. higher learning no longer occupies the top spot in several important categories.

During the height of the Cold War, the Soviet Union launched the Sputnik satellite, sending shockwaves across the American educational landscape. Fear of being outdone by Soviet scientific and technologic advances, the United States focused new resources on educational achievement, especially in the sciences and math. The threat posed today by foreign educational systems overtaking the United States is less obvious. It has come on slowly and methodically and does not have the drama of a tiny, beeping object circling high above our heads and threatening our security. Back then the threat was nuclear annihilation. Today, the threat is global economic irrelevance.

Statistics may help crystallize the threat to U.S. domination of global business. In 2002, about 60,000 students in the United States graduated with engineering degrees. In India and China—the two predominant outsourcing destinations that together comprise one-third of the world's population—more than 300,000 students graduated with engineering degrees. Other Asian countries, such as South Korea, Japan, Taiwan, Singapore, and Hong Kong, share a similar focus on science and technical education. Some commentators speculate that outsourcing is like a universal acid in reverse—it will continue to seep upward unabated and unstoppable into ever-higher-level work, including advanced research and product development.[15]

With the overwhelming numbers of technical graduates abroad, perhaps America is not likely to lead the world in the raw numbers of technically educated workers. That is not necessarily a bad thing. One needs to remember that much of the work done by science and engineering graduates is *applied* rather than *basic research*. And the Asian countries that are excelling in production of technical workers will need each of them to build the next generation of roads, bridges, and telecommunications networks to meet the demands of their burgeoning populations.

The edge in education will not be gained in raw numbers of science and engineering graduates; it is far more likely to go to the country that can take advantage of that low-cost technical labor. Basic research is dedicated to following the trail of scientific advances wherever it may lead. This requires immense funding to enable the greatest minds available the freedom to pursue their interests without worry about commercial potential. Of course, the goal of all federally funded basic research must be commercialization (or, at least, practical application), but that should not be the day-to-day role of those who are responsible for pushing the boundaries of knowledge.

Leadership in the coming age of worldwide outsourcing will go to those countries who produce the breakthroughs in basic research and who develop the entrepreneurs and managers skilled in commercializing the output of those research programs. The United States continues to lead the world in basic research investment and in business/management education. It also has the most nurturing cultural, economic, and political systems to encourage risk takers and entrepreneurs to find ways to bring new products and services to market. The intelligent entrepreneurs today, in whatever country they may call home, will do well to recognize the incredible opportunities for rapid scalability through leveraging global labor resources.

There has been some response in higher education to help domestic companies take advantage of BPO. The Massachusetts Institute of Technology (MIT) entertained a standing-room-only crowd in a first-of-its-kind course on outsourcing during Spring 2004. The course is co-taught, appropriately enough, by Indian MIT professor Amar Gupta. Former dean and economist Lester Thurow is the other professor of record in this class, which is liberally sprinkled with guest speakers from the likes of Accenture and other large outsourcing consultancies. The students run through simulations of outsourcing projects, which include occasional monkey wrenches, such as simulated terrorist threats against offshore ventures.

OUTRAGEOUS PREDICTIONS: WHAT'S LEFT FOR AMERICA?

Shumpeter's famous theory of creative destruction was a popular one during the go-go days of the Internet bubble. The new economy was the engine of destruction during that time, overriding in a few short years the entire economic history of the Industrial Age with its reliable business cycles and bricks-and-mortar business models. Exaggerated beliefs about the staying power of the new economy were part of the reason that a bubble was created, leading to a painful contraction and rebalancing of the economy, expectations, and sound business models. The hype currently surrounding outsourcing, especially offshore outsourcing, is also an exaggeration of its long-term importance.

We predict that there will be some legislative action to regulate offshore outsourcing. However, we do not believe that this action will reverse or markedly slow the movement of business processes to their lowest-cost labor source. Some of the regulations that are likely to be enacted at the federal level include the following:

- *Formal reporting requirements for firms that use offshore outsourcing.* These will probably end up being limited to indicating the number of offshore workers under contract to, or employed by, the firm and the financial amount of the contract. It is likely that a statement in the annual report would satisfy this requirement.
- *Strenuous data privacy rules that indirectly target offshore outsourcing.* Legislators unwilling to be viewed as protectionist but who have a vocal anti-outsourcing constituency will seek indirect means of addressing their concerns. One likely measure is stringent data privacy standards that will impose expensive taxes on BPO buyers and vendors in the form of expensive security safeguards and reporting.
- *Civil rights action aimed at defining a new protected class—the college-educated American.* Such action would make it discriminatory for firms to use offshore labor when similarly qualified individuals are available onshore. The extra cost of the onshore labor would be viewed as an anti-discrimination tax not unlike that imposed on firms that must make reasonable accommodations for disabled workers.

These and other actions are likely to occur in state and federal lawmaking arenas, but there will be nonpolitical movements in the United States to respond to the global outsourcing revolution as well. We have already described the educational initiatives that are underway and those likely to be adopted in the coming years. There will also be massive shifts in entrepreneurial ventures as innovators realize the potential of a global labor force ready and willing to work for unimaginably low wages. Some of these new ventures have already begun to appear. For example, Ryan Kinzy founded his software firm K3 Group with the intent of using Indian labor for development. To his delight, he learned that he could recruit equally qualified developers in Colombia at one-third of the cost of the Indian labor. K3 uses the South American country's highly qualified programming labor pool on an as-needed basis. In addition, being based in Austin, Texas, means that the offshore programmers are working in the same time zone as headquarters staff, enabling real-time communications during normal working hours.[16] Others are eagerly seeking pools of skilled labor in increasingly remote locations, including Southeast Asia,[17] Eastern Europe, and Central America.[18]

Entrepreneurial opportunities abound for individuals familiar with labor-intensive industries with highly specific and specialized functions. Technical analysis, data manipulation and transformation, document design and information mapping, and many other information-related or symbolic analysis work can now be shipped to qualified workers from a desktop computer attached via broadband to the Internet. The domestic entrepreneur has a compelling value proposition—equally qualified workers who will do the same job as domestic firms for 25 to 30 percent less. The major barrier for new ventures seeking to market foreign services to domestic firms is a lack of visibility. For many, the dramatic savings that they can deliver will overcome that initial objection.

CONCLUSION

Each chapter of this book has ended with a "conclusion" section, so we feel an obligation to be consistent and end this chapter in a similar manner. Yet, there is no conclusion to be drawn with confidence about the future of BPO. It is safe for us to speculate that as long as labor rates vary around the world business executives will by dint of bold strategy and competitive pressure find ways to utilize those labor pools to gain an advantage. It is also safe to speculate that labor rates around the world will remain out of balance for at least the next several years.

We are hopeful that American workers who have been displaced by outsourcing will find new ways to use their skills to create wealth for themselves and their families. We are particularly optimistic for entrepreneurs who recognize the unprecedented opportunity to leverage a highly skilled and rapidly scalable global workforce. Those who are able to organize this labor, control it for productivity, and provide leadership-at-a-distance will benefit the most. It is not inconceivable that the United States could witness another entrepreneurial burst akin to the dot-com revolution. The cost-structure disruption potential for entrepreneurs in a number of high-value-added services is present. The spirit to pursue those opportunities will be there if the venture money is willing. Preliminary indications are that the flow of capital to outsourcing-based ventures is only beginning.

Middle managers fearing displacement as a result of outsourcing should re-tool their skill base. Cross-cultural communication, project management, and virtual leadership skills will be paramount to an economy based on BPO. Other professionals that fear displacement should develop similar skills and seek to leverage their base in the United States as an opportunity to put global labor to work.

The post-September 11 world will forever be different from the one that existed before. There is no doubt that BPO is emerging in the shadow of that event. In fact, the lingering fears of global terrorism have likely served to slow the progress of moving service work to foreign labor pools. It is a testament to the strength of the outsourcing phenomenon that it has emerged during these troubled times. As the shackles of fear are lifted in the coming years—and we are confident they will—BPO will be a dynamic force for global economic growth. We envision that national leaders in remote corners of the world will recognize that comparative advantage can now be gained through intellectual assets. Even the most natural resource–impoverished land can prosper if it develops its human capital and makes it available to the global market. Acting on the highest principles of freedom and capitalism—centered on economic self-interest—the entire globe can be connected as regions of labor excellence emerge and develop the capacity to serve increasingly remote regions of demand. We believe that the global economy is trending toward this vision and, barring some unthinkable catastrophe, portends prosperity and freedom for a greater proportion of the world's people. It is difficult to see that as a bad thing.

endnotes

Chapter 1

1. John Krakauer, *Into Thin Air* (New York: Anchor, 1999).
2. "Space Wedding a First for Russia," *CNN* (August 10, 2003).
3. Ibid, p. 81.
4. Nelson D. Schwartz, "Down and Out in White-Collar America," *Fortune* (June 23, 2003), pp. 79–86.
5. William Spain and Andrea Coombes, "Worked Over: Job Exports Seen Constraining U.S. Recovery," *CBS Marketwatch* (August 29, 2003).
6. Matthew L. Sheahan, "Move Over Software, Here Comes BPO," *VCJ* (August 2003), pp. 3–6.
7. "Users of BPO Report High Satisfaction with Existing Relationships," Gartner, Inc. (October 7, 2002), p. 1.
8. Benjamin Beasley-Murray, "Business Process Outsourcing Gains Ground," *Global Finance* (September 2003), pp. 54–56.
9. "BPO Profit Set to Shrink, Says IDC," *Computergram Weekly* (August 5, 2003), pp. 7–8.
10. Daniel Dennett, *Consciousness Explained* (Boston: Little, Brown and Company, 1991).
11. Texas Instruments, accessed October 2003 at *www.ti.com/corp/docs/press/company/2003/c03033.shtml*.
12. Dennis K. Berman, "Profiting from the Broadband Revolution," *Wall Street Journal Reports: Telecommunications* (October 13, 2003), pp. R1, R4.
13. Michael J. Miller, "Rejecting the Tech Doomsayers," *PC Magazine* (July 2002), p. 7.
14. Jodie Kirshner, "A Surge for Broadband," *U.S. News & World Report* (June 30, 2003), p. 17.
15. "DSL Subscribers Almost 26 Million Worldwide," *Computergram Weekly* (August 29, 2002).
16. Paris Lord, "SAR Tops Broadband Use Survey," *Hong Kong Imail* (August 16, 2002).
17. Robyn Greenspan, "Broadband Based on Behavior," *CyberAtlas* (May 19, 2003).
18. "Broadband Worldwide," *eMarketer* (2003).
19. Adam Smith, *The Wealth of Nations* (New York: Prometheus Books, 1991).
20. Gary Hamel and C.K. Prahalad, *Competing for the Future* (Cambridge, MA: Harvard Business School Press, 1996).
21. National Association of Professional Employer Organizations, *www.napeo.org*.
22. "Where the Good Jobs are Going," *Time* (August 4, 2003), pp. 36–38.

23. "Berkshire Discloses Larger ADP Holding," *Reuters* (August 25, 2003).
24. Paul McDougall, "Offshore Outsourcing Moves into the Back Office," *Information Week* (July 14–21, 2003), p. 22.

Chapter 2

1. Richard Barovick, "Outsourcing Export Financing," *World Trade* (October 2003), pp. 58–59.
2. John Harney, "Staking a Claim to Excellence with Offshore Outsourcing," *OutsourcingOffshore.com* (March 2003).
3. Kathleen Goolsby, "Truckloads of Treasures," *Outsourcing Journal* (February 2002).
4. Kim S. Nash, "Sears: The Return on Returns," *Baseline* (January 17, 2003).
5. Leslie Hansen Harps, "Making Dollars and Sense Out of Logistics," *Inbound Logistics* (March 2002).
6. Kit Davis, "Blue Christmas?" *RIS News* (January 2002).
7. Kim S. Nash, "Getting It Back," *Baseline News* (January 2003).
8. Jeffrey Schwartz, "The Art of the Deal," *VARBusiness* (May 26, 2003), pp. 57–59.
9. "The Value of Utility Service Options," *Computer Finance* (February 2003), pp. 2–4.
10. "AMR Warns of Negative Impact of Utility Computing Model," *MultiMedia Futures* (August 8, 2003), pp. 6–7.
11. Much of this discussion has been derived from an online case study of the Kohler–API outsourcing relationship at *www.apioutsourcing.com/cs_kohler.asp*.
12. "Amazon Unit to Offer Outsourced Web Stores," *Computergram Weekly* (June 11, 2003).
13. Lee Copeland, "Borders Turns to Amazon for Outsourcing," *Computerworld* (April 16, 2001).
14. "Amazon.com Launches New Services Subsidiary," *Material Handling Management* (August 2003).
15. Michael Fitzgerald, "Amazon Finds Profits in Outsourcing," *CIO* (October 15, 2002).
16. Linda Rosencrance, "Amazon Outsources Additional Data Center to Equinix," *Computerworld* (July 23, 2003).
17. "Transformational Outsourcing," *InfoWorld* (January 3, 2003).
18. "Accenture and BC Hydro in Agreement Valued at Nearly $1 Billion," *News Release* (February 2003).
19. BC Hydro and Accenture Plan to Offer Services to Utilities Throughout North America," *Creative Resistance* (July 18, 2002).
20. Wesley Bertch, "Why Offshore Outsourcing Failed Us," *Network Computing* (October 16, 2003), pp. 65–68.

Chapter 3

1. "Survey: BPO Moves to Small Business," *Silicon Valley/San Jose Business Journal* (April 2003).

2. "Small Business," *Money* (Fall 2003), p. 93.
3. Michael Hammer and James Champy, *Reengineering the Corporation: A Manifesto for Business Revolution* (New York: Harper Business, 1993).
4. G.W. Keen, *The Process Edge: Creating Value Where it Counts* (Cambridge, MA: Harvard Business School Press, 1997).
5. See for example, Ludwig von Bertalanffy, *General System Theory* (New York: George Braziller, 1968); or Stafford Beer, *The Heart of Enterprise* (New York: John Wiley & Sons, 1979).
6. Jerome Barthelemy, "The Seven Deadly Sins of Outsourcing," *Academy of Management Executive* 17, no. 2 (2003), pp. 87–100.
7. Joann S. Lublin, "What Kind of Managers Target Their Own Jobs in a Restructuring?" *Wall Street Journal* (October 7, 2003), p. B1.
8. Geoffrey Moore, *Managing on the Fault Line* (New York: HarperBusiness, 2002).
9. Bruce Kogut and Nalin Kulatilaka, "Capabilities as Real Options," *Organization Science* (November–December 2001), pp. 744–758.
10. C.K. Prahalad and G. Hamel, "The Core Competence of the Corporation," *Harvard Business Review* (May/June 1990), pp. 79–91.
11. J. Barney, "Firm Resources and Sustained Competitive Advantage," *Journal of Management* 17 (1991), pp. 99–120; K. Conner, "A Historical Comparison of Resources-Based Theory and Five Schools of Thought within Industrial Organization Economics: Do We Have a New Theory of the Firm?" *Journal of Management* 17 (1991), pp. 121–154.
12. Barry M. Staw, "The Escalation of Commitment to a Course of Action," *Academy of Management Review* (October 1981), pp. 569–576.

Chapter 4

1. Nick J. Lavingia, "Improve Profitability Through Effective Project Management and Total Cost Management," *Cost Engineering* 45, no. 11 (November 2003), pp. 22–24.
2. Alex Arthur, "How to Build Your Project Budget," *Management Accounting* (April 2000), pp. 20–22.
3. Charles C. Denova, "The Hawthorne Effect," *Training & Development* (October 1968), pp. 46–49.
4. Many researchers question the validity of the so-called Hawthorne studies and the reliability of the so-called Hawthorne effect. See for example, John G. Adair, "The Hawthorne Effect: A Reconsideration of the Methodological Artifact," *Journal of Applied Psychology* (May 1984), pp. 334–345.
5. Robert Kegan and Lisa Laskow Lahey, "The Real Reason People Won't Change," *Harvard Business Review* (November 2001), pp. 84–91.
6. Arnold B. Maltz and Lisa M. Ellram, "Total Cost of Relationship: An Analytical Framework for the Logistics Outsourcing Decision," *Journal of Business Logistics* 18, no. 1 (1997), pp. 45–65.
7. Keith Regan, "Capellas to Leave HP—for Worldcom?" *E-Commerce Times* (November 12, 2002).
8. Tom Krazit, "HP Integration Team Leader Resigns," *IDG News Service* (November 25, 2003).

9. Mark Jones and Brian Fonseca, "EDS: Outsourcing Still a Money Spinner," *NetworkWorldFusion* (January 18, 2002).
10. Michael Useem and Joseph Harder, "Leading Laterally in Company Outsourcing," *Sloan Management Review* (Winter 2000), pp. 25–36.

Chapter 5

1. Joanne Wojcik, "Formal Process Advised in Vendor Searches," *Business Insurance* (November 16, 1998), p. 16.
2. Vaughan Michell and Guy Fitzgerald, "The IT Outsourcing Market-Place: Vendors and Their Selection," *Journal of Information Technology* 12 (1997), pp. 223–237.
3. Thomas A. Osmond and Beth M. Schnaper, "Trips, Traps and Travails: How to Hire the Right Outsourcing Vendor for Your Organization," *Benefits Quarterly*, Third Quarter (2000), pp. 15–21.
4. Andrew Anderson, "Methodology Removes Guesswork," *Communications News* (August 1, 2003), pp. 38–39.
5. "Keys to Success: Stability of Partner, Maturity of Processes & Industry Focus," *Insurance & Technology* (August 2002), p. 28.
6. Charles A. Weber, John R. Current, and Anand Desai, "VendOR: A Structured Approach to Vendor Selection and Negotiation," *Journal of Business Logistics* 21, no. 1 (2000), pp. 135–167.
7. Ibid.
8. Toby Gooley, "RFPs that Get Results," *Logistics Management* (July 2003), pp. 47–51.
9. "Kellogg's Shows How You Can Outsource Your Entire Recruiting Process," *Human Resource Department Management Report* (September 2002), pp. 1, 11–13.
10. Kerry Massaro, "Managing the Offshore Relationship," *Wall Street & Technology* (October 2003), pp. 10–13.

Chapter 6

1. Randall Poe and Carol Lee Courter, "You Can Go Home Again," *Across the Board* (January 1998), p. 7.
2. "Consultants Claim Demand Is on the Up," *Global Computing Services* (August 1, 2003), pp. 3–4.
3. Jerome Barthelemy, "The Seven Deadly Sins of Outsourcing," *Academy of Management Executive* 17, no. 2 (2003), pp. 87–100.
4. Sung Kim and Young-Soo Chung, "Critical Success Factors for IS Outsourcing Implementation from an Interorganizational Relationship Perspective," *Journal of Computer Information Systems* (Summer 2003), pp. 81–90.
5. " 'Must' Provisions to Consider for Your Outsourcing Contracts," *Supplier Selection and Management Report* (October 2003), pp. 10–12.
6. Farok J. Contractor, "A Generalized Theorem for Joint Venture and Licensing Negotiations," *Journal of International Business Studies* (Summer 1985), pp. 23–50.

7. Mitchell Lee Marks and Philip H. Mirvis, "Making Mergers and Acquisitions Work: Strategic and Psychological Preparation," *Academy of Management Executive* (May 2001), pp. 80–94.

8. Mario Apicella, "Shaking Hands is Not Enough," *InfoWorld* (April 30, 2001), pp. 49–50.

9. Dai Davis, "Service Level Agreements: What Are They? Why Do We Need Them?" *Credit Management* (May 2002), p. 36.

10. Laton McCartney, "How Do You Set Up an Effective SLA?" *Inter@ctive Week* (September 27, 2000), p. 30.

11. Edward M. Lundeen, CPM, CPIM.

12. Both examples from Ann Bednarz, "New Deals Tie Fees to Revenue," *NetWork World* (May 26, 2003), pp. 1, 16.

13. Patrick Thibodeau, "Offshore Risks are Numerous, Say Those Who Craft Contracts," *Computerworld* (November 3, 2003), p. 12.

14. Bart Perkins, "A Reality Check on Going Offshore," *Computerworld* (June 16, 2003), p. 42.

15. "How to Protect IP Before Entering Into New Relationships," *Supplier Selection & Management Report* (April 2003), pp. 2–4.

16. "HIPAA Compliance, ASPs, Outsourcing, and Vendor Relationships," *Medical Benefits* (July 15, 2002), p. 11.

17. Brad Miller, "Outsourcing Aids Compliance," *Bank Technology News* (December 2001), p. 52.

18. Walter Mattli, "Private Justice in a Global Economy: From Litigation to Arbitration," *International Organization* (Autumn 2001), pp. 919–947.

Chapter 7

1. D. Hodgson, "Disciplining the Professional: The Case of Project Management," *Journal of Management Studies* (September 2002), pp. 803–821.

2. Alexa Jaworski, "Fund Managers Share Outsourcing Strategies: Communications Key," *Operations Management* (October 27, 2003), p. 6.

3. "Clients to Blame for Outsourcing Failure," *Global Computing Services* (June 27, 2003), pp. 4–5.

4. Mike Wood, "Don't Be Sunk Offshore," *Electronics Weekly* (September 17, 2003), p. 19.

5. "Enterprises Cannot Manage Multiple Outsourcing Vendors," *Computergram Weekly* (September 4, 2003), p. 4.

6. "Most Change Management Projects Fail," *Accountancy* (January 2003), p. 26.

7. Sidney G. Winter, "The Satisficing Principle in Capability Learning," *Strategic Management Journal* (October/November 2000), pp. 981–996.

8. Mihaly Csikszentmihalyi, *Flow: The Psychology of Optimal Experience* (New York: Harper & Row, 1990).

9. Mark Lasswell, "Fabulists at the Firm," *The Wall Street Journal* (January 9, 2004), p. W11.

10. Warren Bennis, "The Future Has No Shelf Life," *Executive Excellence* (August 2000), pp. 5–6.

11. Roger Gill, "Change Management—Or Change Leadership?" *Journal of Change Management* (May 2003), pp. 307–318.
12. Randy G. Pennington, "Making Changes," *Executive Excellence* (June 2000), p. 11.
13. Kari Reinhardt, "Communicating During Times of Change," *HRProfessional* (February/March 2001), pp. 28–32.
14. Roger T. Sobkowiak, "Lean, Not Mean: RIF Management at The Hartford," *Information Strategy: The Executive's Journal* (Winter 1990), pp. 19–21.
15. Gerald L. Maatman, Jr., "Management Guide on Structuring and Implementing Reductions in Force to Comply with Federal, State and Local Laws," *Labor Law Journal* (Winter 2001), pp. 199–218.

Chapter 8

1. Arielle Emmett, "Building a Synergistic Outsourcing Relationship," *Customer Interface* (January 2002), pp. 24–27.
2. Monika Rola, "Secrets to Successful Outsourcing Arrangements," *Computing Canada* (November 29, 2002), p. 11.
3. These fundamental characteristics have been cited widely in the literature. The authors acknowledge Accenture's White Paper, "Business Process Outsourcing Big Bang," by Jane Linder, Susan Cantrell, and Scott Crist, as an influential source for this discussion.
4. Sean Doherty, "Let's Make a Deal," *Network Computing* (April 15, 2002), pp. 52–56.
5. "Flexibility the Key to Outsourcing Success," *Global Computing Services* (May 17, 2002), pp. 3–4.
6. Thomas Kern and Keith Blois, "Norm Development in Outsourcing Relationships," *Journal of Information Technology* 17 (2002), pp. 33–42.
7. Bob Gunn, "Culture and Control," *Strategic Finance* (December 2002), pp. 15–16.

Chapter 9

1. Jane C. Linder, "Transformational Outsourcing," *MIT Sloan Management Review* (Winter 2004), pp. 52–58.
2. The term *cross-enterprise collaboration* is normally used in supply chain management literature. However, its definition of transparency between organizations with the goal of creating strategic advantages for both firms is pertinent to the BPO relationship. See Donald J. Bowersox, David J. Closs, and Theodore P. Stank, "How to Master Cross-Enterprise Collaboration," *Supply Chain Management Review* (July/August 2003), pp. 18–26.
3. John Storck and Patricia A. Hill, "Knowledge Diffusion Through 'Strategic Communities,'" *MIT Sloan Management Review* (Winter 2000), pp. 63–74.
4. "Transformational Outsourcing—It's All in the Contract," *Global Computing Services* (July 25, 2003), p. 4.
5. "Outsourcing: A Global Success Story," *Logistics Management* (February 2003), pp. 60–62.

6. Shoshanna Zuboff, *In the Age of the Smart Machine: The Future of Work and Power* (New York: Basic Books, 1988).
7. Norbert Turek, "New VPNs for a Global Economy," *Information Week* (August 20, 2000), pp. 57–62.
8. Robert Craig, "Enterprise Repository Solutions," *ENT* (December 13, 2000), pp. 38–39.
9. Daniela Grigori, Fabio Casati, Malu Castellanos, Umesh Dayal, Ming-Chien Shan, and Mehmet Sayal, "Business Process Intelligence," *Computers in Industry* (April 2004), pp. 321–343.
10. "Shared Services: The Benefits & Challenges," *Global Computing Services* (July 25, 2003), pp. 4–6.
11. Judith Platania and Gary P. Moran, "Social Facilitation as a Function of the Mere Presence of Others," *Journal of Social Psychology* (April 2001), pp. 190–197.
12. Martyn Hart, "Call Center Offshoring May Damage Firms," *People Management* (December 4, 2003), p. 7.
13. Linda Punch, "The Global Back Office: Beyond the Hype," *Credit Card Management* (January 2004), pp. 26–32.
14. William W. Lewis, "Educating Global Workers," *McKinsey Quarterly*, 2003 Special Edition, pp. 4–5.

Chapter 10

1. Karl E. Weick and Robert E. Quinn, "Organizational Change and Development," *Annual Review of Psychology* (1999), pp. 361–386.
2. Phillip A. Miscimarra and Kenneth D. Schwartz, "Frozen in Time: The NLRB, Outsourcing, and Management Rights," *Journal of Labor Research* (Fall 1997), pp. 561–580.
3. Roberto Ceniceros, "Moving Operations Overseas Offers Benefits, Challenges," *Business Insurance* (December 22, 2003), pp. 4–5.
4. Lloyd Johnson and Anastasia D. Kelly, "Managing Up, Sideways, and Down," *Corporate Legal Times* (May 2002), p. 12–13.
5. Mike Bates, "Managing Expectations During ISP Installations," *Law Technology News* (August 2001), p. 55.
6. Fred Hererra, "Demystifying and Managing Expectations," *Employment Relations Today* (Summer 2003), pp. 21–28.
7. Michael Useem, *Leading Up* (New York: Crown Publishing, 2001).
8. Rick Sturm, "Managing Up: Dealing with an Exec's Technical Shortcomings," *Communications Week* (June 3, 1996), p. 40.
9. Cade Metz, "Tech Support Coming Home?" *PC Magazine* (February 17, 2004), p. 20.
10. Lucas Mearian, "Bank Group Offers Guidelines on Outsourcing Security Risks," *Computerworld* (January 26, 2004), p. 10.
11. Nigel Howard, "Living with the FTC Safeguard Rules: Industry Tips and Experiences," *Investment Lawyer* (September 2003), pp. 1–7.
12. Paul Hurley, "Outsourcing Information Security: Pros Outweigh Cons," *Energy IT* (March/April 2002), pp. 44–47.

13. Robert K. Weiler, "You Can't Outsource Liability for Security," *Information-Week* (August 26, 2002), p. 76.
14. Marie Alner, "The Effects of Outsourcing on Information Security," *Information Systems Security* (May/June 2001), pp. 35–43.
15. John Kavanagh, "Split Your Outsourcing Contracts to Guard Against Legal Disputes," *ComputerWeekly* (October 14, 2003), p. 76.
16. Part of this discussion is derived from the Sourcing Interests Group Research Report.
17. Kavanagh, *op cit.*, p. 76.
18. "Intellectual Outsourcing: A Tool for Change in the Service Industry," *The Nation* (Thailand), May 5, 2003.

Chapter 11

1. Daniel Henninger, " 'Stop!' Is Not an Option in the New World," *The Wall Street Journal* (February 27, 2004), p. A8.
2. See, for example, Thomas L. Friedman, "Zippies Are Here—Get Used to Them," *Houston Chronicle* (February 22, 2004), p. 3C; "Outsourcing isn't a Threat to America," *Houston Chronicle* (March 7, 2004), p. 3C.
3. Julia Angwin, "Job Losses Pit CNN's Dobbs Against Old Pals," *The Wall Street Journal* (February 26, 2004), pp. B3, B6.
4. Michael Schroeder, "Business Coalition Battles Outsourcing Backlash," *The Wall Street Journal* (March 1, 2004), pp. A1, A10.
5. "E-LOAN Gives Home Equity Customers the Choice to Participate in Indian Outsourcing Program," *PRNewswire* (March 1, 2004).
6. William Safire, " 'Outsourcing' Meets Linguistic Need," *Houston Chronicle* (Sunday, March 21, 2004), p. 6C.
7. John Riberio, "Outsourcing Means Job Creation is a Must, Powell Says," *InfoWorld* (March 16, 2004).
8. Richard S. Dunham, Paul Magnusson, and Alexandra Starr, "Outsource This: The Dems Smell Blood," *Business Week* (March 1, 2004), p. 47.
9. "Offshoring: Is it a Win-Win Game," (San Francisco: McKinsey Global Institute, August 2003).
10. Gary Endleman, "Fall Guy: U.S. Immigration and the Myth of Offshoring," National Association of Software and Service Companies (NASSCOM) Media Room (September 2003).
11. Milton Friedman and Rose Friedman, *Free to Choose* (New York: Harcourt Brace Jovanovich, 1980), pp. 44–45.
12. Cited in Satwik Seshasai and Amar Gupta, "Global Outsourcing of Professional Services," MIT Working Paper 4456-04 (January 2004), pp. 1–2.
13. Michael M. Phillips, "More Work is Outsourced to U.S. Than Away from It, Data Shows," *The Wall Street Journal* (March 15, 2004), pp. A2, A4.
14. Craig Karmin, "Offshoring Can Generate Jobs in the U.S.", *The Wall Street Journal* (March 16, 2004), pp. B1.
15. John Harwood, "Competitive Edge of U.S. is at Stake in the R&D Arena," *The Wall Street Journal* (March 17, 2004), p. A4.

16. David E. Gumpert, "A New Tide in Offshore Outsourcing," *Business Week On-line* (January 14, 2004).
17. Margot Cohen, "Viet Nam, The New Kid on the Block," *Far East Economic Review* (October 2, 2003), pp. 48–49.
18. " 'Offshoring' Drive for Savings Accelerates," *Financial Executive* (September 2003), pp. 52–55.

Index

ABC (activity-based costing) approach, 56
ABN Amro Bank, 27–28
Accenture, 38, 39
Accenture Business Services, 38, 39
Access, 182
Accessibility, 147
Accountability, 196
Accountants, 5
Accounting, 6
Accounts payable, 34–36
ACS. See Affiliated Computer Services, Inc.
Active server pages (ASP), 178
Activities, 56
Activity-based costing (ABC) approach, 56
Administrative safeguards, 198
Administrative section (of RFP), 104
ADP (Automatic Data Processing), 22
Affiliated Computer Services, Inc. (ACS),
    29–30
AFL-CIO, 210
Ahuja, Lalit, 23, 24
Alignment, 114, 168–169
Amazon.com, 36–37
Amazon Services, Inc., 36
American Airlines, 86–87
American Express, 19
American Management Association, 112
Analysis team. See BPO analysis team
Analytic software, 15–16
Aon Consulting, 51
API, 34–36
Applied research, 218
Applied Rights Directive, 117, 118
Aristotle, 112
Arm's length relationship, 157
Arrington, Renee, 55
Asia:
    broadband connectivity in, 13
    education in, 11–12, 217–218
Asia-Pacific region, broadband connectivity
    in, 13

Asimov, Isaac, 47
ASP (active server pages), 178
Assets:
    location of, 81
    ownership of, 80–81
    and vendor relationship, 158
A.T. Kearney Inc., 55
Atos Origin, 118
AT&T, 19, 51
"At will" employment, 191
Audits, security policy, 182
Authentication, 17
Automatic Data Processing (ADP), 22
AXA Financial, 33

Back-office functions, 4
Backups, 182–183, 204
Bangalore (India), 21, 23
Bank Industry Technology Secretariat
    (BITS), 198
Banks, 6
Basic research, 218
BAT. See BPO analysis team
BC Hydro, 38, 39
Benchmarking, 151
Bertch, Wesley, 39–42
BITS (Bank Industry Technology
    Secretariat), 198
Borders (company), 37
BOT (buy-operate-transfer) model, 21
Boyer & Ketchand, LLP, 114
BPM. See Business process mapping
BPO. See Business process outsourcing
BPO analysis and selection, 50–69
    BAT-establishment step of, 50–52
    BPO-opportunity identification step of,
        60–64
    business-case-development step of, 67–68
    core-/noncore-activity identification step
        of, 57–59
    costs of, 73–76

BPO analysis and selection (*cont.*)
  current-state-analysis step of, 53–57
  modeling step of, 64–67
BPO analysis team (BAT), 50–69
  BPO opportunities identified by, 60–64
  business case developed by, 67–68
  core-/noncore-activity identification by,
    57–59
  current state analysis conducted by, 53–57
  establishing a, 50–52
  modeling by, 64–67
  preparation/training of, 52
BPO Life Cycle, x, 71–72, 142–143
BPO project management plan, 136–139
BPO risk-probability matrix, 195–196
BPO Selection Matrix, 60–64
Breadth of relationship, 82
British Leyland, 180
British Petroleum, 19
Broadband Internet, 12–14
Bronstein, Myra, 192
Brooks Automation, Inc., 27–28
BS 7799, 17
BTO. *See* Business transformation
    outsourcing
B2B. *See* Business-to-business
B2C (business-to-consumer), 18
Buffett, Warren, 22
Business case, 67–68
Business continuity, 151, 204
Business model, 68
Business Monitor International, 203
Business practices, 201–202
Business process mapping (BPM), 54–56
Business process outsourcing (BPO), ix,
    3–25
  BTO vs., 38
  criticisms of, 6
  decision making about, 23–25
  definition of, 4
  driving factors of, 9–20
  early adopters of, 19
  GE Capital/Microsoft case studies of, 21
  hot spots of, 4
  labor-cost savings with, 5
  nearshore, 22–23
  number of job shifts with, 5
  offshore, 20, 21
  onshore, 22
  reasons for adopting, 48
  revenues worldwide of, 6

  as socio-technical phenomenon, 7–9
  types of, 20
  and venture capital, 6
Business skills, 155
Business specialization, 18–20
Business-to-business (B2B), 18–19
Business-to-consumer (B2C), 18
Business transformation outsourcing (BTO),
    38–39
Buyer control, 165–166
Buyer's responsibilities, 161–163
Buyer—vendor relationship, x, 154–171
  and assets, 158
  and corporate culture, 158–159
  costs of, 78
  depth/breadth of, 82, 157
  interpersonal, 164–165
  and PMT changes, 163
  and problem identification/resolution,
    163–164
  and profit, 162
  risk factors with, 165–169
  scope of, 157–158
  skills for, 155
  success factors for, 160–162
Buy-operate-transfer (BOT) model, 21

CAL (client access license), 178
Call centers, 119
Canada Life, 122
Capabilities assessment, 103
Capellas, Michael, 87
Case studies (as tool), 105
Cause (term), 199
Certification, 106, 202
Change:
  drivers of. *See* Driving factor(s)
  organizational, 83
  process of, 117
Change management, 135–153
  and BPO project management plan,
    136–139
  and business continuity/benchmarking,
    151
  and corporate culture, 148–149
  and employee communication, 147–148
  and job loss/changeover, 149–151
  principles of, 139–140
  roles of leadership in, 142–147
  vision principle of, 141–142
Changeover, 149–151

Charters:
  BAT, 52
  VST, 98
China:
  education in, 12, 217
  foreign students in U.S. from, 11
  manufacturing/technical outsourcing to, 4
  SARS outbreak in, 204
Civil rights action, 219
Claimpower, Inc., 216–217
Claims processing, 29–30, 126
Clerical workers, 62
Client access license (CAL), 178
Clinton administration, 213
Coalition for Economic Growth and
    American Jobs, 210
Collective bargaining, 191
Colombia, 220
Colton, C. C., 3
Commitment, escalation of, 67
Communication, 55, 144–145, 147–148
Communication skills, 155
Compaq, 87, 118
Comparative advantage theory, 214
Compensation, productivity-based, 30
Competence co-development outsourcing,
    30–32
Competing for the Future (Pralahad and
    Hamel), 18
Competitive advantage, x
Competitiveness, 211–212
Competitors, 85
Computer evidence, 17
Consultants, 74, 75
Contingency plans, 203–204
Contract development, 79–80
Contracts, 112–131
  and data security, 66
  and dispute resolution, 129
  force majeure clauses of, 128–129
  and governance, 123–124
  industry-specific concerns of, 126
  and intellectual property, 124–125
  negotiating, 113–116
  pricing section of, 120–123
  rules of thumb for, 114
  scope-of-work section of, 116–117
  SLA section of, 119–121, 161, 162
  termination of, 126–127
  term of the, 123
  and transition phase, 128

Contractual/legal section (of RFP), 104
Cooperative relationship, 157
Core competences, 4
  elements of, 58
  identification of, 57–59
  and SMEs, 24
  and specialization, 18–19
Corporate culture:
  and change management, 148–149
  and first-time outsourcing, 34
  and vendor relationship, 158–159,
    166–167
Co-sharing risk/reward model, 123
Costs, 70–90
  analysis, 73–76
  contract-development, 79–80
  financial, 73–86
  operating, 83–86
  relationship, 87–88
  strategic, 86–88
  and TCM, 71–72
  transition, 80–83
  vendor-selection, 76–79
Cost-plus model, 122
Cost-reduction BPO projects, 83
Council of Economic Advisers, 213
Creamer, Carlos, 29, 30
Credits, 120
Critical functions, 59
CRM. *See* Customer relationship
    management
Cross-enterprise knowledge management, 180
Culture. *See* Corporate culture
Current state analysis, 53–57
Customers, 197
Customer-centric core competence, 58
Customer mindset, 99
Customer relationship management (CRM),
    22–23
Customer satisfaction, 85, 119
Customer service, 99

Damage (term), 199
Daniele, Diane, 145
Database management system (DBMS), 177
Data centers, 33, 88
Data corruption, 180
Data mining, 177
Data privacy rules, 219
Data Protection laws (UK), 17
Data reconfiguration, 180

Data security, 66
Data sharing, 99
Data storage, inexpensive, 14–15
DBMS (database management system), 177
Deficit, 216
DeLauro, Rosa, 159
Deliverables, 66–67
Dell, 197
Deming, W. Edwards, 135, 211
Democratic Party, 212–213
Depth of relationship, 82, 157
DiamondCluster International, 112
Differential backup, 182, 183
Digital certificates, 17
Digital River, 122
Digital subscriber line (DSL), 13
Directories, 102
Disaster recovery, 204
Dispute resolution, 129
Dobbs, Lou, 210
Downward expectations management, 195
Driving factor(s), 9–20
    analytic software as, 15–16
    broadband Internet as, 12–14
    business specialization as, 18–20
    data storage as, 14–15
    educational attainment as, 10–12
    Internet security as, 16–18
DSL (digital subscriber line), 13
Due diligence, 62, 202
Duty (term), 199

Eastern Europe, broadband connectivity in,
    13
E-business solutions, 36–37
EDI (electronic data interchange), 178
EDS (Electronic Data Systems Corp.), 156
Education, 10–12, 212, 215, 217–218
Einstein, Albert, 154
Electrical engineering, 12
Electronic data interchange (EDI), 178
Electronic Data Systems Corp. (EDS), 156
Electronic protected health information
    (EPHI), 198
Emergent phenomenon, 9–10
Empathy, 55
Employees, 108, 117–118, 147–148
Employment laws, 117, 118, 191–192
Engineering degrees, 12, 212, 217
EPHI (electronic protected health
    information), 198
Equinix Inc., 37

Ernst & Young, 5
Escalation of commitment, 67
Ethics, 125, 150
EU. *See* European Union
Europe:
    broadband connectivity in, 13
    education in, 12
European Union (EU), 17, 117, 118
Exit provisions, 114
Expectations, 195
Extension of buyer's organization, 157

FCG (First Consulting Group), 145
FCG Management Services, 145
Fee structure, 121
Final vendor selection, 108–109
Finance, 6
Financial costs, 73–86
    analysis, 73–76
    contract-development, 79–80
    operating-phase, 83–86
    transition, 80–83
    vendor-selection, 76–79
Financial information, 126
Financial performance metrics, 84
Financial stability, proof of, 106
Findings section (of business case), 68
Fiorina, Carly, 209
First Consulting Group (FCG), 145
First-time outsourcing, 34–36
Fixed-price model, 32–33, 122
Flexibility, 164
FMC Corp., 156
Force majeure, 128–129, 203–204
Ford Motor Company, 19, 211
Foreign students in U.S., 11
Forrester Research, 5
Fosmire, Jill, 156
Framework for Managing Technology Risk
    for IT Service Provider Relationships, 198
Free-trade issue, 213
Friedman, Milton, 214
Friedman, Thomas, 210
FTC (U.S. Federal Trade Commission), 198
Full backup, 182, 183
Functions, 56
Future potential for BPO, 209–221
    and education, 217–218
    and global business environment, 210–211
    and global economics, 213–215
    and global workers, 215–217
    and politics, 212–213

and strategy/competitiveness, 211–212

Gartner Group, 5, 6
GE. *See* General Electric
GE Capital, 21
Gedas, 180
Genco Distribution Systems, Inc., 31–32
General Electric (GE), 18, 19
General requirements section (of RFP), 104
George, David Lloyd, 27
GE Real Estate, 78
Gibran, Kahlil, 93
GLB. *See* Gramm-Leach-Bliley Act
Global business environment, 210–211
Global communications and information
    infrastructure, 3–4
Global economics, 213–215
Global workers, 215–217
Goals, 168–169
Governance, 123–125, 150, 168
Gramm-Leach-Bliley Act (GLB), 126, 198
Granting privileges, 182
Guest worker visas, 193, 194
Gupta, Amar, 218

Hacking, 17
Hardware, 182
Hardware infrastructure, 173–176
Health care information, 198–199
Health Insurance Portability and
    Accountability Act (HIPAA), 17, 66,
    126, 198–199
Help desk vendors, 114
Henninger, Daniel, 210
Hewlett-Packard, 87
Higher education, 10–12, 212, 215, 217
HighTech, 143
HIPAA. *See* Health Insurance Portability and
    Accountability Act
Honesty, 144, 148
Hong Kong, broadband connectivity in, 13
Horizontal management, 196
Hosting services, 36
Hours of operation, 119
HR. *See* Human resources
Human capital risks, 190–194
Human factors, 8–9
Human resources (HR), 5, 51, 202

IBM, 19, 122, 180
IBM Employees' Union, 216
IBM Global Services, 33

IDC, 6
Implementation of BPO project, 76–86
    contract-development phase of, 79–80
    operating phase of, 80–83
    transition phase of, 80–83
    vendor-selection phase of, 76–79
Incentives, 180
Incremental backup, 182, 183
India:
    education in, 21, 217
    employment laws in, 191, 192
    engineering/technical outsourcing to, 4
    foreign students in U.S. from, 11
    and free trade, 213
Indian IT Act (2000), 17
Inflexibility, 167
Information exchange, 165
Information integrity, 180
Information technology (IT) firms, 6
Infrastructure, 172–188
    hardware, 173–176
    knowledge, 178–184
    software, 176–178
    training/support, 184–187
Innovation, 7
Insourcing, offshore, 21
Insurance claims processing, 126
Integration, 169
Intellectual property (IP), 124–125,
    197–200
International Arbitration Association, 201
International Chamber of Commerce, 129
International Court of Arbitration, 129
Internet connectivity, 12–14
Internet security, 16–18
Interviews, 105
IP. *See* Intellectual property
ISO 17799, 17
IT (information technology) firms, 6

Japanese automakers, 19
Job losses, 149–151
Job shifts, 4–6

Kennedy, John F., 70
Kerberos technology, 17
Key functions, 59
Key performance indicators (KPIs), 119
Kinzy, Ryan, 220
Knowledge infrastructure, 178–184
Knowledge of BPO, 74, 75, 85
Kohler Company, 34–36

KPIs (key performance indicators), 119
K3 Group, 220

Labor costs, 5
Labor unions, 210, 216
Language, 114
Latin America, broadband connectivity in, 13
LDV, 180
Leadership, 55, 142–147
Legal risks, 200–201
Lehman Brothers, 109
Letters of credit (LOC), 27–28
Liaison, 196
Life cycle, BPO. *See* BPO Life Cycle
Life Time Fitness, 39–42
Linfoot, Chris, 180
LOC. *See* Letters of credit
Location:
    asset, 81
    hardware, 174
Logical architecture, 53, 107
L-1 visas, 159
Long-list development, 101–102
Lucent, 118

Major League Baseball, 122
Managed-security providers (MSPs),
    199–200
Management. *See* Senior management
Managing on the Fault Line (Geoffrey
    Moore), 58
Mankiw, N. Gregory, 213
Manufacturing, 6, 7
Massachusetts Institute of Technology
    (MIT), 17, 218
Masters' degree in Business Administration
    (MBAs), 21
Medical records, 66
Methodology section (of business case), 67
Metropolitan Life Insurance (MetLife),
    29–30
Mexico, 4
Microsoft, 21
Middleware, 177
MIT. *See* Massachusetts Institute of
    Technology
Model, business, 68
Modeling the BPO project, 64–67
Morale, 88
Mortgage Electronic Registration Systems,
    22–23

MSPs. *See* Managed-security providers
Multiple-service vendors, 158

NAFTA. *See* North American Free Trade
    Agreement
National Labor Relations Act (NLRA), 191
National Labor Relations Board (NLRB),
    191
Nearshore outsourcing, 20, 22–23
Negligence, 199
Negotiation, 113–116
Negotiation skills, 155
New York-Presbyterian Hospital (NYPH),
    145
Nike, 193
NLRA (National Labor Relations Act), 191
NLRB (National Labor Relations Board), 191
North America, broadband connectivity in,
    13
North American Free Trade Agreement
    (NAFTA), 6, 213
NYPH (New York-Presbyterian Hospital),
    145

Objectives:
    project, 64, 65
    team, 52
Obstruction, 146
OCIO (office of the chief information
    officer), 145
ODBC (open database connectivity), 177
Office of the chief information officer
    (OCIO), 145
Offshore insourcing, 21
Offshore outsourcing, 20, 21
    examples of, 28–30
    unsuccessful, 39–42
Offshoring, ix
OLAP. *See* Online analytic processing
Online analytic processing (OLAP), 15–16
Onshore intermediaries, 30
Onshore outsourcing, 20, 22
Open database connectivity (ODBC), 177
Operating phase, 83–86
Organizational change, 83
Organizational culture. *See* Corporate
    culture
Organizational history, 74, 75
Organizational learning losses, 15, 71
Organizational processes, 54
Out-of-compliance performance, 120

Outsourcing. *See* Business process
  outsourcing
Outsourcing fear factor, 36
Ownership, asset, 80–81

Partner mindset, 99
Password policy, 182
Patton, George S., 189
Pay-as-you-go pricing models, 33, 122
Payroll outsourcing, 22
PEO. *See* Professional employment
  organization
Performance-based pricing model, 123
Pew Internet & American Life Project, 13
Philippines, 4
Physical safeguards, 199
Piper, David S., 114
PKI (Public Key Infrastructure), 17
Plan, BPO project management, 136–139
PMT. *See* Project management team
Political issues, 159, 197
Political unrest, 203
Politics, 212–213
Powell, Colin, 213
Precontract stage, 108–109
Preoutsourcing analysis, 35
Preparation costs, 74
"Pressing the value model," 202–203
Pricing, contract, 120–123
Pricing requirements section (of RFP), 104
Privacy laws, 17, 198–199, 219
Problem identification and resolution,
  161–164
Process costs, 60
Process expertise, 99
Process mission criticality, 61
Process names, 56–57
Process productivity, 61
Process swamp, 53, 54
Productivity, 61, 62, 84, 85, 88
Productivity-based compensation model, 30
Product returns system, 31–32
Professional employment organization
  (PEO), 19, 47
Profit, 161, 162
Project management plan, 136–139
Project management team (PMT), 157, 158,
  160–166, 168, 169
Project risks, 194–197
Project team structure, 49–50
Proposal evaluation, 105–106

Public Key Infrastructure (PKI), 17
Pure play vendors, 100

Qualification lists, 99–101
Qualitative measures, 85–86
Quality, 119
"Quality or Else" (TV program), 211

Radiologists, 5
R&D (Requirements and Definitions) study,
  35
Recalibration of SLAs, 161, 162
Recovery, 182–184
Reduction-in-force (RIF), 149–151, 191
References, 106
Referrals, 202
Reich, Robert, 214–215
Relationship. *See* Buyer—vendor
  relationship
Relationship costs, 87–88
Reporting requirements, 219
Republican Party, 213
Request for information (RFI), 102–103
Request for proposal (RFP), 77–79,
  103–105
Requirements and Definitions (R&D) study,
  35
Research, applied vs. basic, 218
Resources, 56
Resource theory, 58
Responsibilities, buyer's, 161–163
Résumés, 106
Return on investment (ROI), 83
Returns processing, 121
Reverse outsourcing, 36–37
RFI. *See* Request for information
RFP. *See* Request for proposal
Ricardo, David, 214
RIF. *See* Reduction-in-force
Risk mitigation, 65–66
Risks, 23, 189–206
  force majeure, 203–204
  human capital, 190–194
  intellectual property, 197–200
  legal, 200–201
  project, 194–197
  relationship, 165–169
  value, 202–203
  vendor-organizational, 201–202
ROI (return on investment), 83
Rooney, Andy, 172

Sabre Holdings, 86
Sabre ticketing system, 86–87
Safeguard Rules, 198
Safire, William, 212
SANS (SysAdmin, Audit, Network, Security)
  Institute, 200
SARS (severe acute respiratory syndrome),
  204
Scalzi, Guy, 145
Scope of work (SOW), 102, 116–117
Sears, 31–32
Security:
  and access limits, 182
  data, 66
  guidelines for, 198
  Internet, 16–18
  issues with, 181
  responsibilities for, 199
Senior management:
  and change, 142–147
  and PMT liaison, 195, 196
  support of, 75
  and Type 1 processes, 61, 62
Service level agreements (SLAs), 86,
  119–121, 167–168, 201
Severe acute respiratory syndrome (SARS),
  204
Shared services, 24, 100
Shareholders, 86
Short-list selection, 106–108
Single-service providers, 157
SLA recalibration clauses, 161, 162
SLAs. *See* Service level agreements
Small to medium-sized enterprises (SMEs),
  23, 24, 32, 47
Socio-technical phenomenon, ix, 7–9
Software, 15–16, 182
Software development, 39–42
Software infrastructure, 176–178
Solidarity, 165
South Asia broadband connectivity in, 13
South East Asia, broadband connectivity in,
  13
SOW (scope of work), 102
Specialization, business, 18–20, 100
Stakeholders, 86
Statement of work. *See* Scope of work
Steering team, 49, 51
Storytelling, 141–142
Strategic BPO, 84
Strategic costs, 86–88
Strategy, 211–212

Subprocesses, 56
Sunk-cost effect, 67
SunTech Data Systems, 23, 24
Suppliers, 197
Support processes, 59, 184–187
Sweat-shop labor practices, 193
Symbolic analysts, 214, 215
SysAdmin, Audit, Network, Security (SANS)
  Institute, 200
System architecture, 175–176

Tape restoration, 182–184
Tape rotation, 182–183
Target.com, 37
Task based costing, 73–74
TCM. *See* Total Cost Management
TCO (Total Cost of Ownership), 71
Teams:
  BPO. *See* BPO analysis team
  developmental stages of, 52
Team approach, ix, 137–139
Technical education, 11, 218
Technical safeguards, 199
Technical workers, 62, 63
Telecommunications, 12–14
Teleconferences, 105, 107–108
Termination indemnity, 192
Termination of contract, 120, 126–127
Term of the contract, 123
Theune, Dan, 34, 35
Third-party professionals, 74, 75, 82, 200,
  201
Three-tier analytic structure, 56–57
Thurow, Lester, 215–218
Ticketing process, airline, 86–87
Tier 1, 56
Tier 2, 56, 61
Tier 3, 56, 57
Time zones, 119
Timing of key events, 65
Tort law, 199
Total Cost Management (TCM), 71–72, 89,
  90
Total Cost of Ownership (TCO), 71
Total quality management (TQM),
  211–212
Trade-Related Aspects of Intellectual
  Property Rights (TRIPs), 124
Training, 85
  BAT, 52
  costs of, 74
  infrastructure for, 184–187

Transfer of Undertakings Protection of
    Employment (UK) (TUPE), 117, 118
Transfer pricing, 73
Transformation outsourcing. *See* Business
    transformation outsourcing
Transition phase, 80–83, 128
Trial period, 109
TRIPs (Trade-Related Aspects of Intellectual
    Property Rights), 124
Trust, 112
TUPE. *See* Transfer of Undertakings
    Protection of Employment
Type 1 processes, 61, 62
Type 2 processes, 62
Type 3 processes, 62
Type 4 processes, 62
Type 5 processes, 62–63
Type 6 processes, 63
Type 7 processes, 63
Type 8 processes, 63

UK. *See* United Kingdom
Unemployment rate, 7
Unions, labor, 210, 216
United Kingdom (UK), 17, 117, 118, 180
United States:
    higher education in, 10–12
    outsourcing specialties of, 4
    unemployment rate in, 7
U.S. Department of State, 203
U.S. Federal Trade Commission (FTC), 198
U.S. Foreign Corrupt Practices Act (1977),
    201–202
U.S. Labor Department, 7
U.S. Supreme Court, 191
Unit-pricing model, 122
Upward expectations management, 195

Valstad, Clay, 32
Value risks, 202–203
Van Natta, Owen, 37
Variable-price outsourcing, 32–33
Variable-pricing model, 122
Vendor-organizational risks, 201–202
Vendor presentations, 107
Vendor relationship. *See* Buyer—vendor
    relationship

Vendor selection, 93–111
    case study of, 95–96
    costs associated with, 76–79
    final step of, 108–109
    long-list development step of, 101–102
    proposal-evaluation step of, 105–106
    qualifications-establishment step of,
        99–101
    RFI step of, 102–103
    RFP step of, 103–105
    short-list step of, 106–108
    team-appointment step of, 96–98
Vendor selection team (VST), 94, 96–98
Venture capital community, 6
Virtual private network (VPN), 178
Visas, 159, 193, 194
Visibility, 147, 220
Vision, 141–142
VPN (virtual private network), 178
VST. *See* Vendor selection team

Walden Books, 37
Wal-Mart, 193
WAN (wide area network), 177
WARN (Worker Adjustment and Retraining
        Notification Act), 117
Watchmark Corp., 192
Weighting system, 100, 101
Welch, Jack, 18
Western Electric, 76
Western Europe, broadband connectivity in,
    13
Wetware, 179
Wide area network (WAN), 177
Worker Adjustment and Retraining
        Notification Act (WARN), 117
The Work of Nations (Robert Reich),
    214–215
WorldCom Inc., 156
World Trade Organization, 124

Xerox, 94

Zandi, Mark, 7
Zogby poll, 213
Zupnick, Hank, 78

9 780471 655770